1980

Writing the Research P

795

Writing the Research Paper
A Guide and Sourcebook

Marsha Hirsch Cummins

BRONX COMMUNITY COLLEGE

Carole Slade

BAYLOR UNIVERSITY

HOUGHTON MIFFLIN COMPANY   Boston
Dallas   Geneva, Ill.   Hopewell, N.J.
Palo Alto   London

Library of Congress Catalog Card Number: 78-69613
ISBN: 0-395-27259-9

Acknowledgment is made to the following sources of facsimile materials:

Page 81
Readers' Guide to Periodical Literature © 1974, 1975. Material reproduced by permission of The H. W. Wilson Company, publisher.

Page 82
Readers' Guide to Periodical Literature © 1975, 1976. Material reproduced by permission of The H. W. Wilson Company, publisher.

Page 82
Readers' Guide to Periodical Literature © 1973, 1974. Material reproduced by permission of The H. W. Wilson Company, publisher.

Page 86
© 1975 by The New York Times Company. Reprinted by permission.

Contents

Two Sourcebook for a Paper

Preface

Writing the Research Paper is designed to teach the skills students need for writing research papers throughout their college careers. These skills are explained, illustrated, and reinforced one by one so that students who have never had the experience of writing a research paper will be able to enjoy success.

Among the unique features of this text are the exercises that accompany each explanation; the presentation of the writing of the research paper as an extension of essay writing; the emphasis on the process of writing and on critical reading; and the Sourcebook, a collection of research materials on a single subject.

To allow students to approach their research projects with confidence, the book begins by relating the process of writing a research paper to the research and writing skills students already possess. To build on their knowledge, the text offers exercises that involve review of skills as well as practice and mastery of each new technique involved in writing research papers at the college level. These exercises give students satisfaction in completing small units and thus help to ensure that they will successfully complete an entire paper.

Students and instructors will find that the text reinforces the concepts taught in composition and basic writing courses through its treatment of the research paper as one type of essay and its emphasis on the use of essay-writing techniques. After reviewing the principles of expository writing, students evaluate their own essay writing in relation to the particular kinds of writing skills the research paper requires.

Writing the Research Paper demonstrates the interrelation of all the processes the research project requires. From the note-taking stage to the final draft, the writing of clear and logical prose is stressed; an entire chapter is devoted to writing and revising the rough draft. Another substantial section in an early chapter is devoted to the use of critical-reading skills in the evaluation of research materials, while a later chapter demonstrates how students can apply these skills to their own writing. Requirements of form, such as documentation, are presented as they occur naturally in the writing process to allow students to develop an understanding of their function and necessity.

Most importantly, this textbook contains within its covers a miniature library in the form of the Sourcebook (Part Two). The theme of the Sourcebook is television, a subject which can be approached from the point of view of many disciplines. Students planning careers in almost any field—psychology, engineering, history, drama, or journalism, for example—may work with the subject as it relates to their own interests.

The articles in the Sourcebook were selected to cover a wide range of aspects of the subject of television and to represent a variety of writing styles, levels, and approaches. Students are encouraged to evaluate the form and content of the selections and to practice all their research skills on Sourcebook materials. Students will thus gain experience in using research materials that will enable them to make productive use of their time in the library.

Instructors may ask students to write one or more short papers using the Sourcebook exclusively. At the same time, a comprehensive chapter on library resources is included so that students may extend their research beyond the Sourcebook, either to other materials on television or to another subject.

For their many helpful suggestions and criticisms, we wish to thank Dr. Nahma Sandrow and Dr. Bernard L. Witlieb of the English Department and Prof. Jean Kolliner of the Library Department of Bronx Community College; Shannon Burns of the University of Arkansas, Little Rock; Richard Dillman and Alan Dubrow of the University of Oregon; and Teoman Sipahigil of the University of Idaho. We also gratefully acknowledge ideas and encouragement from our students and colleagues at Morgan State College, New York University, Bronx Community College of the City University of New York, and Baylor University, as well as from fellow-members of the CUNY Association of Writing Supervisors.

M.H.C.
C.S.

One

Guide to Research and Writing

1
From the essay to the research paper

What do I already know?

Writing a research paper can sound like a formidable task. Indeed, like other important activities, producing an accurate and well-written paper requires time and attention. This book gives you the skills necessary to write a research paper successfully even if you have never done formal research before.

Part One consists of chapters that explain each step in the process of writing a research paper and provide exercises for practicing each skill. Part Two constitutes a Sourcebook, a collection of readings excerpted from articles and books on the subject of television. The Sourcebook serves two purposes. First, it provides examples of the concepts presented in Part One; and many of the exercises in Part One are based on selections from the Sourcebook. Second, the Sourcebook functions as a miniature library on the subject of television.

If your instructor wishes, you will use this Sourcebook exclusively to do your research for a short research paper of 1,000 words or fewer. Alternatively, your instructor may ask that you use the Sourcebook as the basis for more extensive research at a library. Ten pages or 2,500 words is the average length of a research paper.

You should first understand what a research paper is. In this chapter you will see the ways in which the processes involved in writing a research paper are similar to and different from the kinds of writing and research you already know how to do. You will then be ready to define the research paper and to begin your own paper by formulating a preliminary controlling question to guide your thinking and research.

Writing the Essay

You have probably written many essays or compositions for high school and college classes. *The research paper is a type of essay.* You will, therefore, be able to apply many of the skills you have developed for writing essays—outlining, formulating a controlling idea, and paragraphing, for example—when you write your research paper. For this reason, a review of your essay-writing techniques will prepare you to begin working on your research paper. Also, it is always a good idea to organize your own thoughts on a subject before you begin reading other people's ideas.

Assignment

Write an essay of approximately 500 words on the subject of television. Select one aspect of the topic as a focus for your essay. When you have completed your essay, turn back to this page to examine your writing.

MODE OF COMMUNICATION

You should first consider the mode, or way, you chose to communicate in your essay. If you presented details you received through sensory perception, perhaps aural or visual, you probably wrote an essay of *description*. If you related a story about an experience involving television, you wrote an essay of *narration*. If you attempted to persuade your reader to take a particular position on an issue, you wrote an essay of *argumentation*. If you explained or provided information about television, you wrote an essay of *exposition*. An essay often employs more than one of these modes of communication, yet one mode usually dominates.

Choose and write down the word that best describes the way you communicated in your essay. (Description, narration, exposition, argumentation.)

The research paper is an essay of exposition. Although it may contain elements of description, narration, or argumentation, its primary method of communication is expository. That is, the principal goal of every research paper is the explanation of a subject. If you determine that your essay is primarily expository, you can continue using the same mode of communication in your research paper. If your essay consisted primarily of another of these modes, you will have to set that mode aside and change to exposition for your research paper.

POINT OF VIEW

A writer's point of view is his or her attitude toward the subject. You are undoubtedly aware of the ways in which your attitude toward a person can affect your behavior, including the words and gestures you use to communicate with that person. In the same way, a writer's point of view on a subject affects every aspect of the writing: word choice, tone, sentence structure, and punctuation. In writing your research paper, you should strive to have an objective point of view. After reading the following sections, you will be able to decide whether your point of view in your essay was objective or subjective.

Subjective Point of View

An essay written from a subjective point of view deals with a topic through the writer's own experiences, observations, impressions, or feelings. The focus is primarily on the writer rather than on any external event or topic. The writer often seeks to evoke emotion, to recreate his or her own feelings in the reader. The following excerpt of an essay by Michael Arlen illustrates the use of the subjective point of view. Arlen writes about his personal experience of the 1968 Democratic convention in Chicago when demonstrators were confined to Lincoln Park and beaten by the police.

It's common knowledge by now, to be sure, how Daley and the Democrats combined to cut down the television coverage of the events in Chicago by managing the electrical-workers' strike so that there wasn't any time left to provide the networks with mobile hookups—that, plus preventing the networks' mobile trucks from parking at key places on the streets, and making things generally as difficult and restrictive as possible. Still, it's hard to realize, just sitting there in one's living room and looking at the screen, the extent to which one's bird's-eye view of actuality can be diminished, altered, censored in this country, in the year 1968, by a combination of officialdom and sheer brute force. It has truly been very ugly here, and I do not mind being so personal about it because there was something very special in the air in Chicago this week and I have been reading the newspaper stories about it, with their now almost conventional narrations of "thumpings" and "thwackings," and I have been looking at the television, and even the television, which did as well by all of us as I think it humanly could have, couldn't quite give it out as it really was.[1]

Michael Arlen's account of these events is subjective because he relates primarily his own experiences and reactions. He uses suggestive words like *ugly* and *sheer brute force,* which, in addition to describing the event, carry emotional weight. If you wrote about your experience of television or your feelings about it, you probably wrote an essay with a subjective point of view.

Objective Point of View

The focus of an essay written from an objective point of view is a subject external to the writer. He or she attempts to keep feelings or personal experiences out of the discussion. The writer's primary purpose is to inform the reader about the topic. In the following passage, Marshall McLuhan explains his now well-known concept of "hot" and "cool" media. Because he seeks to be objective, his language is neutral rather than suggestive. His purpose is to inform the reader about the differences among the media rather than to raise the reader's passions about one medium or another.

There is a basic principle that distinguishes a hot medium like radio from a cool one like the telephone, or a hot medium like the movie from a cool one like TV. A hot medium is one that extends one single sense in "high definition." High definition is the state of being well filled with data. A photograph is, visually, "high definition." A cartoon is "low definition," simply because very little visual information is provided. Telephone is a cool medium, or one of low definition, because the ear is given a meager amount of information. And speech is a cool medium of low definition, because so little is given and so much has to be filled in by the listener. On the other hand, hot media do not leave so much to be filled in or completed by the audience. Hot media are, therefore, low in participation, and cool media are high in participation or completion by the audience. Naturally, therefore, a hot medium like radio has very different effects on the user from a cool medium like the telephone.[2]

As the preceding passage demonstrates, taking an objective point of view does not mean that you forgo having your own ideas; it does mean that you express them as unemotionally and impersonally as possible.

[1]Michael J. Arlen, *Living-Room War* (New York: Viking Press, 1969), pp. 239–40.
[2]Marshall McLuhan, *Understanding Media* (New York: New American Library, 1964), p. 36.

Choose and write down the word that describes the point of view of your essay. (Subjective, objective.)

If you wrote an objective essay, you will be able to use the same point of view in writing your research paper. If your essay was subjective, you will want to change to the objective point of view for your research paper.

STRUCTURE

As you study your own essay, you will also want to examine its form, or structure. An essay normally consists of three parts: the introduction, the body, and the conclusion. The structure of a research paper is exactly the same.

Introduction

The essay-writer uses the introduction to capture the reader's interest and attention. The introduction may begin with an anecdote or a provocative question and often includes a statement about the significance of the subject explored in the paper. In addition, the *controlling idea,* a sentence that delimits the scope and content of the entire essay (also called a *thesis statement*), normally appears in the introduction.

Can you find the controlling idea in the following introductory paragraph of an essay on cable television?

Cable television is a medium still in its infancy. It presently reaches into less than 15% of the television homes in America, and, for most of these homes, cable's only purpose is to retransmit programs originating from broadcast stations. If allowed to grow, however, cable could have far-reaching effects, not only on the way Americans receive information but on their patterns of daily living as well.[3]

Even though you do not have the entire article here, you should be able to recognize the final sentence of the paragraph as the controlling idea, the idea the author will prove and demonstrate in succeeding paragraphs.

Now answer the following questions about your own essay.

[3]"Cable Television and Content Regulation: The FCC, the First Amendment, and the Electronic Newspaper," *New York University Law Review,* 51 (Apr. 1976), 133.

Does my essay have an introduction?

yes   no

☐ ☐

Does my essay have a controlling idea?

yes   no

☐ ☐

Write out the controlling idea of your essay.

_____

_____

_____

The Body

Paragraphs that develop and support the controlling idea make up the body of an essay. A *paragraph* is a unit of related sentences about one thought or subject generally from 100 to 250 words in length. Each paragraph contains a generalization that serves the same purpose within the paragraph as the controlling idea serves for the entire essay; that is, it delimits the content of the paragraph. This generalization, often called the *topic sentence,* may be either stated or implied through the gradual development of the idea in the paragraph. Just as each of the topic sentences in an essay must relate to and support the controlling idea, each sentence in a paragraph must support the stated or implied topic sentence.

The basic methods of developing the topic sentence of a paragraph are *supporting details, illustration, definition, comparison and contrast,* and *analysis.* After you read the following examples and explanations of each method, you should be able to determine the methods of development you used to support each of the stated or implied topic sentences in the body paragraphs of your essay.

Development by *supporting details* is the listing or enumeration of the events in a series, the steps in a process, statistics, or the elements of description to support a topic sentence. In paragraph 10 from an article in the Sourcebook, Arthur Nielsen develops the topic sentence (the first sentence) with details about the process his firm uses to determine the number of viewers watching a given program.

[10] We keep tab by connecting automatic recorders (Audimeters) to a cross section of the Nation's TV sets. These Audimeters are placed out of

sight—in closets, basements, etc.—and by electronic "photographs" on film, record minute-by-minute whether the sets are on or off, and to what channel they are tuned. This record is kept 24 hours a day, week in and week out, and the film records are mailed back to our production center twice a month, when the sample home receives a fresh film magazine.

(For other examples of paragraph development by supporting details consult the Sourcebook: selection 2, paragraph 5; selection 3, paragraph 17; selection 11, paragraph 4.)

Illustration is the use of specific examples or instances to clarify a point and to support the topic sentence of a paragraph. In the following excerpt from selection 16 in the Sourcebook, James Baldwin uses several examples to support the generalization in his topic sentence (the first sentence in the passage).

[1] Someone once said to me that the people in general cannot bear very much reality. He meant by this that they prefer fantasy to a truthful re-creation of their experience. The Italians, for example, during the time that De Sica and Rossellini were revitalizing the Italian cinema industry, showed a marked preference for Rita Hayworth vehicles; the world in which she moved across the screen was like a fairy tale, whereas the world De Sica was describing was one with which they were only too familiar. (And it can be suggested perhaps that the Americans who stood in line for *Shoe Shine* and *Open City* were also responding to images which they found exotic, to a reality by which they were not threatened. What passes for the appreciation of serious effort in this country is very often nothing more than an inability to take anything very seriously.)

(For other examples of development by illustration, or example, consult the Sourcebook: selection 10, paragraphs 9 and 21.)

Definition, the stating of the meaning of a term, can be used to develop an entire paragraph or as an introductory sentence for a paragraph or essay. Definition acquaints the reader with terms or concepts that may be unfamiliar or used in unique ways. A term may be defined in several ways. An example may serve as a definition: " 'All in the Family' is an example of a situation comedy." You might use a synonym to define a term: "A dissolve is a slow cross-fade." In either case, the example or synonym must be familiar to the reader or it will not function to define the term. If your reader does not know what a slow cross-fade is, he or she will not learn what a dissolve is from your definition. A formal definition, usually the most accurate way to define a term, involves first placing the term in a class and then distinguishing it from all other things in that class: "An antenna [the term] is a metallic device [the class] for radiating or receiving radio waves [the distinguishing detail]." Here the distinguishing detail separates the antenna from all other metallic devices.

In the following excerpt from the Sourcebook, Horace Newcomb defines the term *sports*. He begins with a formal definition in the first sentence to explain how he will use the term and then extends the definition with analysis (see page 11) and supporting details.

[1] ... Sports, as games involving human beings, embody almost every aspect of popular entertainment. The idea of conflict is central. Legitimate violence is present in varying degrees in all athletic contests. Ultimately the sporting event as game focuses on the aspect of problem-solving, that pattern we have seen in all the entertaining forms of the popular arts. But unlike the socially oriented problems that form the content of most television programming, the sports game is much more like combat. Instead of value conflicts, generational differences, and human interaction, we have the basic tests of skill and strength. To maneuver the team down the field without losing the ball, to control play so that the opposing team achieves no runs for its hits, to loop the ball into the basket as the last buzzer sounds—these are the conflicts that have thrilled vast numbers of fans in the most traditional ways and that thrill millions more on television.

(For other examples of paragraph development by definition, consult the Sourcebook: selection 11, paragraph 9; selection 3, paragraph 16.)

Comparison and contrast, the demonstration of similarities and differences between two things, is used to clarify the meaning of one or both of them. In the following paragraph the author uses comparison to demonstrate the similarities between the states of consciousness produced by watching television and by taking a drug such as alcohol.

Not unlike drugs or alcohol, the television experience allows the participant to blot out the real world and enter into a pleasurable and passive mental state. The worries and anxieties of reality are as effectively deferred by becoming absorbed in a television program as by going on a "trip" induced by drugs or alcohol. And just as many alcoholics are only inchoately aware of their addiction, feeling that they control their drinking more than they really do ("I can cut it out any time I want—I just like to have three or four drinks before dinner"), people similarly overestimate their control over television watching. Even as they put off other activities to spend hour after hour watching television, they feel they could easily resume living in a different, less passive style. But somehow or other while the television set is present in their homes, the click doesn't sound. With television pleasures available, those other experiences seem less attractive, more difficult somehow.[4]

The subject of the following paragraph from selection 5 in the Sourcebook, as Gerald Lesser states in his topic sentence, is the

---

[4]Marie Winn, *The Plug-In Drug* (New York: Viking Press, 1977), p. 21.

contrast, or difference, between traditional teaching and educational television.

[7] Television differs from traditional teaching in some major ways. Traditional teaching depends primarily upon oral language; television combines the visual as well as auditory means. Television moves, in contrast to the more static techniques in schools and classrooms. Traditional teaching tries to control the level and pace of the materials presented to children, giving them what we believe they need, organized and sequenced into progressive steps, followed by appropriate reinforcements. Television does not meet these standard criteria, usually being more helter-skelter and richer in surplus meanings. Some children learn very well from traditional techniques; others need an alternative like television.

(For other examples of paragraph development by comparison and contrast, consult the Sourcebook: selection 1, paragraph 11; selection 4, paragraphs 10 and 11; selection 9, paragraph 13.)

Analysis, another method of paragraph development, is the examination of a subject through dividing it into its parts (division) or grouping the parts into categories (classification) for the purpose of understanding the whole. In the following excerpt from selection 8 the Sourcebook, Les Brown analyzes the success of television comedian Flip Wilson by dividing his act into its component parts.

[6] Why did Wilson catch on, and not [Don] Knotts and [Tim] Conway? First, because he had never been a second banana and could conduct a show of his own without seeming out of character. Second, because his source of humor was not white society but black, and in that sense it *was* original for television, other Negroes in the medium having had to pretend the races had a common culture. Third, he was a one-man repertory company, having developed two characters outside his own stand-up comedy identity, the Reverend Leroy of the Church of What's Happening Now and the Harlem chatterbox Geraldine Jones, both satirical types and so distinctly Negro they had no credible co-ordinates in white society. Fourth, his comedy was not an ethnic argument; rather than sentimentalizing Negro-American culture it seemed to mock it. And fifth, it did mock it.

(For other examples of paragraph development by analysis, consult the Sourcebook: selection 8, paragraph 7; selection 3, paragraph 25.)

EXERCISE 1.1

(1) Number each paragraph in your essay. (2) In the left-hand columns following, write the numbers of the paragraphs that make up the body of your essay. (3) In the center column, write the topic sentence for each of the body paragraphs. If any of your

topic sentences is implied rather than stated, write the implied topic sentence. (4) In the right-hand column indicate the method of development you used: supporting details, illustration, definition, comparison and contrast, or analysis. If you combined these methods in any paragraph, write down all the methods you used. You may wish to ask your instructor to guide you in completing this exercise.

Body Paragraph Number	Topic Sentence	Method(s) of Development
_____	_____	_____
	_____	_____
	_____	
	_____	
	_____	
_____	_____	_____
	_____	_____
	_____	
	_____	
	_____	
_____	_____	_____
	_____	_____
	_____	
	_____	
_____	_____	_____
	_____	_____

_____

_____

_____

_____ _____ _____

_____ _____

_____

_____

_____ _____ _____

_____ _____

_____

_____

_____

In reviewing this exercise you should consider whether or not you have overused one method of development. If so, you will want to think about varying the methods of paragraph development in your research paper. Also, you should examine each paragraph to be sure that it supports and develops the topic sentence. Repetition of the same idea does not constitute adequate development of a paragraph.

The Conclusion

The conclusion ties everything in the essay together, often by summing up the ideas that have been presented. The writer sometimes reinforces the controlling idea by stating it again in different words or suggests an appropriate attitude the reader might adopt. The following conclusion to a book chapter states the significance of the information presented in the chapter.

In the end, cable must grow as conventional television has grown: on the basis of its own accomplishments. As it takes on an identity of its own, the current debate over distant signals and the passion it arouses, as well as the disputes concerning the rights over local broadcast signals, will come to appear insignificant stages in the growth of a total television system. The recommendations made here for the period of transition are intended primarily to be as equitable as possible to all the parties concerned during the difficult period when that total system is gradually taking shape.[5]

Now consider your own essay.

yes no

Does my essay have a conclusion? ☐ ☐

Unity and Coherence

An essay should have *unity;* that is, every sentence and paragraph in the essay should contribute to the development and support of the controlling idea. If you are reading an essay about movie directors who began their careers in television, you would be surprised to find a paragraph on movie stars who disliked acting for television programs. Such a paragraph would destroy the unity of the essay.

In addition, an essay should have *coherence,* which means that the essay offers an orderly and logical arrangement of ideas. The reader can rightfully expect a discussion of the history of variety shows on television to proceed in *chronological* order. If, for example, the writer, in the middle of a discussion of variety shows in the 1960's, suddenly and illogically discusses a 1940's program, he destroys the coherence of the essay.

yes no

Does my essay have unity? ☐ ☐

yes no

Does my essay have coherence? ☐ ☐

Look back over all of your responses in this review of your essay. You may find that you need assistance from your instructor or study and practice on particular aspects of essay-writing. As

[5]The Sloan Commission on Cable Communications, *On the Cable: The Television of Abundance* (New York: McGraw-Hill, 1971), p. 62.

you read the Sourcebook, you can learn writing techniques by noticing the ways professional writers develop their ideas. Try to analyze the structure, mode of communication, method of paragraph development, and point of view of the selections you read.

Doing Research

Now that you have compared the writing skills you have with those you will need for the research paper, you are ready to measure the research skills you have against those you will need. Although you may not have undertaken formal research before, you probably do informal research all the time.

INFORMAL RESEARCH

If you wish to find out how your favorite baseball player is hitting this season, you will turn to the sports page of the newspaper. If you are undecided about what to add to your fall wardrobe, you might thumb through the fashion section of a magazine or newspaper. This kind of searching for information is informal research. Informal research can be even more purposeful. In a discussion, if an issue is in dispute, you might consult a reference work, such as a dictionary or an encyclopedia, to settle the disagreement.

FORMAL RESEARCH

Although informal research is a first step toward formal research, it differs significantly from formal research because of its smaller scope. The goal of informal research is usually to find one piece of information; the goal of formal research is to attain a thorough understanding of a subject. Because achieving this goal involves reading, comprehending, and evaluating a number of sources with different approaches and attitudes, formal research requires a more open mind. Also, the process of formal research can be much lengthier because it involves careful reading, analysis, and extensive recording of information in note-taking. You probably will discard some of the information you find as you refine the focus of your paper in the course of your work; but such modifications indicate that you are conducting your research with an open mind.

Whereas informal research relies on chance encounters of sources or may stop with consultation of one source, formal research requires an organized, systematic search for the existing information on a subject. Chapter 3 presents the skills necessary to conduct this kind of research in a library. (The library can extend the range of sources for this research paper and is essential for other research papers you may undertake.) Formal research also requires careful analysis and critical evaluation of many sources with different approaches and attitudes toward the same subject.

Formal research also requires careful *documentation,* the citing of the source of information or of evidence you use. When you write a research paper, you effectively say to your reader, "Let me show you what I think and how I have used other people's ideas to arrive at my position." To be able to demonstrate what went into your thinking, you must be scrupulously careful to document by crediting every source of your ideas, whether you use the exact words of the sources or put their ideas into your own words. To ensure that you will be able to give such credit in the final draft, you will have to follow carefully the procedures for gathering and organizing this information at each stage of the process of writing the paper. These are presented in Chapters 2, 4, and 5.

The formal research project on which you are embarking requires *secondary research,* the use of works or studies by others on your subject. You will not be asked to do *primary research,* direct or personal study of the subject, nor should you attempt to do it. At this stage you should be forming your ideas from the studies of those more expert in the field than you are. You may be tempted, for example, to do primary research by watching several detective shows and analyzing their content or by conducting a survey of student opinion about detective shows rather than reading what others have said or written about them. If primary research is to have value, however, the researcher must be thoroughly acquainted with all the secondary material on the subject and the techniques necessary for the particular type of research. A knowledge of statistics would be a prerequisite for meaningful survey-taking, for example. Thus, while you may wish to include a few of your own observations about television, you should rely on secondary sources in formulating and supporting your controlling idea.

THREE TYPES OF RESEARCH PAPERS

After conducting your formal research, you might write one of the three types of research papers: a report, a thesis, or a proposal. The type you choose may depend on the nature of your subject and the outcome of your research, or your instructor may decide with you which of the three you will write.

The Report

The report involves gathering as much information as possible about the subject. *The purpose of the report is to present a thorough discussion of all aspects of a subject.* A report might explain all the current developments in cable television, for example.

The Thesis

The thesis involves investigating and understanding the subject and presenting a thorough explanation of it, but it goes one step further. The thesis judges, or evaluates, the information gathered. *The purpose of the thesis is to come to a conclusion about the subject.* In a thesis, a writer, having studied cable television, might conclude that cable television, properly developed, could offer the public access to broadcast channels and allow greater diversity in programming than currently exists.

The Proposal

The proposal explains the subject as the report does, comes to a conclusion as the thesis does, but it takes the additional step of advocating a position or course of action. *The purpose of the proposal is to convince the reader to adopt a particular position.* The following excerpt from an article by a former federal communications commissioner is an example of a proposal on the subject of cable television.

Cable television offers greater diversity among commercial television programs—at the moment, mostly movies, sports, and reruns—but it can also offer another advantage: public access. The FCC has indicated that cable systems should be encouraged and perhaps ultimately required to offer channels for lease to any person willing to pay the going rate. In the *Red Lion* case last year, the Supreme Court upheld the FCC's fairness doctrine and, noting the monopolistic position most broadcasters hold, suggested that "free speech" rights belong principally to the audience and those who wish to use the station, not the station owner. This concept—which might raise administrative problems for single stations—is easily adaptable to cable television.

If someone wants to place a show on a single over-the-air broadcast station, some other (generally more profitable) program must be cancelled. A cable system, by contrast, can theoretically carry an unlimited number of programs at the same time. We therefore have the opportunity to require cable systems to carry whatever programs are offered on a leased-channel basis (sustained either by advertising or by subscription fee). Time might even be made available free to organizations, young filmmakers and others who could not afford the leasing fee and do not advertise or profit from their programming. Now is the time to guarantee such rights for your community. City councils all across the nation are in the process of drafting the terms for cable television franchises. If your community is at present considering a cable television ordinance, it is your opportunity to work for free and common-carrier "citizens' access" to the cables that will one day connect your home with the rest of the world.[6]

Your instructor will specify which of these types of research papers he or she wishes you to write, or whether you are to make the choice yourself.

Defining the Research Paper

You should now be able to define the research paper. You might wish to review the preceding sections on mode of communication, point of view, structure, and research before formulating your definition.

My definition of the research paper:

_____

_____

_____

_____

Now compare your definition of the research paper with this one:

$$(1) \quad (2) \quad\quad\quad (3)$$
A research paper is an *expository essay* with an *objective point of*
$$(4) \quad\quad\quad (5)$$
view in which the writer presents *documented information* gained

[6]Nicholas Johnson, "What Do We Do about Television?" *Saturday Review,* 53 (July 11, 1970), 27. © Saturday Review, 1970. All rights reserved.

$$(6) \qquad\qquad\qquad\qquad (7)$$
from *formal research* for the purpose of *understanding a subject,*
$$(8)$$
forming a conclusion about a topic, or *convincing the reader to*
$$(9)$$
adopt a particular position.

Your definition may not coincide exactly with this one, but that isn't important. What is important is that you understand the key elements of the definition. Check your definition to see how many of the nine concepts numbered in the preceding definition you have included.

Choosing a Subject

One way to find a subject for your research is to formulate some questions you would like to answer. Since you probably wrote your essay on an aspect of television that interests you, you might begin the process there. You can begin your formulation of questions by turning your controlling idea and each of your topic sentences into questions by using one of the words which form questions: *who, why, what, where, when,* or *how.* If, for example, one of your topic sentences were "Television can be very educational for children," you might produce the following questions from it: "How does television educate young children?" "Which television programs are the most educational?" "Who has worked on television programs for children?" Then other related questions would begin to occur to you: "Have any studies been done on the subject?" "Do children learn negative as well as positive things from television?" One of the questions you derive from your own essay may prove so interesting that you will want to try to answer it by doing research.

In addition, as you read through the excerpts from books and articles on television included in this chapter, perhaps you became interested in another aspect of the subject, one which you did not deal with in your essay. You may thus have some new ideas about television, which you can turn into questions.

EXERCISE 1.2

A. Use the topic sentences or the controlling idea in your essay to formulate five questions you *might* be able to answer by doing research.

1. _____

   _____

2. _____

   _____

3. _____

   _____

4. _____

   _____

5. _____

   _____

B. Before you decide on a question to guide your research, you should do some preparatory reading to determine whether secondary sources are available on your subject. Since you will be using the Sourcebook for part or all of the research for this project, you should read over the table of contents for Part Two, the Sourcebook, and then look over all of the articles there quickly just to get an idea of the nature of the material. This early reading will prevent you from formulating a preliminary controlling question on which you may not find secondary sources.

After scanning the contents of the Sourcebook, formulate two questions regarding any aspect of the subject of television on which you might like to do research.

1. _____

   _____

2. _____

   _____

Assignment

Read carefully the first four articles in the Sourcebook. The material in these selections will serve as the basis for the exercises in this chapter and Chapter 2. Also, they will give you ideas about possible subjects for research.

Write down three questions you think can be answered by using the first four articles in the Sourcebook.

1. _____

_____

2. _____

_____

3. _____

_____

THE PURPOSE AND NATURE
OF THE CONTROLLING QUESTION

The preliminary controlling question gives direction to your reading and note-taking, helping you to avoid unnecessary work in the limited time you have to complete your assignment. At the same time, you should be prepared to change your question should the evidence you find in your research require it. In the course of your research you will develop an answer to your controlling *question*. That answer will be the controlling *idea* for your research paper.

The nature of the preliminary controlling question will differ depending on the type of research paper you plan to write—a report, a thesis, or a proposal. In fact, the controlling question often determines the type of research paper that will result from answering it.

If you were to ask the question "What kind of plots do situation comedies have?" your question would most likely lead to a report explaining or describing these plots. If you were to begin with the question "Are the characters in situation comedies generally stereotypes?" and then to find that they are, you might write a thesis presenting information concerning stereotypes in situation comedies and a conclusion suggesting reasons they dominate that type of program. If you were to ask "What actions can be taken to eliminate ethnic stereotypes in situation comedies?" your question would probably lead to a proposal advocating a particular course of action.

THE SCOPE OF THE CONTROLLING QUESTION

A controlling question must have the appropriate scope. In other words, the controlling question must be one for which you have the necessary expertise and for which materials are available. Questions that are too vague or broad, too narrow, too localized or provincial, biased, or too specialized or technical do not lead to a controlling idea that can be developed.

A question that is too vague or broad will not sufficiently limit your possibilities. The question "Has television affected us?" is both vague and broad. We don't know who the "us" are. If *us* refers to all viewers of television, the subject is too vast to say anything significant about in one paper. Narrowing the subject to a smaller group, such as children, would give clearer direction to the research. It would be even more productive to consider a particular aspect of television in relation to children—such as the nature of the medium or its value to advertisers. The idea "affected" should be qualified or narrowed to indicate a specific effect, such as psychological, social, or educational.

A question that is too narrow may lead to a paper of limited interest and significance. In addition you may not find sufficient information to develop a paper. The problem of a narrow question may be solved by expanding its scope. The question "What role models exist for American Indians on televised situation comedies?" might be extended to "What role models will children from minority groups find in dramatic series on television?"

A question that is too localized or provincial cannot be answered with secondary research. "What are the television viewing habits of students at Brookside College?" would be a fine topic for primary research, but it would not be a good topic for the secondary research required for a college research paper, since it is unlikely that sufficient material on the subject exists.

A question that is biased—that is, one containing a conclusion formulated before you have begun your research—eliminates the possibility of doing an objective study if the unstated opinion on which the question is based is not also explored. The question "Why are women presented as stereotypes in television advertising?" assumes that women actually are stereotyped. Until that assumption is explored and demonstrated to be true, the question will prohibit open-minded research.

A question that is too specialized or technical may demand knowledge you cannot acquire in the time you have for your project. Unless you have some background in physiology, psychology, and statistical sampling methods, you would want to reject the question "What has research determined about the effects of television viewing on the listening patterns of preschool children?" You would probably find material on this subject too difficult.

The two exercises below will help you to formulate a preliminary controlling question of the appropriate nature and scope.

EXERCISE 1.3

The selections in the Sourcebook are research papers of various types. Complete the following assignments for selections 2, 3, and 4 in the Sourcebook: (1) determine the type of research paper (report, thesis, or proposal); (2) find the controlling idea for the selection; (3) formulate a possible controlling question for which the controlling idea is an answer.

As a model for your work, these tasks have been performed on selection 1, the Boorstin reading.

A. Selection 1, pages 201–07

1. Type of research paper: Thesis (Because the author comes to a conclusion about the material.)
2. Controlling idea: "It [television] extended simultaneous experience, created anonymous audiences even vaster and more universal than those of radio, and incidentally created a new segregation." (Stated in paragraph 3.)
3. Possible controlling question: How has television transformed the social and community life of Americans?

B. Selection 2, pages 209–14

1. Type of research paper:

_____

_____

_____

2. Controlling idea:

_____

_____

_____

3. Possible controlling question:

_____

_____

_____

C. Selection 3, pages 215–24

1. Type of research paper:

_____

_____

_____

2. Controlling idea:

_____

_____

_____

3. Possible controlling question:

_____

_____

_____

D. Selection 4, pages 226–32

1. Type of research paper:

_____

_____

_____

2. Controlling idea:

_____

_____

_____

3. Possible controlling question:

_____

_____

_____

EXERCISE 1.4

Indicate whether you consider the following controlling questions
appropriate, too vague or broad, too narrow, too localized or provincial, biased, or too technical or specialized. If you decide a
question is appropriate, add whether the resulting paper would be
a report, thesis, or proposal. Be prepared to defend your position,
since more than one response is possible in some instances.

1. What image of Mexican-Americans emerges on television?

_____

2. How has television affected American taste in sports?

_____

Choosing a Subject   25

3. Does television cause violent behavior?

_____

4. What attitude is conveyed about civil liberties on television police dramas?

_____

5. Does the editing process distort television news?

_____

6. Should the United States follow the example of Great Britain with regard to ownership of television channels?

_____

7. What is the future of cable television?

_____

8. Should the television industry be operated for profit?

_____

9. Why is Carol Burnett funny?

_____

10. What is the relationship between mass culture, tastes of minorities, and television?

_____

11. What factors influence decisions about programming?

_____

12. Is American television as advanced technically as European television?

_____

13. Why do so many British programs appear on American public television?

_____

14. What is educational television?

_____

15. What are the differences between the media of film, television, and videotape?

_____

16. How are television ratings used?

_____

17. How can the technology of television be utilized in health-care services?

_____

18. What effect has television had on the careers of comedians?

_____

19. What effect does heavy television viewing have on children?

_____

20. What are the implications of the phrase "the medium is the message"?

_____

Your Preliminary Controlling Question

You are ready to formulate your preliminary controlling question
if you can answer Yes to the following questions.

Did my preliminary reading indicate that there is
enough secondary material available on my chosen
subject for a research paper? (You may wish to check
with your instructor.)

yes   no
☐ ☐

Does my question properly limit the scope of my research, so that the subject is not too broad or vague, too
narrow, too localized or provincial, too biased, too technical or specialized?

yes   no
☐ ☐

My preliminary controlling question:

_____

_____

_____

_____

_____

Indicate whether the question should lead to a report, thesis, or
proposal.

_____

To be completed when you begin Chapter 4:

yes   no

Did your research lead to modifications in your preliminary controlling question?

☐ ☐

State the controlling idea to be used for the outline and the rough
draft of your paper.

_____

_____

_____

To be completed when you reach Chapter 5:

State the controlling idea for the final draft of your paper.

_____

_____

_____

_____

2
Deciding which material to use

How shall I record information?

After you have formulated your preliminary controlling question, you are ready to begin your research. This chapter discusses three processes that are essential in doing research: preparing a working bibliography, reading critically, and recording information accurately.

Preparing a Working Bibliography

In your research paper you will have to demonstrate the foundations and reasons for your thinking, being scrupulously careful to distinguish between your ideas and those you have found through research. You will have to credit the sources of ideas you find whether you use the exact words of the sources or put their ideas into your own words. Not giving this credit, either by intentionally or unintentionally allowing your reader to think another person's idea is your own, is a kind of theft called *plagiarism*.

To avoid plagiarism you will have to keep a careful record of the sources you have read and the ideas you have found in them. This process begins with the development of a *working bibliography,* an alphabetical list of sources you plan to look over or read. From the working bibliography you will eventually compile your *final bibliography,* an alphabetical list of those works you actually consulted or used. (See pages 137–38 for a description of the types of bibliographies.)

THE EQUIPMENT

To prepare a working bibliography you will need 4 × 6 inch index cards and a manila envelope to carry them in. Some researchers use 3 × 5 inch cards; but those are so small that they may prevent you from recording all the necessary information. You can also use the 4 × 6 inch cards for taking notes.

You may wonder why a notebook or slips of paper would not suffice. The reason is that cards provide greater flexibility and greater durability. Developing a bibliography is a continuing process. You may wish to add to your list of sources even while you are writing the paper. If several sources were already entered on a page, you would destroy the alphabetical order with each new addition, and then you would have to waste time hunting for a source. Also, cards are sturdier and less likely to be misplaced or destroyed than slips of paper.

BASIC BIBLIOGRAPHY FORMS

The two types of sources you will work with most often are *books* and *articles in periodicals* (journals or magazines published at intervals). The basic bibliography forms for these sources are illustrated here. Variations of these forms are used when additional information, such as the name of a co-author or editor, is

Book: Single Author, Basic Form

needed or when the source is other than a book or article, such as a television program. (The form for articles represents a streamlined version of the MLA format; it may be used for articles in most journals and magazines regardless of differences in the frequency of their publication or systems of pagination. Appendix A is a listing of the bibliography forms for the sources you are likely to encounter in your research. See points 20 and 21 for a complete discussion of the forms for articles.)

Books

Author entry	Last name first (for alphabetization); followed by a period.
Title entry	Includes any subtitle given on the title page; is underlined and followed by a period.
Facts-of-publication entry	Includes city of publication followed by a colon, name of the publishing company (can be shortened provided the name remains clear) followed by a comma, and the date of publication or copyright followed by a period.
Notes to yourself	Use brackets for any additional information, such as the name of the library and the book's call number or a short description of the book.

Articles in Periodicals

Author entry	Last name first (for alphabetization); followed by a period.

Author entry — Title entry — Facts-of-publication entry —
Baldwin, James. "Black man in America." WFMT Perspectives, 10 (Dec. 1961), 25-30.

Articles in Periodicals: Basic Form

Title entry	Title and any subtitles; followed by a period and enclosed in quotation marks.
Facts-of-publication entry	Name of periodical underlined and followed by a comma; volume number in arabic numerals; date—day, month (abbreviated) or season, and year—in parentheses, followed by a comma; inclusive page numbers without abbreviation for *page(s)*, followed by a period.

THE SYSTEMS

Bibliography cards should contain all the information you need to locate sources throughout the process of your research project. Later, you will transfer information from your bibliography cards to entries on your bibliography page to give your readers essential facts about the sources of your words and ideas, thus allowing them to locate your sources for themselves. Fortunately, each writer does not have to devise a system for condensing and presenting this information. Groups doing research in various disciplines have developed systems for the rest of us in the form of *style sheets*. In addition to bibliographical forms, style sheets cover such matters as note forms and general principles of style and format.

This textbook follows the style sheet of the Modern Language Association of America, *The MLA Handbook*. The systems of other disciplines in the humanities and social sciences resemble that of the MLA, but there are variations among them. (See, for example, the note pages of the selections 5, 10, 12, and 14 in the Sourcebook.) Systems used in the physical and biological sciences sometimes differ greatly from those used in the humanities. (See Appendix B for a discussion of documentation in the sciences.) Your instructor or school may have specific requirements. Whenever you write a research paper, you should find out which style sheet is preferred.

COMPLETENESS AND ACCURACY

You should make a bibliography card for every possible source of information on your subject: books, journal and magazine articles, newspaper articles, letters, records, films, television programs, lectures, interviews, and videotapes. You usually begin to build a bibliography at the card catalog and in the reference room of the library. In the case of this research paper, you have a short bibliography from the Sourcebook; but if you plan to extend your bibliography beyond the material in the Sourcebook, you will want to read Chapter 3, which discusses the use of the library.

Try to take down all the information necessary to avoid having to backtrack. Leaving out a date or page number may mean an extra trip to the library. When you are preparing bibliography cards, you should have a copy of the appropriate style sheet with you to consult for the proper forms. You are not expected to memorize these forms. What a researcher must know, however, is where to find them. Your style sheet for this paper is contained in Appendix A.

EXERCISE 2.1

Use the bibliography forms in Appendix A and the two basic forms given earlier to complete these exercises.

A. Prepare a bibliography card for each of the selections in the Sourcebook. Use the original facts of publication given on the first page of each selection and the original pagination, which is indicated within the selection box. That is, assume that you are working with the selections in their original published form rather than as a part of the Sourcebook. For example, your card for selection 9 would read as illustrated on page 35. This entry differs from the basic book form in that it has three authors. To determine the correct form you would turn to the bibliography forms in Appendix A and look up the section on books with three authors. You will also find other variations of the two basic forms in Appendix A.

B. Prepare a bibliography card for information received as a result of each of the following experiences.

1. After sending a letter asking questions about women in television journalism to Barbara Walters, a newscaster at American Broadcasting Company, you receive a letter from her dated August 1, 1978.
2. You listen to a record by a famous news correspondent, Edward R. Murrow, made in 1957 for Columbia Recording Company and entitled *Year of Decision: 1943* with the number CPS-3872.
3. You read a summary of a five-volume study published by the Government Printing Office for the Surgeon General, United

Minow, Newton N., John Bartlow Martin, and Lee M. Mitchell. *Presidential Television*. New York: Basic Books, 1973.

A Bibliography Card for Selection 9

States Public Health Office, in 1972 in Washington, D.C., and called *Television and Growing Up: The Impact of Televised Violence.*

4. You watch a six-part series called "Scenes from a Marriage," directed by Ingmar Bergman for Swedish television in 1973. You watch it on an American Public Broadcasting station in the week of January 16, 1978. Liv Ullmann played the starring role.

5. You watch a documentary called "Fireman," which appeared as a segment of "Who's Who" on February 8, 1977, on the Columbia Broadcasting System. Howard Milkin produced it and Dan Rather narrated it.

Reading Critically

Once you have developed a working bibliography, you can begin to examine the sources you have listed in it to choose those which will be helpful to you in answering your preliminary controlling question. To select useful sources, you have to read critically, which means recognizing sources that are appropriate and well-reasoned and avoiding those that are inappropriate or flawed by faulty reasoning.

INITIAL APPRAISAL

The process of evaluating a source begins even before you read the text with an appraisal of the date of publication, the author's qualifications, and the level of the material.

Date of Publication

In certain fields developments occur so quickly that information becomes obsolete. In the case of some subjects, such as the plays of

Shakespeare, previous knowledge may not necessarily be out of date. In areas of rapid growth or change, however, such as medicine, science, technology, education, and the social sciences, you will want to be sure that your material represents current knowledge and thinking. Television is one of these rapidly developing fields. You would not, for example, use a 1950's study of television-viewing habits in a report today unless you were doing a study of the 1950's or using the information for a comparison and contrast. Viewing habits have changed so markedly that a study done almost thirty years ago would tell you little or nothing about the present.

Author

When you are relatively inexperienced in a field, it is wise to begin research by consulting the work of an expert. You can discover whether a writer is an authority in an area in several ways. A short biographical sketch of the author is often included at the beginning or end of a selection along with a list of the author's other works. You can consult *Who's Who in America* or a similar reference work for such information. (See Chapter 3 for a discussion of biographical reference works.) The work of a person respected in a field is often cited by others in their texts and bibliographies, and, therefore, you should note the names you encounter. In fact, reading the bibliographies and notes of your sources is a good way to find valuable additions to your working bibliography.

In examining the qualifications of an author, you may find that he or she has expressed opinions on a subject outside of his or her recognized area of expertise. If so, you might give less credence to these views than to those of an expert or to those the author expresses *within* his or her area of expertise. It may be interesting, for example, to learn the opinions of a successful novelist about the effects of television on the reading habits of Americans. Unless the novelist has done some serious study of the subject, however, his or her opinion, although possibly interesting, is not necessarily expert.

You also want to know if the author's attitude toward the subject in question might be affected by a personal relationship to the subject. The writer may have a bias for or against certain ideas because of a political ideology, personal experience, or religious beliefs, to name only a few possible reasons for bias. A writer may also have a stake or investment called a vested interest, in presenting ideas in a certain light that might preclude objectivity.

The producer of a television program might stand to benefit financially from a favorable assessment of that program; thus, his comments should be considered with his personal interest in mind. You do not have to avoid materials by authors with a bias or a vested interest, but you should learn to recognize the writer's point of view.

Consider the possible differences in expertise, bias, and vested interest you might find in the writing or statements of the following persons: Fred Friendly, an ex-president of the news division at CBS, who was fired after a disagreement with his superiors about the amount of coverage the network could afford to give to the Vietnam War; Frank Stanton, president of CBS; and Edward J. Epstein, a Harvard graduate student and free-lance writer, who never worked for CBS.

EXERCISE 2.2

A. Answer the following questions about selection 2, by Thomas Elmendorf, in the Sourcebook.

1. How does the author's mention of the resolution by the American Medical Association function in paragraphs 24, 25, and 26?

_____

_____

_____

2. Does Elmendorf express opinions on a subject outside his area of expertise? Explain your answer.

_____

_____

_____

_____

B. Read the paragraph on the credentials and qualifications (at the beginning of each selection) of each of the authors named below.

Determine (a) the expertise of the author and (b) any possible reason for bias. (c) Read the articles and determine the authors' perspectives on their subjects. Do you find any bias? If so, where?

1. Boorstin, selection 1

   a. _____

   _____

   b. _____

   _____

   c. _____

   _____

2. Epstein, selection 3

   a. _____

   _____

   b. _____

   _____

   c. _____

   _____

3. Gerbner and Gross, selection 4

   a. _____

   _____

   b. _____

   _____

c. _____

_____

Level of the Material

Before you begin a careful reading, you should read quickly, or scan, the material to determine whether the level of the discussion and writing is appropriate. You might begin by asking yourself what kind of audience the writer is addressing. You may use sources directed toward both professional and lay, or nonprofessional, readers. As the variety of styles and levels of the selections in the Sourcebook indicates, you can use a wide range of materials. You will probably want to avoid using highly specialized or very low-level sources, however. In a professional journal, for example, you may find writing directed to a specific professional audience. If the vocabulary is technical, the work is probably not intended for the lay person or beginning scholar and is probably inappropriate for your research. In other magazines, you may find material that is sensational, based on hearsay and gossip rather than on fact or substantiated opinion. Articles in magazines such as *The National Enquirer* and *TV Star Parade* often fall into this category and are probably inappropriate for your research.

THE DIFFERENCE BETWEEN FACTS AND OPINIONS

When you have found material that is timely, authoritative, and written at the appropriate level, you can begin an analysis of its content to determine what use, if any, you wish to make of it in developing and writing your research paper. In your reading you will encounter two kinds of statements: facts and opinions. All reasoning is based on facts or opinions or some combination of them; it is necessary to be able to distinguish between the two.

A *fact* is a statement that can be verified. It has happened or is true. It is possible to find out whether the statement is correct by consulting the appropriate source or by direct observation. If the statement is found to be incorrect or false, it is not a fact. Consider, for example, the following statement: "Three earth tremors occurred this morning in Omegaville." By consulting a newspaper or a geological survey station, you could ascertain the truth or falsity of this statement. If the statement proved to be false—if you were to find that only two earth tremors occurred in

Omegaville or that they happened yesterday rather than today—this statement would not be true and therefore not a fact.

An *opinion* is a conclusion, a judgment, or an inference based on facts and/or opinions. No matter how sound an opinion may be, it cannot be verified or proven to be correct. "Omegaville is a dangerous place" is an opinion. Even if there is no question in your mind that Omegaville is dangerous because of the frequent occurrence of earthquakes, this statement is an opinion because it cannot be verified.

A *conclusion* is an opinion that involves interpretation of facts or opinions. "Because Omegaville has had several earthquakes in the last ten years, the construction of buildings over ten stories should be banned there" is a conclusion based on facts about the incidence of earthquakes in Omegaville.

A *judgment* is an opinion that expresses approval or disapproval. "The state commission's recommendation that the construction of skyscrapers in Omegaville be continued is irresponsible" is a statement that, however reasonable, is an opinion.

An *inference* is an opinion that makes a statement about the unknown based on the known. "Measurement of stress along the fault indicates that an earthquake is likely to occur soon in Omegaville to relieve the pressure" is a prediction, based on known behavior of earthquakes, about the future, which is unknown. The statement is therefore an opinion.

Many statements involve combinations of fact and opinion, and you will have to determine which portion of a statement is fact and which is opinion. In some cases, the whole of a statement may be an opinion even though it contains some facts: "Since two previous earthquakes in Omegaville were preceded by earth tremors, the area should be evacuated immediately." The statement about the two previous earthquakes might well be a fact, but the conclusion about evacuation derived from the fact makes the entire statement an opinion.

On the other hand, the whole of a statement may be a fact even though it contains some opinions: "One resident, Mr. Kelley Jones, said that there is no reason to panic and that everyone should stay put." That Kelley Jones did or did not make the statement expressing his opinion can be verified. If he did, the entire statement is a fact.

EXERCISE 2.3

The following exercise tests your ability to distinguish between facts and opinions. All of these sentences are taken from articles in the Sourcebook and represent the kinds of statements you will encounter in your research. Fill in the blank beside each sentence with the word *fact* or the word *opinion*. If you decide that the statement is an opinion, indicate whether it is a conclusion, judgment, or inference by adding *c, j,* or *i* after the word *opinion*.

_____ 1. "The age group most involved, with the greatest number of both victims and arrests, is 20 to 24." (Elmendorf, selection 2)

_____ 2. "We feel that television dramatically demonstrates the power of authority in our society, and the risks involved in breaking society's rules." (Gerbner and Gross, selection 4)

_____ 3. "More than half of all characters on prime-time TV are involved in some violence, about one-tenth in killing." (Gerbner and Gross, selection 4)

_____ 4. "The report said, 'People who watch a lot of TV see the real world as more dangerous and frightening than those who watch very little. Heavy viewers are less trustful of their fellow citizens.' " (Gerbner and Gross, selection 4)

_____ 5. "By enabling him to be anywhere instantly, by filling his present moment with experiences engrossing and overwhelming, television dulled the American's sense of his past, and even somehow separated him from the longer past." (Boorstin, selection 1)

_____ 6. "But art and ideas come out of the passion and torment of experience; it is impossible to have a real relationship to the first, if one's aim is to be protected from the second." (Baldwin, selection 16)

_____ 7. "In World War II the British, Americans, Canadians, and others made beachheads at Normandy in 1944 and pressed eastward, toward Berlin." (Maloney, selection 9)

_____ 8. "Increasingly television will begin to enter the daily activity patterns of our seasonal and life-cycle existence." (Kalba, selection 12)

_____ 9. "Advertisers in the children's television market are heavily concentrated in such products as cereals, candies, snack foods, toys, and until recently, vitamins." (Melody, selection 13)

_____ 10. "Television and film, as well as radio, tapes, and records, have contributed to a radical transformation in our perception of the world—from a visual, print base to an auditory base." (Schwartz, selection 17)

Reasoning from Facts

In your reading you will encounter combinations of facts and opinions. When a writer uses facts as the basis of his or her opinions, the researcher has to evaluate the soundness of the relationship between the facts and the conclusion, judgment, or inference based on them. There are different kinds of facts as well as different methods of reasoning with them, and you should be familiar with proper—and improper—ways of reasoning from facts.

Statistics You will often encounter facts in the form of statistics or numerical data in your research. Because statistics are often problematic for the layperson, you should be very cautious about them. The issues concerning statistics discussed here arise in connection with selections in the Sourcebook.

Any graphs or tables in the text should be explained in prose form; you should be wary of unexplained graphs and tables. Also, when an author refers to the results of a study, the statistical data from the study should be included. If a study was inconclusive, the author should inform the reader that the facts uncovered were insufficient evidence from which to draw a conclusion.

Precise use of statistics also requires that they be presented in the *context* of the facts surrounding them. The information that approximately 3 million television sets were tuned to a particular program is meaningless unless you know its context: the number of people estimated to be tuned in to other channels at the same time, the usual audience for similar programming at the same hour and season, and other surrounding facts. Only in relation to its context does the statistic become meaningful.

Variables are factors, in addition to the factor under study, that may affect the result of the study if they are not controlled or removed. In a study attempting to determine the effect of television on declining attendance at movie houses, variables might include increased crime in theater districts, a change in the types of movies shown in theaters, and rising admission charges. A reliable study will mention variables and the ways in which the researcher controlled or attempted to control them.

Statistical inference, the drawing of a conclusion about a whole population based on a small sample, is perhaps the most difficult area of statistics for the layperson to understand. This difficulty arises because such calculation involves knowledge and use of statistical tables and because the size of the sample involved, usually less than 5 percent of the whole, seems very small. In fact, it is possible for a statistician to reach a conclusion about the whole based on a sample of less than 1 percent in some cases, but this conclusion is always subject to some uncertainty, which the researcher must acknowledge.

The procedure of statistical inference works this way. First, a sample representative of the whole must be isolated for study. The more heterogeneous or varied the population under scrutiny, the more difficult it is to obtain a representative sample. The most representative sample is a *random sample,* or one in which every member of the population has an equal chance of being included. After the sample is determined to be representative, a statistical table is used to determine the probability that a conclusion made about the sample will be valid for the whole. The larger the sample, no matter how large the whole is, the greater the probability that the statistical inference will be valid for the whole. It is the size of the sample, not its proportion to the whole, which determines degree of reliability. Hence, pollsters can predict with high reliability the outcome of national elections in which 40 million people vote by using a sample of between 2,000 and 5,000.

Take, for example, a study attempting to find out what percentage of television sets in Omegaville are color without examining each set. If the sample consists of 10 sets, the researcher uses the number of color sets in the sample of 10 to predict the percentage of the whole. Given a representative sample, if 7 of the 10 sets are color, the researcher would find in a statistical table that he could predict with a reliability of 95 percent that between 35 and 93 percent of the television sets in Omegaville are color sets. This large degree of uncertainty makes such a statistic almost useless. A sample of 100 sets would be more useful. If 70 of the 100 sets were color, the researcher would find in the tables that he could predict with a reliability of 95 percent that between 60 and 79 percent of the sets in Omegaville were color, regardless of the total number of sets involved. This prediction is accurate enough for many purposes. If a more precise prediction were needed, the size of the sample would have to be increased. While no study can ever predict with absolute certainty, the larger the sample, the more reliable the conclusion drawn in the process of statistical inference.

When you encounter the use of statistical inference in your reading, you should be sure that the researcher has included information about the size of the sample and the degree of reliability of his study.

EXERCISE 2.4

A. Answer the following questions for selection 4, by Gerbner and Gross, in the Sourcebook.

1. Are the statistics presented in their context? If so, describe the context.

_____

_____

2. What attempt was made to obtain an adequate sample and a group to which to compare it?

_____

_____

_____

3. Do the authors explain any difficulties they encountered?

_____

_____

_____

4. What variables were taken into consideration?

_____

_____

_____

5. Does textual explanation accompany tables and graphs?

_____

_____

_____

6. Is the study conclusive? If so, in what ways?

_____

B. Answer the following questions for the selection 2, by El-mendorf, in the Sourcebook.

1. What is the difference between the use of statistics in para-graphs 2 and 3?

2. Is the context given for the statistic about the annual rate of increase in murders between 1960 and 1974 (paragraph 3)? If so, what is it?

3. How do the statistics presented in the first seven paragraphs affect your response to this statement: "We of the medical pro-fession believe that one of the facts behind violence is televised violence" (paragraph 8)?

C. Evaluate the use of statistics in both selections (2 and 4). After taking into consideration the qualifications of the authors and the audience for whom each selection was intended, decide which article has the more careful use of statistics.

_____

_____

_____

D. Check the aspects of the process of statistical inference that Nielsen discusses in selection 7 in the Sourcebook.

_____ context

_____ probability

_____ size of sample as it affects reliability

_____ representative sample

_____ sample under 5 percent of the whole

E. Answer the following questions using selection 8, by Brown, in the Sourcebook.

1. With which of the preceding aspects of Nielsen's procedure of statistical inference does Brown take issue?

_____

_____

_____

2. On what grounds?

_____

_____

_____

Cause and Effect A demonstration that one fact resulted in the occurrence of another is cause-to-effect or effect-to-cause reasoning. Support for the statement "The televising of professional football has brought about changes in the game" would involve effect-to-cause reasoning. After showing that the game had changed, the writer would attempt to show that television was a cause, perhaps by citing facts such as the rearranging of season schedules to coincide with prime viewing hours and changes in the pace of the game to provide for advertising time. Other factors (variables) may have caused changes in the game of football, however, and the researcher must be careful not to attribute the effects of these factors to television. Improvements in equipment, increased professionalism in college athletics, and better training techniques have probably also caused changes in professional football, and these changes may not be linked to television.

Often it is difficult to isolate the precise cause of an effect. Think of all the factors to be considered in answering the question "Does television cause violent behavior?" You can probably think of a number of other possible causes of violent behavior—unemployment, poverty, war, family background—that would have to be considered before a valid conclusion could be reached about the unique effect of television. The researcher should try to examine all available facts and draw conclusions from them about effects and likely or possible causes. You as a reader have to determine whether the conclusions are convincing.

With many kinds of subjects absolute causality (cause established beyond any doubt) cannot be demonstrated because the facts are difficult to obtain. In such cases researchers may use *causal generalization,* a prediction of probable causality by using findings about a small sample to generalize about the larger group of which it is a part. Often statistical inference is used for causal generalization. The 1964 Surgeon General's report on the relationship between lung cancer and cigarette smoking was based on this kind of reasoning. After experiments were conducted on representative samples, the results indicated that it is probable that cigarette smoking can cause cancer and does increase the risk of cancer. Reliable studies of this kind preface the conclusion with phrases such as "in my opinion" and "appear to."

Fictionalized Facts A difficult kind of writing to evaluate is that based on facts derived from solid research but fictionalized to appeal to the imagination. In the process of fictionalizing, that is, adding details or forms usually associated with creative writing, the facts which support the opinions can be obscured. The writer may cast the material into dialogue that sounds accurate but cannot be checked; or the writer may create action sequences that would be irrelevant if the sole purpose of the work were to relate facts in support of the writer's opinion.

The danger of fictionalized facts is that they are often accepted uncritically as correct because they appeal to emotions rather than to reason. They direct the reader away from the issues to actions, speech, physical appearance, or issues often unrelated to the subject but about which the reader is likely to have strong feelings. If the reader is unwary, these feelings interfere with his or her evaluation of the material.

The Selling of the President 1968 by Joe McGinniss uses this fictionalizing technique. The facts about Richard Nixon's use of television in his 1968 campaign for the Presidency are presented in an offhand manner as a part of a narrative, as the following excerpt demonstrates:

It was about this time that the results of the Semantic Differential Test came in. Treleaven and Garment and Shakespeare went into the big meeting room at Fuller and Smith and Ross and watched a tall, thin, frowning man named John Maddox explain what all of it meant.

"The semantic differential is the most sensitive instrument known to modern marketing research," he said. Then he pointed to a big chart on a slide screen on the wall. Running down the chart were twenty-six pairs of adjectives or phrases such as weak–strong, wishy-washy–firm, stuffed shirt–sense of humor, tense–relaxed, stingy–generous, and on like that. . . .

John Maddox explained that he had gone all through the country asking people to evaluate the presidential candidates on the scale of one through seven, and also asking them to evaluate the qualities an ideal President would have. If they thought Humphrey, for instance, was very generous they would give him a seven on the stingy–generous line; if they thought he was not much of either they would give him a three or a four. Maddox had plotted what he called the Ideal President Curve, which was the line connecting the points that represented the average rating in each category as applied to the ideal. Then Maddox plotted curves for Nixon, Humphrey and Wallace. The gaps between the Nixon line and the Ideal line represented the personality traits that Nixon should try to improve. It was considered especially important, Maddox said, that Nixon close the "Personality Gap" between himself and Humphrey.

"It is of substantial significance, we believe," Maddox wrote later in a report, "that the widest gap of all is the 'cold–warm.' "[1]

McGinniss presents facts in dialogue, setting, and physical characteristics and actions of the people involved. Few facts are presented, however. If you use sources like this one, you should be careful not to be swept away by the author's ability to write an enthralling, fast-moving story; you must distinguish between fact and fiction.

EXERCISE 2.5

1. What facts are contained in the preceding excerpt from McGinniss's book that could be used in a research paper?

[1]Joe McGinniss, *The Selling of the President 1968,* (New York: Simon and Schuster, 1969), pp. 77–78.

_____

_____

_____

_____

2. What details about the speaker are given?

_____

_____

_____

3. What effect do these details have on the reader?

_____

_____

_____

4. Do the details affect your perception of the facts? If so, how?

_____

_____

_____

Reasoning from Opinions

While it is true that everyone is entitled to his or her opinion, not all opinions are equally sound. If facts are available, a writer should base conclusions, judgments, and inferences on them. Often you will find subjects on which it is impossible to reason from facts, however. These are subjects beyond proof or on which it is impossible to obtain factual proof at the present time. For example, the answers to the following questions cannot be proven factually now for various reasons: "Who was the first human?" "Is there a God?" "Is sexuality the basis of human motivation?"

Any conclusion about such issues must rest not on facts, but on other opinions. You certainly do not want to reject ideas that are beyond proof; but you should seek to discover all the assumptions—that is, opinions—on which such conclusions are based, and you should then ask yourself whether these assumptions are reasonable.

Assumptions When you encounter conclusions drawn from opinions or assumptions, you should evaluate the conclusions by examining the accuracy of the assumptions on which they are based. If you find assumptions in the reasoning unacceptable, you have to reject any conclusion to which they lead.

Selection 1, by Daniel Boorstin, in the Sourcebook includes both reasoning from facts and reasoning from opinions, as do most source materials you will encounter. Statements such as "Television watching became an addiction comparable only to life itself" and "[Television] left the nation more bewildered than it dared admit" are conclusions based on assumptions about what constitutes addiction and bewilderment. You may choose to accept these assumptions because Boorstin is considered an expert on American life and because many people share his opinions. On the other hand, you may reject his conclusion if you question the assumptions that life is addictive and that our attachments to life and to television are comparable or if you do not feel that "bewildered" is an accurate description of Americans' reaction to television. Reasoning from opinions requires a reader to question each opinion and its underlying assumptions carefully.

Analogy Analogy is a form of comparison that uses an extended simile or an extended metaphor. A simile is a stated comparison ("You are like a ray of sunshine"); a metaphor is an implied comparison ("You are the sunshine of my life"). Both employ a comparison between two things that are basically dissimilar, but that have at least one attribute in common. Human beings and the sun are in different classes, yet may share attributes such as warmth and radiance. Such comparisons are opinions, for they are not verifiable. An analogy usually indicates a number of similarities between two basically different things. These similarities may be either stated or implied, and often the reader must discover those not stated.

Analogy is effectively used to clarify a new or difficult concept by comparing it to something easier to understand or more familiar to the reader. In the following paragraph the author uses an analogy to explain the concept of mass culture.

Mass culture is fabricated by technicians and profit-seeking administrators who find that the mass status of the people requires less trouble and less imagination, and yields higher return on investment. The analogy to industrial production is obvious: The bigger the volume and the fewer the styles or models, the bigger the profits.[2]

Cover the right-hand column that follows. Then, using television programming as an example of mass culture, see how many points of similarity you can find in the analogy, including both parallels stated by the author and those suggested by the analogy. Ask yourself which attributes of mass culture (television programming) correspond to the characteristics of industrial production.

Industrial Production	Mass Culture
1. big volume	1. large audience
2. few models	2. few types of programs, for example, situation comedies, detective shows
3. interchangeable parts	3. standardized plots for each model
4. production line	4. quantity writing and producing by many different people
5. profit	5. profit

An analogy such as the preceding one can be an effective explanatory device, but the analogy is a weak method of reasoning. Since each point of similarity involves an opinion, an analogy is a series of opinions leading to a conclusion. A *false analogy* results when any of these opinions is unsound or inaccurate. (The reader has to evaluate the implied as well as the stated parallels before accepting the analogy as sound.) Also, because analogies do not include differences between things, they can be simplistic and misleading. They should generally be used for clarification rather than argumentation.

The following analogy is used to convey the importance of television in American life, or, in effect, for argumentation. This passage from *Time* compares American television viewing to the events surrounding the visit of Alex Haley, author of *Roots,* to the African village of his ancestors and thus indicates that television provides essential information about our own lives. In analyzing the analogy, you have to ask yourself whether the two elements of it are in fact alike or comparable.

[2]Harry Skornia, *Television and Society* (New York: McGraw-Hill 1965), p. 139.

Without a doubt, the medium had much to do with the impact of the message. Haley learned about his earliest ancestors from an elderly Gambian *griot* (storyteller), a living repository of oral history who sat him down in the tiny village of Juffure and recited for him the centuries-old saga of his West African clan dating back seven generations to the warrior Kunta Kinte. Modern Americans learned about Haley's lineage in much the same way—huddled in a semicircle in their living rooms around that electronic-age *griot,* the television set.[3]

Cover the right-hand column and see how many of the parallels implied by the analogy you can discover.

Alex Haley	American Television Viewer
1. *griot*	1. television set
2. village	2. living room
3. sitting face to face	3. sitting before an electronic device
4. *griot's* history of Haley's ancestors	4. the dramatization of another person's history

EXERCISE 2.6

A. Is there any essential difference in the preceding analogy that weakens any implied point of similarity? To begin, you might ask yourself what role your television set plays in your life. Review each of the four points, deciding whether the implied parallels are actually similar.

1. _____

2. _____

3. _____

4. _____

yes no

Is the analogy sound? ☐ ☐

yes no

Is the analogy false? ☐ ☐

[3]"Why 'Roots' Hit Home," *Time,* 109 (14 Feb. 1977), 69.

B. Read the following analogy from selection 1, by Boorstin, in the Sourcebook (paragraph 10) and compare it to the above analogy from *Time*.

Television was a one-way window. The viewer could see whatever *they* offered, but nobody except the family in the living room could know for sure how the viewer reacted to what he saw. Tiny island audiences gathered nightly around their twinkling sets, much as cave-dwelling ancestors had clustered around their fires for warmth and safety, and for a feeling of togetherness. In these new tribal groups, each child's television tastes were as intimate a part of family lore as whether he preferred ketchup or mustard on his hamburger. With more and more two-TV families (even before 1970 these were one third of all American households) it became common for a member of the family to withdraw and watch in lonely privacy. Of course, broadcasters made valiant and ingenious efforts to fathom these secrets, to find out what each watcher really watched, what he really liked and what he really wanted. But the broadcasters' knowledge was necessarily based on samples, on the extrapolation of a relatively few cases, on estimates and guesses—all merely circumstantial evidence.

1. Are the two analogies related in any way?

2. Is Boorstin's tone serious or humorous?

3. Which elements of the analogy brought you to your conclusion in answering the preceding question?

4. The analogy from *Time* and the one from Boorstin reach opposite conclusions. What are they?

_____

_____

_____

5. Which conclusion do you agree with? Why?

_____

` _____

EXERCISE 2.7

A. Determine the method of reasoning in each of the following passages, labeling each method as statistical inference, cause and effect, causal generalization, assumption, or analogy. A passage may contain more than one of these methods of reasoning.

B. Indicate whether you find the reasoning process sound or unsound.

1   A sample of 900 (primarily) third-grade children in Columbia County, New York, were first tested in their classrooms in 1959–60, and 252 were questioned again in 1964–65. The authors had the children rate each other on aggression and interviewed the parents as well. Boys' television habits established by the age of eight were found to influence aggressive behavior through childhood and the adolescent years. "The more violent the programs preferred by boys in the third grade, the more aggressive is their behavior, both at that time and ten years later." They further concluded "the effect of television violence on aggression is cumulative."[4]

Method of reasoning:

_____

Reasoning, sound or unsound:

_____

[4]Monroe M. Lefkowitz, et al., "Television Violence and Child Aggression: A Follow-Up Study," in _Television and Social Behavior_ by the Surgeon General's Committee on Television and Social Behavior (Washington, D.C.: GPO, 1972), pp. 35–135. (Summary)

2 Seymour Feshback reported on an experiment among 129 Los Angeles elementary school children. The children were split into matched groups and shown different types of violence. A control group watched baseball and circus films, a "fantasy aggression" group watched war films, and a "real aggression" group saw police actions involving campus riots. Feshback found no conclusive evidence for his hypothesis that aggression would be lessened or unaffected when dramatic content functioned as fantasy. He did find some backing for the hypothesis in a second experiment with 60 children, who showed more aggressive response to aggressive television content when they thought it was real than when it was described as fantasy.[5]

Method of reasoning:

_____

Reasoning, sound or unsound:

_____

3 Just as the lungs of a chain smoker are demonstrably different from a nonsmoker's lungs, is it not possible that the brain of a twelve-year-old who has spent ten thousand hours in a darkened room watching moving images on a small screen is in specific ways different from the brain of a child who has watched little or no television? Might not the television child emerge from childhood with certain left-hemisphere skills—those verbal and logical ones—less developed than the visual and spatial capabilities governed by the right hemisphere?[6]

Method of reasoning:

_____

Reasoning, sound or unsound:

_____

Reading critically, then, means investigating the authority and nature of the material before you begin reading and then as you

[5]"Reality and Fantasy in Filmed Violence," in *Television and Social Learning,* ed. John P. Murray, et al., Vol. II of *Television and Social Behavior* (Washington, D.C.: GPO, 1972), pp. 318–45. (Summary)
[6]Marie Winn, *The Plug-In Drug* (New York: Viking Press, 1977), p. 43.

read, evaluating the way facts and opinions are used. You should also remember to apply the same critical principles to your own thinking and writing.

Recording Information Accurately

You may have thought that modern methods of reproducing material have made note-taking a thing of the past. Duplicating machines do provide researchers with a valuable, if costly, tool. Reproducing material from a source in a library allows you to check and recheck your understanding and use of it. Owning a copy of a source, however, does not take the place of taking notes, which is an active process and the best means of learning and organizing other people's ideas for yourself.

GENERAL PRINCIPLES OF NOTE-TAKING

When you have determined that material will be useful for your paper, you are ready to take notes on it. You should keep a few basic principles in mind as you record information.

Thorough Understanding

You should be certain that you understand a passage thoroughly before you take notes on it, looking up words unfamiliar to you in the dictionary and rereading the passage several times if necessary. You cannot correctly represent the author's idea if you do not understand it. Furthermore, if you use a quotation in your paper which you do not understand, you may say something that you don't intend. In the following example, the writer, desiring strong support for the conclusion, attempted to use an expert opinion for that purpose.

> The evidence demonstrates that television crime shows treat the law with contempt. They do not make any attempt to present accurately police and court procedures. As law professors Stephen Arons and Ethan Katsh point out in their article "How TV Cops Flout the Law," "the line between television logic, police logic, and judicial logic is becoming all but indiscernible."[17]

Because the writer chose to quote a sentence that contained one word unfamiliar to him (*indiscernible*), he contradicted part of his own conclusion. The writer should have looked up the word he did not understand while he was taking notes.

One Idea to a Card

The ideas in your paper should be in your control and follow an order you select. The information you take down as notes from many different sources during your research will be used to support those ideas. While it can often be somewhat difficult to isolate one idea or concept, if you try to follow the principle of writing only one idea down on each card, you will be able to arrange your supporting evidence according to your own plan. As you outline and write, you will be taking one idea from one source, then turning to another, and perhaps later returning to still another idea from the first source. If all the ideas from one source were on a single sheet of paper, you would lose the capacity to rearrange those ideas easily. Moreover, if you take down more than one idea on a card, you will inevitably follow someone else's organization and logic. Your notes from another source will reflect yet another way of thinking. You then run the risk of simply stitching together the ideas of one source and another and destroying the unity and coherence of your paper.

Accuracy

Accuracy, close attention to detail, is essential in all phases of writing a research paper, particularly in note-taking. Leaving off a number or omitting a phrase or even a syllable can distort information. Consider the effect of accidentally omitting "Only the first episode of the new series" from the following sentence: "Only the first episode of the new series *Carrying On* uses a fresh approach to race relationships, avoiding the stereotypes found in so many situation comedies." That phrase qualifies or limits the rest of the sentence and cannot be omitted without changing the meaning completely.

METHODS OF NOTE-TAKING

You are ready to begin taking notes when you are satisfied that you understand the material. Since you already have bibliography cards with complete information for identifying each source, you need only write a brief indication at the top of each note card. The author's last name and the page or pages from which you take the information usually suffice. (See the sample note cards on page 59.) If you are using more than one work by the same author, you will have to add part or all of the title to distinguish the two. You should enter this information on *every* note card, even those that are continuations. (Imagine dropping your cards and finding twenty cards that read only "cont." at the top.) You should also write only on one side of a card so that you can see all the information you have at one time by spreading your cards out on a table.

There are a variety of ways to take notes: direct quotation, summary, outline, and combinations of these such as outline-summary. You should choose the one best suited to the material. Whichever method you use, you should always distinguish between the words and ideas of the source and your opinions or comments about them.

Direct Quotation

When you quote directly, you take down the exact words of the source. You should use this method primarily when the language of the passage is unique or necessary to communicate its full meaning, including tone and mood, or when you might want to use the author's words to give strength to your own conclusions. Use quotation marks to open and close any passage you quote directly. If a quotation contains a quotation, an interior quotation, you should use single quotation marks to indicate the interior quotation.

On the note card illustrated the researcher quotes the passage directly because it is the conclusion to Epstein's complex argu-

Double quotation marks for entire quotation

Epstein, p. 180

"Rather than recording the actual flow of events, network news follows predetermined lines, from the developing of a story line to the photographing of selected aspects of the happening to the final editing. Since each of the participants in the process—the cameraman, sound recorder, correspondent, editor and producer—has relatively fixed ideas of what material is wanted

Quotation from Original Source

Single quotation marks for interior quotation

Double quotation marks for entire quotation

Brackets for researcher's comment

> Epstein, p. 180 (cont.)
> for each type of story, the 'reality'
> produced tends to be shaped, if
> not predetermined, by this web of
> expectations."
>
> [EE's conclusion]

ment (Sourcebook, selection 3) and represents a unique way of approaching the subject.

When you wish to add anything to a direct quotation, you use brackets [ ], and when you wish to delete or omit anything from a direct quotation you use an ellipsis, three spaced periods (. . .). You will use brackets when you add clarifying comments or identifying names, often to refer to something the writer has explained and which you are not taking down on your note card. You should generally avoid using the ellipsis with direct quotation, particularly at the note-taking stage, because deletions can cause distortions.

Study the example of the proper use of brackets and the ellipsis. The original material is on page 214 of the Sourcebook.

When you use direct quotation to record a passage in which the author quotes someone else, you should indicate that you are taking down a quotation on your card so that you can give credit to both the author and the person being quoted. If the author gives the source of the quotation either within the text or in a note, you should add this information to your card as well. (See illustration.)

Paragraph symbol indicates a new paragraph in the original source

Researcher's explanation added in brackets

Ellipsis for deletion from original

Period ends sentence; three ellipsis points show the sentence continues in the original

> Elmendorf, p. 766
> ¶ " That [the evidence that children
> imitate TV violence] is why the
> American Medical Association . . .
> has declared violence on TV an
> environmental health risk. . . ."

Use of Brackets and the Ellipsis

Epstein, pp. 164-65
[Quotes Sander Vanocur, NBC Commentator]
"Network news is a continuous loop: there are only a limited number of plots — 'Black versus White,' 'War is Hell,' 'America is falling apart,' 'Man against the elements,' 'The Generation Gap,' etc.—which we seem to be constantly redoing, with different casts of characters."

Quotation of a Source Containing a Quotation

You do not want to use direct quotation exclusively when you are taking notes. Because it involves copying the words of others, there is the danger of copying without digesting and understanding the material. The use of other methods, summary and outline, often help you to grasp the meaning of the ideas in your sources at the note-taking stage.

Summary

A summary is a statement in your own words of information in a source. This method of note-taking helps you to understand the material because you must analyze carefully to be able to restate and summarize. Even though you express the ideas in your own

Epstein, pp. 175-78
Film editors follow several basic principles: they eliminate all flawed footage and sound, as much that is not action as possible, and any footage that doesn't illustrate the story. Editors are much less autonomous than correspondents. Coming under the control of the producer, they are likely to conform to the policies of the producers and executives. Sometimes the producer or a correspondent even supervises the actual cutting.

Summary

words, you record the author's name and page number or numbers so you can give proper credit in your paper.

If you refer to the source (pages 215–24 in the Sourcebook) for the summary card illustrated, you will find that the writer was careful not to take even a short phrase directly from the original.

Outline

An outline is a schematic list of the major points in an argument or explanation with ideas of equal importance in parallel position. (See Chapter 4, pages 110–15, for a detailed discussion of outlining.) Outlining is the quickest way to take down information if you want only the basic ideas and pattern of development in the material or if you think you might want to summarize the entire article in your research paper. You should be certain to take down enough information so that you can decipher the note later.

On the outline note card illustrated the researcher added information in brackets to provide clarification. The outline briefly identifies the major points covered in selection 3, giving an overview. More detailed notes on these ideas would be necessary if they were to be used in a paper.

Combination of Methods

It is possible to use quotation, summary, and outline in various combinations such as partial quotation and outline-summary.

Partial quotation is a combination of the words of the researcher and the words of the source or direct quotation, even in the same sentence, as in the example shown.

Epstein, pp 152-78
I Story lines that govern news filming
   A. "Dialectical model" [balanced, non-political]
   B. "Ironic model" [the news joke]
   C. "National news package" [Combines local stories]
   D. "Action story"
   E. "Nostalgia model"
II Principles that govern news editing
   A. Elimination of inferior film
   B. "Heightened visual effects" [action]
                                    (cont.)

Brackets indicate researcher added information for clarification.

Quotation marks indicate phrase originated with source, not researcher.

Outline

> *Epstein, p. 164*
> *The real flow of events, the news,*
> *is manipulated to result in "illustra-*
> *ting a limited repertory of story*
> *lines with appropiate pictures."*

Partial Quotation

> *Epstein, pp 178-80*
> *Reconstructing news stories alters*
> *the image of reality in several*
> *important ways.*
>   *1. Makes events seem resolved,*
>   *ordered, and clear cut*
>   *2. Makes reality seem filled with*
>   *frenetic, hectic action*
>   *3. Makes reality seemed filled*
>   *with visual facts - only what*
>   *makes a good film*

Outline-Summary

The *outline-summary* combines the outline with the re-searcher's restatement of the source's ideas as explanation. On the note card shown here the researcher begins with a sentence that clarifies the short outline that follows.

EXERCISE 2.8

A. Study the following examples of notes improperly recorded from selection 1 in the Sourcebook. Decide whether the distortion in each note results from improper use of ellipsis, inaccurate summary, material out of context, or misinterpretation of the material.

B. Rewrite each note so that it accurately reflects Boorstin's original meaning. Use the same method attempted in the distorted note.

1. Television, according to Daniel Boorstin, is a "one-way window" that allows us to see without being seen. (paragraph 10)
   Type of distortion:

   _____

   Correction of the note:

   _____

   _____

   _____

2. Daniel Boorstin argues that television is exciting, "focusing interest on the exciting, disturbing, inspiring, or catastrophic instantaneous *now*." (paragraph 13)
   Type of distortion:

   _____

   Correction of the note:

   _____

   _____

   _____

3. "Successful programming offered entertainment . . . instruction . . . political persuasion . . . and advertising." (paragraph 17)
   Type of distortion:

   _____

   Correction of the note:

   _____

NOTES FROM ORAL AND VISUAL SOURCES

Taking notes from any material that you have the opportunity to hear only once, such as a lecture, film, television program, recording, or tape, demands special techniques. You want to take down the main ideas in whatever abbreviated form you will understand. Immediately afterward add all the details you can recall and transfer the notes to cards.

The Interview

You must always request permission for an interview by letter or telephone. Explain your project and the importance of the interview to it. If you wish to use a tape recorder, you should ask permission first.

You may have noticed that interviewers on forums like talk shows are prepared. They know something about the person or the subject. You should prepare yourself by writing questions on separate cards so that you can take down the major points of the response, following the same rules that you use for any unrepeatable experience.

Your questions should direct the session to the area you wish to know about, but you should also allow the person to explore the subject in his or her own way, for you may not have anticipated every facet in your prepared questions.

The Letter

If you write to someone for information, you should explain your project and the use you plan to make of any information you obtain. You will want to acknowledge any response.

DIVISION OF NOTES BY SUBTOPIC

To avoid working in a haphazard manner, you should have an idea of what aspects of the subject you will explore and in what order. You can accomplish this by dividing your preliminary controlling question into smaller parts, or subtopics, and listing them in the order in which you think you should investigate them. In this way, you create a very simple and temporary outline, which you can refine and change as you progress in your research.

You should try to complete the note-taking from one source before you begin another. After finishing for a given day, you should read through your cards and arrange them in a temporary order. You can pencil in subtopic heads at the top of each card. This does not mean you are committed to a particular order or organization;

you may continually reorganize your material and change your outline.

At the beginning of each note-taking session read over your notes from the previous session to see which subtopics need more attention and which remain to be investigated to answer your controlling question.

When you feel that you have gathered enough material to answer the question you formulated at the end of Chapter 1, or any version of the question which develops in your research, you are ready to turn your controlling question into a controlling idea and to use your note cards, divided by subtopics, to construct an outline—processes discussed in Chapter 4.

3
Going to the library

How can I find out more?

To have a successful college career and to be able to continue your education after college you must be capable of learning on your own outside the classroom. One of the best places to teach yourself is the library.

In this chapter you will learn how to locate books and articles on any subject and how to find information you need in general and specialized reference works and other library resources. You may use these skills to find materials to supplement the articles on television in the Sourcebook; or if your instructor has assigned a research paper based exclusively on the Sourcebook, your work in this chapter can serve to acquaint you with the library for the other papers you will write in college.

Discovering Books on a Subject

Your search for research materials usually begins in the library. In this case you have already begun your research with the

Sourcebook readings, and going to the library will be the second phase of your research. There are two schools of thought about the best place in the library to begin developing a bibliography. Some researchers prefer to start their library work in the reference room with indexes or with bibliographies (see pages 80–88), others choose to use the card catalog first. Unless you have a good deal of experience in the particular subject area, you will probably find it more practical and productive to begin by consulting the card catalog to determine which books on your topic the library can supply.

THE CARD CATALOG

The *card catalog,* usually kept in cabinets with rows of numbered drawers, is an alphabetized list on separate cards of all the books owned by your library. Most books are represented in the catalog on at least three cards: a subject card (books of fiction do not have this card), an author card, and a title card. Some libraries alphabetize all of these cards in one catalog (called a dictionary catalog), while other libraries divide the cards for their collection into two separate catalogs, an author and title catalog and a subject catalog (called a divided catalog).

Alphabetization of the Card Catalog

Regardless of the catalog arrangement, the cards are always filed in alphabetical order. You can thus use the catalog as you would use a dictionary. A few special rules on alphabetization apply to card catalogs, however.

1. The definite and indefinite articles—*a, an, the*—are omitted from alphabetization in a card catalog. All other words, even short ones, are alphabetized.
2. Abbreviations are alphabetized as if they were spelled out in full.
3. *Mc* and *M'* are alphabetized as if they were spelled *Mac.*
4. Your library may use either of two methods of alphabetization: word-by-word system or letter-by-letter system.

If *The Good Earth* precedes *Goodbye, Columbus,* your library uses the word-by-word system: each word is considered a complete unit. (Note that the article *the* is not considered in the process of alphabetization.) If a longer word (*goodbye*) contains a shorter word (*good*), the entry for the longer word will be found following the conclusion of all names or titles beginning with the shorter word. The subject card for New York would precede that for Newfoundland.

If *Goodbye, Columbus* precedes *The Good Earth,* your library uses the letter-by-letter system: all words in a title are alphabetized together as if they were one long word.

The following exercise will help you to master these rules.

EXERCISE 3.1

1. Underline the letter by which you would look for the title card of the book *The Electronic Mirror* by Sig Mickelson.
2. Underline the letter by which you would look for the title card of the book *To Kill a Messenger: Television News and the Real World* by William Small.
3. Number the following titles in the order they would appear in a card catalog.

_____ *Mr. Sammler's Planet*

_____ *Mist*

_____ *A Misunderstanding*

4. Place the following surnames in the proper alphabetical order.

_____ McLoughlin

_____ MacLure

_____ McLuhan

5. Does the title card for *The Good Earth* come before or after that for *Goodbye, Columbus* in your library's card catalog?

_____

6. Does your library use word-by-word or letter-by-letter alphabetization?

_____

Subject Card

The subject card will generally be the one most useful to you in the beginning stages of your research, since you might not know the names of specific authors or titles. Subject headings are typed

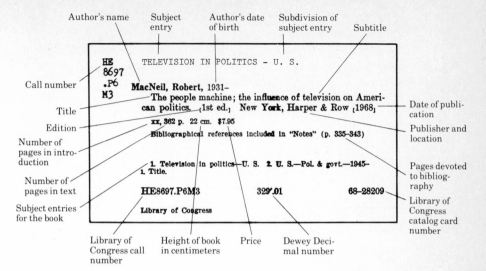

Figure 3-1   Subject Card

across the top of a catalog card in red ink or capital letters. If a book includes any special features such as illustrations, maps, or appendixes (supplemental chapters dealing with related subjects), these will also be noted on the catalog card.

Study the subject card illustrated, filed in the *t*'s under "Television in politics," noting the kinds of information you can find on it.

The subject may be divided into several areas or fields. In the case of the card above, "Television in politics" is a subdivision of the subject "Television." These subdivisions may either help you to limit your subject or provide you with the books most pertinent to your narrowed topic. Subdivision cards are filed in alphabetical order following the cards on the general subject. In the case of historical subjects, subdivision cards are filed in chronological order.

EXERCISE 3.2

List all the subdivisions of the subject "Television" in your library's card catalog.

_____   _____

_____   _____

_____   _____

Another way to discover sources on your topic is to use *cross-reference cards,* entries filed behind subject and subdivision cards

```
┌─────────────────────────────────────────────┐
│                                             │
│                                             │
│                                             │
│           Television in education           │
│                                             │
│                 See also                    │
│                                             │
│          Closed-circuit television          │
│                                             │
│                                             │
│                                             │
│                                             │
└─────────────────────────────────────────────┘
```

Figure 3-2 Cross-Reference Card

that designate closely related subjects with the phrase "See also," as in the sample card shown.

Particularly at the beginning of your research, you should follow up any of the subject headings suggested by cross-reference cards as well as by the alternate subject headings listed at the bottom of catalog cards. (See Figure 3.1.) In addition, you should try to think of subject headings yourself. For example, under the subject "Media—electronic" you might encounter a book not filed under "Television." Your ingenuity in using the subject catalog can add a fresh perspective to your research.

EXERCISE 3.3

1. Look up Daniel Boorstin's book *The Americans,* which contains a chapter on television. Under what subject headings is this book filed in your library's card catalog?

   _____ _____ _____

   _____ _____ _____

2. List five subject headings under which you might encounter the titles of books that relate directly or indirectly to the topic television.

   _____ _____

   _____ _____

   _____

HE
8697
.P6
M3

MacNeil, Robert, 1931–
The people machine; the influence of television on American politics. [1st ed.] New York, Harper & Row [1968]

xx, 362 p. 22 cm. $7.95

Bibliographical references included in "Notes" (p. 335–343)

1. Television in politics—U. S. 2. U. S.—Pol. & govt.—1945–
I. Title.

HE8697.P6M3 329′.01 68–28209

Library of Congress

Figure 3-3 Author Card

Author Card

Like subject cards, author cards can be used to help you discover books on your subject. Suppose you find one book by an author, Marshall McLuhan, for example, under the subject heading "Television." Some of his other books, while perhaps not dealing exclusively with television and thus not indexed under "Television," might contain a chapter or section dealing with the subject. Under the name heading "McLuhan" you would find entries for all books by him which your library holds.

If you compare the author card shown above to the subject card for the same book (page 69), you will see that the two are identical except for the omission of the subject heading on the author card. You would find the author card under "MacNeil."

Title Card

If you know only the title of the book you need, you can locate it by consulting the title card, filed alphabetically by the name of the book. You would find the title card shown on page 72 under the letter *p*.

As you decide which books in the card catalog you wish to consult, you should write out a bibliography card for each book on a separate 4 × 6 inch card. In the case of your research paper on television these cards will supplement those you already have for articles in the Sourcebook. When you make a bibliography card from the card catalog, remember to record the name of the library as well as the call number, since you might work in more than one library and call numbers for the same book could be different in different libraries. Before you leave the card catalog, it is a good

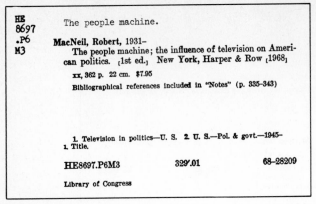

Figure 3-4   Title Card

idea to check each of your bibliography cards carefully for completeness and accuracy to avoid having to retrace your steps.

LOCATION OF BOOKS

The key to locating any book in the library is the *call number,* the code of numbers and letters in the upper right-hand corner of the catalog card and marked on the spine of the book and often inside the back cover.

The first row of letters or numbers in a call number reflects one of two methods of classifying books: Dewey Decimal, a numerical system based on a tenfold division of subjects, or Library of Congress, a newer system that combines letters and numbers to des-

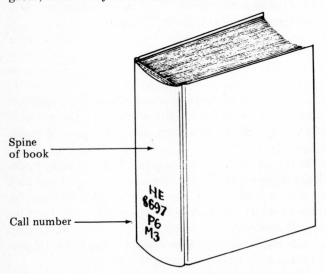

Spine
of book

Call number

Figure 3-5   Book Spine Showing Call Number

ignate classes and divisions of subjects. Additional lines of letters and numbers may indicate the author's last name, special collections or buildings where the books may be shelved, or information for librarians' use. You will need the entire call number to locate a book.

Your library may allow you direct access to the shelves of books. If so, it has what are called *open stacks*. In this case you will search for books yourself. Every library posts or distributes a guide to its stacks indicating the location of books by call numbers. By following the directions, you can easily find most books on your own. If your library does not allow you to enter the area where the books are shelved, it has *closed stacks*. In this case, you will fill out a call slip provided by the library and submit it at the loan desk.

EVALUATION OF BOOKS

When you have located books on your subject, you should make a preliminary judgment about which of them you might want to read and study carefully. By examining the essential elements of a book (which are described on the following pages) you can make a decision about its usefulness for your purposes.

The *title page,* always on the right-hand side of the book, includes some or all of the following information: the title; a subtitle, which explains or narrows the title; the author's name; the author's credentials; any co-authors, editors, illustrators, or translators involved in the production of the book; the name of the publisher; the location of the publisher. You can often gauge the nature of a book by the qualifications of the author or editors, as you learned in Chapter 2. Also, the orientation and reputation of the publisher sometimes provide information for a preliminary assessment. A book published by a large university press often tends to be scholarly, while one published by a church-affiliated press might present a theological or religious approach to a subject.

The *copyright page,* the reverse side of the title page, includes the date of publication, the dates of previous editions, the name and location of the publisher, and in recent books a reproduction of the Library of Congress catalog card for the book, which gives both Library of Congress and Dewey Decimal call numbers. The date is a guide to the relevance of the information for your particular subject. The number of previous editions may indicate the book's popularity or success. When you have a choice, you should use the most recent edition of a book.

The *dedication,* an expression of the author's admiration or affection for a member of his family, a friend, or a person in his field, is sometimes valuable in determining the orientation of the book. You might recognize the name or you might consult a biographical reference work (see page 90) for information about the person. The *epigraph,* one or more quotations with which the author chooses to complement or explain his work, can also be an important guide to the book's approach to the subject. The dedication and the epigraph are usually found on pages immediately following the title page, although not every book includes these features.

The book may have a *preface, foreword,* or *introduction,* introductory pages preceding the text and written by the author or by an authority in the field, which will help you to evaluate the quality of the book, the author's approach to the subject, and the intention of the book. These prefatory sections are numbered in small roman numerals to distinguish them from page numbers in the body of the text.

The *table of contents,* a list of chapters and other subdivisions of the book, indicates which areas of the subject the book covers and how much space is devoted to each. If you have already narrowed your research paper topic, you may find one or two chapters that are pertinent; and you may be able to ignore or skim the others.

The *index,* an alphabetical listing of key terms, names, and places with pages on which references to them are found, is usually the final section of a book. Consulting the index is a convenient and quick way to determine whether or not a book deals with your topic.

The *bibliography,* the list of books the author read as sources for his or her own book, can indicate the depth of the research and provide additions for the bibliography of your paper, books you may not have encountered in the card catalog. The bibliography is usually found near the back of a book. An *annotated bibliography* is a bibliography that includes a short description or assessment of each book it lists.

Notes (called footnotes when they are placed at the bottom, or foot, of a page), are annotations to the text that serve several purposes: providing the source of the information which the author has gathered from others (documentation), supplying further bibliographical references, or adding materials which cannot be worked smoothly into the text. An examination of the notes to a book may indicate the thoroughness with which the author has substantiated his conclusions.

When evaluating books you will also want to look for special features, such as illustrations, charts, diagrams, a glossary (list of definitions of terms or concepts), or appendixes (supplemental chapters dealing with related subjects) before deciding whether to devote time to the chapters that constitute the body of the book.

Finally, you should utilize the techniques you learned in Chapter 2 to evaluate the text itself, determining the level of writing and discerning possible reason for bias in the author, for example.

EXERCISE 3.4

Answer the following questions by analyzing the book *News from Nowhere* by Edward Jay Epstein. You can probably find this book in your library. (Perhaps your instructor will have had it placed on reserve.) The paperbound edition is also readily available in stores. Your instructor might request that you answer these questions or similar ones about another book.

1. Turn to the title page of *News from Nowhere*. What kinds of information do you find there?

_____

_____

_____

_____

2. Can you make any inferences about the book from this information?

_____

_____

3. What information about *News from Nowhere* do you learn from the copyright page?

_____

_____

4. To whom is *News from Nowhere* dedicated?

_____

If you do not recognize the name, look it up in *Who's Who in America*. What position does this person hold?

_____

5. What does the epigraph of *News from Nowhere* tell you about the book's point of view?

_____

6. How is the epigraph related to the title of the book?

_____

_____

_____

7. Who wrote the preface to *News from Nowhere?*

_____

_____

8. Why did Epstein decide to do this study?

_____

_____

9. What does he feel are the difficulties of such a study?

_____

_____

_____

10. Why did he select network news as his subject?

_____

_____

_____

11. Which network does he concentrate on and why?

_____

_____

_____

12. What are the sources of his information?

_____

_____

_____

13. When was the research done?

_____

_____

14. What "central problem" does he believe he is addressing?

_____

_____

_____

15. How are the chapters in _News from Nowhere_ grouped?

_____

_____

_____

16. To which of the sections does the author devote the most pages?

_____

17. On what pages is the index found in *News from Nowhere?*

_____

18. If you were doing a research paper on television advertising time, would you find information for it in *News from Nowhere?*

_____

19. On what pages does the longest passage dealing with the Fairness Doctrine appear?

_____

20. Is the bibliography of *News from Nowhere* annotated?

_____

Epstein organizes his bibliography according to types of sources. What are the categories of his sources?

_____

_____

21. What conclusions can you make about the book from the bibliography?

_____

_____

_____

22. Where are the notes placed in *News from Nowhere?*

_____

_____

23. Where did Epstein find the statistics he cites on page 4, line 2?

_____

24. What is the source of the statistics cited on page 31, lines 34 and 36?

_____

_____

25. What purpose does the note to page 201, line 8, serve?

_____

_____

_____

26. What is the purpose of the note to page 175, line 1?

_____

_____

Using General Reference Works to Gather Information

In the broadest sense, a *reference work* is any work you consult for information. In its narrower definition, reference work means particular kinds of materials found in libraries: indexes, dictionaries, encyclopedias, biographical dictionaries, atlases and gazetteers, yearbooks, and handbooks. You turn to a reference work when you are seeking a specific piece of information. You would rarely, if ever, want to read the entirety of a reference work, for they are not written to be read straight through. A *general reference work* is designed in level and approach for an audience of students and lay persons and is usually broad in scope. Reference works are generally grouped together in one section of the library and may not be taken out of the library. You can usually locate them by looking up the title or subject in the card catalog. General encyclopedias are sometimes filed under the heading "Encyclopedias" in the subject catalog.

If you should encounter difficulties when searching for reference works or for any other library materials, you may wish to consult the librarian, whose desk is often located near the reference section.

INDEXES

Index is a general term that refers to any alphabetical listing of names and topics. Rather than supplying information, an index indicates where information is located. A card catalog is in fact simply an index of all the materials available in the library. Also, as you know, many books contain indexes, which list the persons and subjects treated in the book. The word *index* can also designate a kind of reference work, a book that lists materials from a variety of sources. Especially in the case of magazines and newspapers, for which it would be impossible for you to consult every issue, reference indexes are indispensable in locating information on your subject.

Indexes to Journal and Magazine Articles

For many subjects, journal and magazine articles may be even more help to you than books, since they are likely to be more recent and more limited in scope. Finding these articles often requires more time and persistence than locating a book; but once you learn to use reference indexes, you will be able to look up articles easily. The following list of indexes to journal and magazine articles includes those indexes that are most likely to be available to you.

Readers' Guide to Periodical Literature. 1900–   . This index does precisely what the title suggests: It guides you (the reader) to literature in article form in periodicals (publications that appear at regular intervals). Periodicals are generally called magazines if they are of a popular nature (*Time* and the *Atlantic,* for example), or journals if they are specialized or intended for a professional audience (the *Harvard Business Review* and *UNESCO Courier,* for example). The periodicals indexed in the *Readers' Guide* cover a broad range of fields; most are written for the general public. Because not all the articles listed in the *Readers' Guide* are written at a level appropriate for a college research paper, you will have to determine the suitability of material you encounter by using the guidelines presented in Chapter 2.

A good way to begin using the *Readers' Guide* is to look up a subject under the heading you have been working with in the card catalog. The main heading is often subdivided into specific aspects of the topic and/or cross-references, which lead you to other entries. The *Readers' Guide* uses numerous abbreviations to shorten its entries, and you will find a key to them at the beginning of each volume. Study the entry from the *Readers' Guide.*

Most articles are listed twice in the *Readers' Guide,* once in a subject entry and once in an author entry. Articles *about* an author are listed *after* those *by* him (see Figure 3.7). Stories and novels are listed by title and author (see Figure 3.8).

Issues of the *Readers' Guide* appear twice monthly, making it possible for you to locate current materials. Every three months these issues are cumulated into one alphabet in a larger booklet,

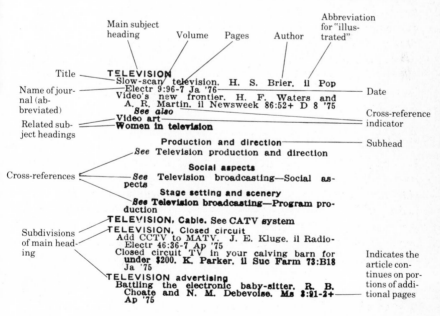

Figure 3–6   Excerpt from *Readers' Guide*

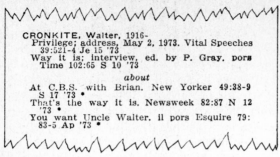

Figure 3–7

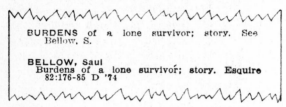

Figure 3–8

and approximately once a year these booklets are again cumulated into a permanent volume. When you are searching for very recent articles, you must look at the paper pamphlets shelved after the bound volumes.

EXERCISE 3.5

Answer the following questions about the *Readers' Guide*. Some of these will require that you use volumes in your library.

1. Study the following entry:

Wages of TV and appliance technicians. H.B. Williams. il Mo Labor R 97: 53–5 Jl '74

a. What is the title of the article?

_____

_____

b. Write out the full name of the journal.

_____

_____

c. In which volume of the journal did this article appear?

_____

d. On which pages can this article be found?

_____

e. What is the date of the magazine in which this article appeared?

_____

f. Is this article illustrated?

_____

2. Give the meaning of the following abbreviations used in the *Readers' Guide*.

abr_____

bibliog_____

bibliog f_____

no _____

por _____

Mr_____

rev _____

sec_____

3. Find an entry for any article that appeared within the last six months on "Television in education."

_____

_____

4. List the subdivisions of the subject heading "Television programs" in any recent volume of the *Readers' Guide.*

_____   _____

_____   _____

_____   _____

Poole's Index to Periodical Literature. 1802–1906. This index of
American periodicals published between 1802 and 1906 provides
a valuable extension to the *Readers' Guide.* Articles in each of the
seven volumes are indexed by subject; an author index is supplied
in an additional volume. With the *Readers' Guide* and *Poole's*
you can locate periodical literature from the beginning of the
nineteenth century to the present.

Nineteenth Century Readers' Guide. 1890–1899. This extension
of the *Readers' Guide* indexes by author and subject selected
periodicals (fifty-one of the nearly five hundred published at the
time) from the final decade of the nineteenth century.

Essay and General Literature Index. 1900– . This index will
lead you to essays and articles collected or anthologized in books.
Although the books themselves would be listed in a card catalog,
the articles they contain would not be, and you would need to turn
to this reference work to find mention of them.

Index to the Little Magazines. 1949– . During the last several
decades, numerous little magazines have come into existence to
supplement major publications by printing creative work or
essays, often with controversial points of view. Journals of
scholarly, literary, and political criticism, such as the *Denver
Quarterly,* and magazines publishing fiction and poetry, such as
Epoch, are indexed here.

Book Review Digest. 1905– . You can locate evaluations of
current books or information about the critical reception of a book
at the time of publication in the *Book Review Digest,* an index
with summaries of book reviews from approximately seventy
periodicals. In some cases, the summary alone will provide you
with enough information; if not, you can look up the entire review
in the appropriate periodical.

Social Sciences Index. 1974– . *Humanities Index.* 1974– .
[formerly combined as the *Social Sciences and Humanities
Index* (1965–1974) and previously entitled the *International
Index* (1907–1965)]. These indexes are more specialized and
scholarly than the preceding indexes; but because they cover a

broad range of fields, they are helpful for research papers even in freshman-level courses.

The *Social Sciences Index* covers the fields of anthropology, economics, environmental science, geography, law and criminology, medical sciences, political science, psychology, public administration, and sociology. The *Humanities Index* includes the fields of archaeology, classical studies, area studies, folklore, history, language and literature, literary and political criticism, performing arts, philosophy, religion, and theology.

In many areas, these indexes overlap and complement one another; you may need to consult both of them. For example, "Television" is a subject entry in both indexes. The *Social Sciences Index* includes subdivisions such as "Television and politics" and "Television and the aged," while the *Humanities Index* contains entries such as "Television and literature" and "Television authorship." The subdivision "Television and children," however, appears in both indexes although the articles cited in each will have different perspectives.

When you find an article on your subject in any of these indexes, you should write out a bibliography card for it, as you learned in Chapter 2. Periodicals may be shelved along with books and thus located with a call number, which can be found in the card catalog under the name of the periodical. Some libraries shelve periodicals separately in alphabetical order and provide a pamphlet or listing to indicate whether the library owns the periodical you seek and where it is if the library does (or the call number you need to find it). You should record this information on your bibliography card.

If your library does not own the periodical you need, you can consult *union catalogs,* reference works that list the holdings of books and/or periodicals in one or more libraries. A national union catalog listing 55,000 periodicals, the *Union List of Serials in Libraries of the United States and Canada* (1965) can tell you which libraries own the periodical you need and the dates of the issues they hold. This work is supplemented by *New Serial Titles, 1950-1970.* Also, cooperating or affiliated universities and colleges may have their own union catalogs. The *State University of New York List of Periodicals* is an example of such a union catalog.

Indexes to Newspapers

Newspapers are extremely important sources of information for many research papers, particularly those dealing with current events or people in the news and historical subjects.

New York Times Index. 1851–   . The *New York Times* is the nation's most comprehensive newspaper, with broad and detailed coverage of national and international news. Therefore, it is the newspaper most likely to provide news stories or commentary on your topic.

The *New York Times Index,* a subject index in alphabetical order, provides efficient access to the paper's articles. The index alone can even be useful. First, it can guide you to articles in newspapers that are not indexed; since you can discover when a particular event occurred or was under discussion in the *New York Times,* you can then look through concurrent issues of other newspapers. Also, included for each article is an *abstract,* a short descriptive summary, which is a helpful research tool in itself. By reading through the abstracts for a particular period you may be able to discern a trend in ideas or points of view being expressed during a given time. In some cases, these abstracts can supply all the information you need, as the detailed abstract from the *New York Times Index* shown here illustrates.

After reading an abstract such as this, you may decide to read the entire article. Newspapers, with the possible exception of editions only a week or two old, are stored on microfilm. By greatly reducing the amount of space required to store printed materials, this invention makes it possible for even the smallest library to own a complete set of the *New York Times* back to 1851. See page 102 for information on using microfilm.

The Newspaper Index. 1972–   . This relatively new index can guide you to articles on your subject in *The Chicago Tribune, The*

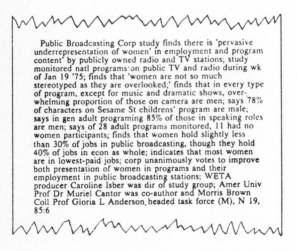

Public Broadcasting Corp study finds there is 'pervasive underrepresentation of women' in employment and program content' by publicly owned radio and TV stations; study monitored natl programs·on public TV and radio during wk of Jan 19 '75; finds that 'women are not so much stereotyped as they are overlooked;' finds that in every type of program, except for music and dramatic shows, overwhelming proportion of those on camera are men; says 78% of characters on Sesame St childrens' program are male; says in gen adult programing 85% of those in speaking roles are men; says of 28 adult programs monitored, 11 had no women participants; finds that women hold slightly less than 30% of jobs in public broadcasting, though they hold 40% of jobs in econ as whole; indicates that most women are in lowest-paid jobs; corp unanimously votes to improve both presentation of women in programs and their employment in public broadcasting stations; WETA producer Caroline Isber was dir of study group; Amer Univ Prof Dr Muriel Cantor was co-author and Morris Brown Coll Prof Gloria L Anderson.headed task force (M), N 19, 85:6

Figure 3–9   Excerpt from *The New York Times Index*

Los Angeles Times, The New Orleans Times-Picayune, and *The Washington Post,* four of the nation's important newspapers from various regions.

BIBLIOGRAPHIES

After using the card catalog and the appropriate indexes to periodicals, you may wish to build a more extensive list of works for possible consultation. In this case, you can turn to a bibliography, a reference work that provides lists of books on a subject or leads you to lists of books within articles or other books.

General Bibliographies

Organized by subject, general bibliographies provide lists of bibliographic information on a wide range of topics.

Bibliographic Index: A Cumulative Bibliography of Bibliographies. 1937– . Triannual. This is a subject index to bibliographies, including those published separately as books and those that appear within other works. Besterman, Theodore. *A World Bibliography of Bibliographies.* 1965. 5 volumes. This work includes only bibliographies published as separate books.

Union Catalogs

Some union catalogs, lists of the holdings of one or more libraries, deal exclusively with books. (See page 85 for union catalogs of periodicals).

Library of Congress Catalog—Books: Subjects. 1950– . This subject index of books catalogued by the Library of Congress includes nearly every book published in the United States and Canada as well as a large percentage of books published abroad.

The National Union Catalog: A Cumulative Author List. 1956– . This catalog organizes books by author and gives information about which libraries own them.

If your library does not own a book you are seeking, you may find that a nearby library does. Most libraries have an *interlibrary loan* service, which allows you to request books and periodicals from any library in the United States or Canada.

Trade Bibliographies

American trade bibliographies include only books published in the United States and currently for sale. You may find that you can save yourself a good deal of time by purchasing one or two of the books most essential to your research.

Subject Guide to Books in Print. 1957– . This reference work, which is published annually, may provide you with titles in print on your subject along with the publisher, series, price, edition, and date of publication.

Books in Print. 1948– . This two-volume work indexes books in print by author and by title. An accompanying volume, *Paperbound Books in Print,* lists titles currently available in paperback form.

DICTIONARIES

The purpose of a dictionary is to provide information concerning words. An unabridged dictionary attempts to include all of the words in a language, while an abridged or general dictionary contains a selection of words. One of the most widely used unabridged dictionaries is *Webster's Third New International Dictionary of the English Language.* In addition, some dictionaries are devoted to particular aspects of the language, such as historical development, usage, or slang. A few of the most useful and important of these are described here.

Historical or Etymological

Murray, Sir James Augustus Henry, et al., eds. *The Oxford English Dictionary [OED].* 1933. 12 volumes with a supplement. This extraordinary work traces the history, or etymology, of every word introduced in the English language since 1150. It provides quotations from various periods to illustrate the evolving meanings of more than 500,000 words. In 1971, the *OED* was issued in a two-volume compact edition set in miniature type, which is read with the aid of a magnifying glass.

Slang

Wentworth, Harold, and Stuart Flexner. *Dictionary of American Slang.* 1967. This work includes vulgarisms and American expressions absent from the *OED.* It defines more than 21,000 terms and expressions and includes the date of origin and illustrations of usage in quotations.

Synonyms and Antonyms

Roget's International Thesaurus. 1962. This system of classifying groups of related words was developed by Peter Mark Roget (1779–1869). An index at the back directs you to the appropriate section, where groups of synonyms are listed according to part of speech.

Usage

Fowler, Henry Watson. *A Dictionary of Modern English Usage.*
1965. This work will answer your questions about correct use of
words and about disputed spellings. The orientation of the work is
British usage.

Follett, Wilson. *Modern American Usage: A Guide.* 1966. This
guide focuses on American usage of words and phrases.

Quotations

Bartlett, John. *Familiar Quotations.* 1968. You can find quotations to introduce your paper or illustrate your ideas by using this
reference work indexed by subject, author, and key words of quotations and verses judged by the editors to be "familiar or worthy
of being familiar."

You will also find dictionaries designed for a variety of other
purposes, from solving crossword puzzles to creating rhymes.
Also, your library very likely owns a wide range of foreign language dictionaries.

ENCYCLOPEDIAS

An *encyclopedia* is a comprehensive work attempting to cover all
branches of knowledge. Thus, you are likely to find an encyclopedia entry on nearly any subject on which you may be writing a
paper. The encyclopedia can be helpful to you at the beginning of
your research by giving you an overview of the subject or suggesting subdivisions of it which you might develop. Some encyclopedias provide a bibliography at the end of the entries or in a
separate volume. You should be careful, however, not to rely too
heavily on the encyclopedia for information. Your instructor may
even prefer that you avoid using the encyclopedia altogether for
college papers, since the apparent completeness of the entries
may inhibit your looking for other materials. An encyclopedia can
be useful in supplying basic facts on a subject, but you will need to
look in books and articles for interpretation and opinions on your
subject. The most reputable encyclopedias have signed articles;
that is, the author's name or initials appear at the end. This identification of the author means that you can ascertain the person's
qualifications for writing the entry.

Because of the enormous cost involved in producing an encyclopedia, new editions are published rather infrequently. Most encyclopedias are kept up to date with annual supplements, which you
should consult for the latest information.

Encyclopedia Americana. This is an especially comprehensive encyclopedia in both scope and depth with strengths in scientific, technological, and geographical coverage. For rapid reference work it is preferable to the *Encyclopaedia Britannica*. The final volume contains an index (volume 30 of the 1975 edition).

Encyclopaedia Britannica. Generally acknowledged to be the most scholarly of American encyclopedias, the *Britannica* has particular strengths in art, history, literature, and the biological sciences. With the 1974 edition a new system of organization was introduced, dividing the encyclopedia into three sections: *Propaedia, Micropaedia,* and *Macropaedia.* The *Propaedia* is a one-volume outline of knowledge designed to provide an overview of the entire scheme and to place each topic within it. For example, "Television" is a subdivision (as are "Radio" and "Satellites") of the category "Technology of information processes and of communication systems." The *Micropaedia* contains complete entries for small or narrow subjects, and for large subjects, its entries direct the reader to particular volumes and pages of the *Macropaedia,* where subjects are covered in great detail.

Collier's Encyclopedia. Less difficult in style and content than the *Britannica* or the *Americana, Collier's* is geared to high school and college curricula. The final volume contains an index, bibliography, and study guide.

BIOGRAPHICAL REFERENCE WORKS

A variety of biographical reference works can provide you with information about people who are or have been prominent or famous. These sources are often called *biographical dictionaries* because the entries are arranged alphabetically. In order to consult the appropriate biographical dictionary you usually need to know the person's nationality and whether the person is living or dead. Any additional information you have may help lead you to the proper source, since many biographical references are restricted by nationality, region, or profession.

Living Persons

International Who's Who. 1935–   . This biographical dictionary, updated and published annually, contains profiles of persons of prominence in many fields and has an international scope. Other biographical dictionaries of the same type include the original work of this kind, *Who's Who* (Great Britain and the Commonwealth), as well as *Who's Who in America, Who's Who in the East, Who's Who of American Women,* to list only a few.

Deceased Persons

The most accessible source of information on a deceased person of some prominence is often an encyclopedia. In addition, a number of retrospective biographical works exist, many of which are organized by nationality. One of these is the *Dictionary of American Biography*. 1944–1973. The twenty-one volumes of the *DAB* provide lengthy signed articles on some 15,000 persons significant in American life who died prior to 1935. *The Dictionary of National Biography* is an equivalent work for Great Britain.

A very useful guide to biographical information in books, periodicals, and newspapers is the *Biography Index* (1946–   ), which is published quarterly and cumulated annually. This index includes persons both living and dead, listing them by name and profession, and is international in scope.

ATLASES

The name for a collection of maps derives from the name of Atlas, the Greek god condemned by Zeus to bear the world on his shoulders. In addition to maps, an atlas may include material such as rainfall and vegetation charts, mileage tables, and population statistics. Recent atlases contain maps of the moon and of outer space. Historical atlases, which provide maps showing political boundaries and relationships at various times, are an important companion to the study of history and political science.

General

Bartholomew, John W., ed. *The Times Atlas of the World, Comprehensive Edition*. 1971. This highly regarded atlas gives balanced coverage to all areas of the world in good, clearly detailed maps. The index contains 200,000 names, which refer the reader to sections of individual maps.

Historical

The New Cambridge Modern History. 1970. The final volume of this historic work is an atlas that includes maps from the Renaissance to the end of Second World War.

ALMANACS AND YEARBOOKS

Almanacs and yearbooks are annual compilations of facts and statistics, usually published in paperbound form. Almanacs, which originally served as calendars providing information such as weather forecasts and tide tables, have been expanded so that they now function as a kind of small encyclopedia. Yearbooks are often devoted to particular fields and aim to bring the reader up to date concerning the year's developments.

The World Almanac and Book of Facts. 1868– . This is one of many almanacs providing factual and statistical information on a wide range of subjects.

The Statesman's Yearbook. 1864– . The subject of this yearbook is the governments of the world. It provides data on fields such as education, population, commerce, and agriculture.

EXERCISE 3.6

Consult the appropriate reference work in your library to answer the following questions or to find the required information. Write down the name of the reference work in which you located the information when the source is not indicated in the question.

1. Look up the word *cloister* in *Webster's Third International Dictionary.* What kinds of information do you find there about the word?

   _____

   _____

2. Look up the word *cloister* in the *Oxford English Dictionary.* What additional information do you find?

   _____

   _____

3. Write down a quotation on the subject of loyalty. Also list your source.

   _____

   _____

   _____

4. What did the early English word *goderheal* mean? What is the source for your answer?

_____

_____

_____

5. What does the slang expression "one on the country" mean?

_____

The expression "one on the city"? Indicate the source of your information.

_____

_____

_____

6. Find out about John Chancellor's experience in print and broadcast journalism. List your source.

_____

_____

_____

7. Read the section on history in the entry "Television" in the *Encyclopaedia Britannica* or the *Encyclopedia Americana* and then answer the following questions.
   a. What is the definition of television?

_____

_____

b. In what year was the earliest proposal for color television made?

_____

c. In what year did commercial television broadcasting begin in the United States? In most other countries?

_____

8. Near what lake is the city of Puno, Peru, located? List some facts about this lake. Also list your source.

_____

_____

_____

9. Who won the Academy Award for best actress in 1966 and for acting in what motion picture? List your source.

_____

_____

_____

10. What does the Swahili word *kidividivi* mean? Indicate your source.

_____

_____

11. List the subdivisions of the heading "Television" in the latest *Social Sciences Index.*

_____

_____

12. Find out how much the paperbound version of Daniel Boorstin's *The Americans* costs. What source did you use?

_____

_____

13. In what publications did book reviews of Maxine Hong Kingston's novel *The Woman Warrior* appear when it was published in 1976? List your source.

_____

_____

_____

14. Locate a bibliography on some aspect of television in the *Bibliographic Index*. Record the entry here.

_____

_____

_____

Becoming Acquainted with Specialized Reference Materials

When you need intensive, exhaustive treatment of a subject, you will want to use specialized reference works. Nearly every field of study has a series of reference works that can be useful to you, particularly for upper division courses or for work in your major. Specialized reference works are of the same kinds as general reference works; that is, you will find indexes, dictionaries, encyclopedias, biographical dictionaries, and so forth, designed for each field.

Specialized works are filed in the card catalog under author (or editor), title, and subject. You can discover reference works in a field by looking up the subject. Subject entries are divided by type of reference work, as in "Comparative literature—Bibliographies" or "Education—Encyclopedias." In addition, you can consult guides to specialized reference works. One of these is *Guide to Reference Books* (1976) by Eugene P. Sheehy, which is available in the reference sections of most libraries.

Those works published monthly or quarterly are usually cumulated into volumes annually or biannually. Some encyclopedias and handbooks are updated periodically by supplements in book or pamphlet form.

The following list of specialized reference works can serve as an introduction to the large number of works available for each subject. The list includes one or two of the most useful indexes and most respected encyclopedias or handbooks in each of several fields in which you may be taking courses. Scholars in the same field may hold different opinions about the value of a reference work; and as your knowledge in a field grows, you will develop your own judgments about reference books. You should ask your instructors to recommend additional reference works in their fields.

Anthropology

Abstracts in Anthropology. 1970– . Quarterly. Provides subject and author indexes and abstracts of works in anthropology. International in scope.

Art

The Art Index. 1929– . Quarterly. Indexes journal articles and other publications by author and subject; covers both fine and applied arts.

Encyclopedia of World Art. 1959–1968. 15 volumes. Includes discussions with illustrations of a wide range of artists, periods, and forms of art.

Biology

Biological Abstracts. 1926– . Semimonthly. Provides abstracts from articles in five thousand periodicals for all of the biological sciences, including biochemistry, agriculture, nutrition, and other fields, both theoretical and applied. International in scope.

Gray, Peter, ed. *The Encyclopedia of the Biological Sciences.* 1970. Includes definitions and explanations of biological subjects for both the student and the scientist.

Business and Economics

Business Periodicals Index. 1958– . Monthly except July. Subject index to publications in business, economics, accounting, advertising, and related fields.

Index to Economic Journals. 1961– . Indexes articles in major economics journals from 1886 to 1959. Supplemented by the *Index of Economic Articles.* 1960– .

Greenwald, Douglas, et al., eds. *McGraw-Hill Dictionary of Modern Economics.* 1973. Defines terms from economics and allied fields; provides lists of reference sources.

Chemistry

Chemical Abstracts. 1907– . Weekly. Provides abstracts of articles from twelve thousand journals and offers entries on books, conferences, and dissertations. Published by the American Chemical Society. International in scope.

Mellon, Melvin Guy. *Chemical Publications, Their Nature and Use.* 1965. A guide to reference sources in chemistry with chapters devoted to sample research problems for students. Author, subject, and title indexes.

Education

The Education Index. 1929– . Monthly, except July and August. Indexes by author and subject over two hundred periodicals as well as books, pamphlets, and other materials on all aspects of education.

Research in Education. 1966– . Published by the United States Office of Education. Contains abstracts of research reports and projects in education and provides information on obtaining the materials through the computerized Educational Resources Information Center.

The Encyclopedia of Education. 1971. 10 volumes. Includes articles by experts on history, theory, research, philosophy, and structure of education in the United States.

Engineering

Engineering Index. 1906– . Monthly. Indexes by subject and is divided into the various areas of engineering. International in scope.

Perry, Robert H., ed. *Engineering Manual.* 1967. Provides information for both students and engineers on the standard fields of engineering.

Film

Film Literature Index. 1973– . Quarterly. Indexes by title and director reviews in film journals.
  New York Times Film Reviews. 1903–1970. Includes the complete texts of reviews from the *New York Times.*

Geography

Fullard, Harold. *The Geographical Digest.* 1963– . A yearbook providing brief entries on changes and developments in the field of geography.
  Deffontaines, Pierre, ed. *The Larousse Encyclopedia of World Geography.* 1965. Includes, with maps and illustrations, articles on nations grouped by geographical area.

Geology

Bibliography of North American Geology. 1919– . Annual. Cumulated in four volumes covering approximately a decade each, it lists books and articles for the study of the geology of North America.
  Dictionary of Geological Terms. 1962. Defines for students and teachers terms concerning rocks, minerals, and fossils. Published by the American Geological Institute.

History

Historical Abstracts: Bibliography of the World's Periodical Literature, 1775– . 1955– . Quarterly. Covers political, intellectual, and social history of nations (except the United States and Canada). Annual indexes by author and by subject.
  America: History and Life: A Guide to Periodical Literature on the United States and Canada. 1964– . Quarterly. Abstracts of books and articles covering the pre-Columbian period to the present. Subject index.
  Johnson, Thomas H. *The Oxford Companion to American History.* 1966. Concise entries on people and events of United States history with some bibliographies.
  Adler, Mortimer J. *The Negro in American History.* 1969. 3 volumes. A study of blacks in American life from 1493 to 1968.

Linguistics

Language and Language Behavior Abstracts. 1970– . Quarterly. Abstracts of articles with author, subject, and periodical indexes. International in scope.

MLA International Bibliography, volume III. (See following section, Literature).

Literature

MLA International Bibliography of Books and Articles on the Modern Languages and Literatures. 1921– . Annual. Each volume contains three sections (I—English and American literature, II—Other world literatures, III—Linguistics) with author and subject indexes and a key to abbreviations. Includes books and articles; international in scope.

Watson, George, ed. *The New Cambridge Bibliography of English Literature.* 1969–1974. 4 volumes. Covers works by and about British and Commonwealth authors writing from 600 to 1950 with an extensive bibliography.

Spiller, Robert E., et al., eds. *Literary History of the United States.* 1963. A history of American literature with a bibliography indexed by author, subject, and title.

Feder, Lillian, ed. *Crowell's Handbook of Classical Literature.* 1964. Provides definitions and interpretations of authors, figures, and locations occurring in classical literature and mythology.

Mathematics

Mathematical Reviews. 1940– . Monthly. Includes reviews of all types of publications in the field of mathematics. International in scope. Published by the American Mathematical Society.

Burington, Richard Stevens. *Handbook of Mathematical Tables and Formulas.* 1973. Provides information for work in mathematics for students and professional mathematicians.

Music

Music Index: The Key to Current Music Periodical Literature. 1949– . Monthly. Indexes by subject and author more than two hundred periodicals in the fields of music and dance.

Scholes, Percy A., ed. *The Oxford Companion to Music.* 1970. Includes definitions of musical terms, the history of music and of musical instruments, discussions of forms and schools of music, and biographical information on composers and musicians. Illustrated.

Philosophy

The Philosopher's Index: An International Index to Philosophical Periodicals. 1967– . Quarterly. Indexes by subject and author eighty American and foreign journals of philosophy.
Edwards, Paul, ed. *The Encyclopedia of Philosophy.* 1973. 4 volumes. A comprehensive work covering philosophical topics and theorists for students and specialists.

Physics

Science Abstracts. 1898– . Monthly. Covers the fields of physics, electronics, and computers by abstracts from a wide range of publications.
Handbook of Chemistry and Physics. 1914– . Revised annually. Provides tables of chemical and physical information.
Besancon, Robert M., ed. *The Encyclopedia of Physics.* 1974. Offers short introductory articles on the history, symbols, and terminology of physics.

Psychology

Harvard University. *The Harvard List of Books in Psychology.* 1971. An annotated bibliography of books arranged by branches of psychology considered "important and valuable in psychology at the present time."
Psychological Abstracts. 1927– . 2 volumes per year. Includes summaries of publications in psychology and related fields and has an author-and-subject index.
Eysenck, H. J., ed. *Encyclopedia of Psychology.* 1972. Contains definitions of terms, historical surveys, descriptions of research, analyses of schools of psychology, and bibliographies.

Religion

Religious and Theological Abstracts. 1958– . Provides abstracts of articles in Jewish, Christian, and Muslim publications.
Religious Periodicals Index. 1970– . Quarterly. Indexes articles in American periodicals representing a range of denominations and viewpoints.

The Interpreter's Dictionary of the Bible. 1962. 4 volumes. An encyclopedia of names, terms, and subjects found in the Bible. A basic reference work for students and scholars.

Science and Technology—General References

Jenkins, Frances Briggs. *Science Reference Sources.* 1969. A bibliography of science reference sources arranged by subject and by type of material.

Science Books: A Quarterly Review. 1965– . Evaluations published by the American Association for the Advancement of Science, of scientific materials.

McGraw-Hill Encyclopedia of Science and Technology. 1971. 15 volumes. An encyclopedia of the sciences for the general reader. Illustrated. Updated in yearbooks.

Social Sciences—General References

International Encyclopedia of the Social Sciences. 1967. 17 volumes. Focuses on the development and expansion of the social sciences in the 1960's. Includes a detailed index and bibliographical material.

White, Carl M., et al., eds. *Sources of Information in the Social Sciences: A Guide to the Literature.* 1973. Deals with works on history, geography, economics, business administration, sociology, anthropology, psychology, education, political science, and geography.

American Behavioral Scientist: The ABS Guide to Recent Publications in the Social and Behavioral Sciences. 1965– . Annual. An annotated bibliography, indexed by author, subject, and title, of articles, books, and reports.

Sociology

Sociological Abstracts. 1952– . 5 issues per year. Abstracts classified by fields in sociology and indexed by subject and author.

Mitchell, G. Duncan, ed. *A Dictionary of Sociology.* 1968. Defines terms for beginning students of sociology.

Using Non-Book Library Resources

In addition to books and journals, most libraries provide a variety of non-book materials for your research. The most frequently used of these resources are audio-visual materials and documents, but non-book materials may also include pamphlets, photographs, videotapes, stamp collections, and works of art.

AUDIO-VISUAL MATERIALS

Audio-visual materials include a wide range of resources: photographs, microfilm, microfiche, slides, filmstrips, films, records, tape recordings, and transparencies. These materials may be cataloged with books or separately. Usually they are housed in a separate place with a special catalog. You should not overlook the possibility of using audio-visual materials, which are increasing rapidly in both quantity and quality and are now available on nearly every subject.

Microfilm is the audio-visual material you will probably use most frequently for a research paper. A *microfilm* is film in strips or rolls that contains microscopic photographs of the pages of a book, newspaper, magazine, or other form of print. Microfilm is a practical way of storing large quantities of information, such as the back issues of newspapers. Also, since books and magazines have a limited physical life, putting them on microfilm is a way of preserving them. To read microfilm you need to use a machine that magnifies the image on the film to a readable size. Your library will provide you with such a machine along with instructions for using it.

A *microfiche* works on the same principle as microfilm, but pages, as many as eighty, are reproduced on a small card rather than on a length of film. Most libraries have facilities for making full-sized print copies from microfilm and microfiche.

You can find information about audio-visual materials available on your subject either in the card catalog or in reference guides such as the following.

National Information Center for Educational Media. *Index to 8mm Cartridges.* 1971.
_____. *Index to 16mm Educational Films.* 1972.
_____. *Index to 35mm Educational Filmstrips.* 1972.
_____. *Index to Educational Video Tapes.* 1972.
_____. *Index to Educational Audio Tapes.* 1972.
Roach, Helen. *Spoken Records.* 1970.
Schwann Record and Tape Guide. Monthly.

These volumes are indexed by subject and generally include numerous cross-references. You can determine the running time, price, and producer and find a brief description of the material in these sources; but you will usually need to consult the catalog of the company that produced the audio-visual material for a complete description of the level, scope, and purpose of the presentation. In addition, the *National Union Catalog* and the *Library of Congress Catalog* have supplemental volumes for some audio-visual materials; these supplements provide information on availability of the materials in libraries.

GOVERNMENT PUBLICATIONS: DOCUMENTS

Any publication authorized or printed by a local, state, or national governing body is called a *document*. United States government publications cover a wide range of areas: records of committee and Congressional proceedings, rules and regulations, results of studies and research, projections of future trends, analyses of institutions, and any other reports prepared by government agencies. The United States Government Printing Office generally publishes these documents and offers them free or at cost to libraries and to the public.

Government publications may be shelved separately or integrated with other library materials. Since no single method of arranging documents applies to all libraries, you may wish to consult a librarian about their location. Information on ordering documents from the U.S. Superintendent of Documents can be found in each volume of the indexes listed here.

The Monthly Catalog of the United States Government. 1898–
A listing of all government publications including the title, date, length, purpose and availability of the document.

Congressional Information Service [CIS] Index to Publications of the United States Congress. 1970–   . Monthly. An index with abstracts of House and Senate documents, reports, hearings, and special publications.

Boyd, Anne Morris, and Rips, Rae E. *United States Government Publications.* 1949. Describes the nature of the publications of the various branches of government. An introduction to the various kinds of documents.

NEW METHODS OF INFORMATION RETRIEVAL

The amount of printed material is increasing rapidly. In the year 1900, 10,000 periodicals were being published; today there are more than 100,000 periodicals published. The Yale University Library has estimated that if it continues its present acquisitions policies, it will have 200 million books by the year 2040, which will fill 6,000 miles of shelves and require 80 acres for the card catalog.[1] To deal with this problem, libraries are placing more and more materials on microfilm. Some libraries have begun to keep their card catalogs on microfilm. Another method for coping with the expanding amount of material involves computer reference services. In the fields of business, economics, sciences, social science, technology, and law, computerized reference services are available in some libraries. At present, these services are quite expensive and primarily useful to graduate students and professionals. The technology of libraries will be changing rapidly in the next decades, however, and your research techniques will evolve with it. In the meantime, if you wish to do research and to learn on your own, there is no substitute for knowing how to use the tools of the library—its card catalog and reference works.

[1]William A. Katz, *Basic Information Sources,* Vol. I of *Introduction to Reference Work,* 2nd ed. (New York: McGraw-Hill, 1974), p. 26.

4
Writing the rough draft

How do I bring everything together?

Researchers are often reluctant to stop taking notes and go on to writing the rough draft. Even if you do not feel that you have discovered everything that exists on your subject, you are probably ready to begin writing your rough draft when you are able to answer your controlling question, in other words, when you have refined and stated your controlling idea.

After formulating your controlling idea, the first step is organizing the information you have recorded in a way that supports your controlling idea. This organization involves dividing your cards by subtopics, a process you began while taking notes, and developing an outline based on a logical arrangement of these subtopics. The outline will guide you during the writing of the rough draft. Neither of these tasks can be completed independently of the other, for they overlap and complement each other. You may find, for example, that you need to rework your outline; and revision of the outline will likely result in shifting your note cards. Even during the process of writing the rough draft you may need to reorganize your outline.

A sample research paper appears on pages 145–97. It will serve as a model for your own paper and will be referred to in this chapter to demonstrate the process of organizing, outlining, and writing a rough draft.

EXERCISE 4.1

1. Read and study the sample research paper, including the title page, the outline, the notes, and the bibliography. As you read the paper, record the numbers of the paragraphs where you locate the following features. Keep in mind that the methods of paragraph development can also be methods of development for the whole research paper.

Features   Paragraph Number(s)
    Controlling idea   _____

    Introduction   _____

    Body paragraphs   _____

    Conclusion   _____

Methods of Development
    Supporting details   _____

    Illustration   _____

    Comparison and contrast   _____

    Definition   _____

    Analysis   _____

2. Is this research paper a report, a thesis, or a proposal?

_____

Refining and Stating the Controlling Idea

The process of answering your controlling question in the form of a controlling idea normally goes through several phases as your research progresses. The development of the controlling question for the sample research paper illustrates this process. After discovering in some preliminary reading that the audience of soap operas includes not only fellow college students but also a Supreme Court judge, and that soap operas have a larger audience than any other type of television program, the writer, whose curiosity was aroused about the reasons for this popularity, decided on the following as a preliminary controlling question:

Why do so many people watch soap operas?

After some additional reading about the nature of soap operas and other television programs, the writer refined the question.

What unique qualities of soap operas enable them to appeal to a large and varied audience?

In the course of doing research the writer formulated a tentative answer, or a preliminary controlling idea.

Soap operas appeal to people because they deal with the family, a source of universal concern and fascination.

This preliminary controlling idea presented further questions: "How do soap operas treat the family?" and "What effect does this treatment of the family have on viewers?" More research provided answers to these auxiliary questions and enabled the writer to refine the controlling idea; the controlling idea became a complete response to the initial question.

The unique form of soap operas and their concentration on family themes provide viewers with emotional, moral, and educational resources for dealing with their own family lives.

You can see that the process of refining and stating the controlling idea involves several phases. You also probably changed your controlling question and preliminary controlling ideas as you did research.

Assignment

Turn back to Chapter 1, page 28. Write down the controlling idea that you now intend to use to develop your outline and to write your rough draft.

Dividing the Notes into Categories

You began the process of organizing your notes when you divided your preliminary controlling question into smaller parts, or subtopics, and then listed them in an order for investigation. This simple and temporary outline enabled you to place a notation or heading—the subtopic—on each note card. When taking down the note illustrated, the writer of the sample research paper annotated it to indicate that it might be used to substantiate the researcher's assertion that the content of soap operas involves the family.

You can begin to divide your note cards into categories by using the subtopics and headings you noted while doing research or refining your controlling question. Remember that these subtopics are preliminary and tentative. If you find that any idea on a note card should be used in a way different from your original intention, you can simply cross out the subtopic you first entered and substitute a new one, as the altered card on page 109 illustrates.

Content - family

Phillips, p. 117
" On all my shows, I try to present a family in the round — the life-giving strength that comes from a secure family unit, and the destructiveness its members can unconsciously wreck on one another. Nancy Hughes, the real heroine of 'As the World Turns' (as Chris, her husband is the real hero), is a devoted mother, a loving wife, a creative homemaker. ..."

Note Card with Subtopic as Heading

Content—family
Contrast with
Situation Comedies

Adler, p. 83

" This [the soap opera] is not
the evening's entertainment, which
one watches, presumably with members of the family; not the shared
family-situation comedies, which
(with the important exception of 'all
in the Family') are comfortable
distortions of what family life is
like."

Note Card with Subtopic Changed

If possible, work at a large table where you can spread out your note cards to see at a glance exactly what information you have. Then you can place together the cards that belong in the same category. After analyzing the note cards, the writer of the sample paper organized them into the following subtopics of the general topic:

Audience
Women characters
Definition of the program
  type
Form
Advertising
Production costs
Parodies
Viewers' reactions

Content
Artistic value
Educational nature
Controversy on fantasy versus
  reality
Values presented
Comparison with situation
  comedies
Nature of television

You should read through all of your note cards several times both during and after the organization process to be sure that you have placed them properly. If you find that you have taken down more than one idea to a note card, you should make another card to separate the material that belongs in another category. You may also want to make duplicates of some cards and place them in two categories to provide yourself with the possibility of using the idea in either one.

Developing an Outline

After dividing your note cards into subtopics you are ready to begin developing your outline. In formulating your outline you are making decisions that establish the ideas you will discuss and the way they will relate to and support the controlling idea. Outlining is a process of determining the logical relationships between the ideas in your paper. It is essential that you understand those relationships before you begin to write. It can be tempting to cut short the outlining procedure on the assumption that the

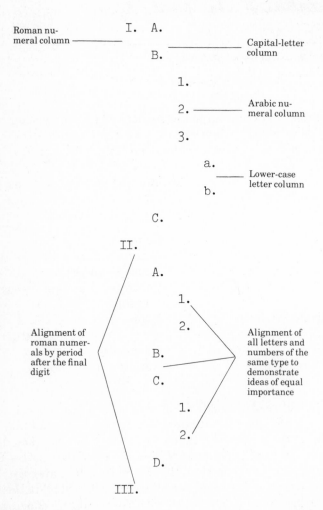

Structure of an Outline

paper will flow once you begin writing, but you will only be delaying the time when you will have to construct a coherent and logical plan of organization—an outline.

PRINCIPLES OF OUTLINING

An outline is an arrangement of ideas by numerals and by letters that demonstrates the logical relationship of the ideas, their relative importance, and the order in which they are developed in the paper. Ideas with equal importance are designated by the same kind of numeral or letter. That is, all ideas designated by large roman numerals (I, II, III) are equal in importance and they are of more importance than those ideas indented below them under the headings A, B, and C. The same relationship of subordination holds between the capital letters and their subdivisions (1, 2, 3). If a category is divided, it must have at least two subdivisions, since the concept of a division implies at least two parts. Study the mechanics and structure of the skeleton of an outline shown on page 110.

TYPES OF OUTLINES

The two types of outlines are a topic outline and a sentence outline. A topic outline uses a word or phrase to indicate each idea. In a sentence outline each idea is presented with a complete sentence. Study the portions of topic and sentence outlines for the same paper shown here.

Topic outline:

    I. TV programs using existing forms

        A. News program

        B. Variety show

   II. TV programs representing new forms

        A. Drama documentary

        B. Talk show

The topic outline is effective because it allows both the writer and the reader to discern the structure of the paper easily. Headings in a topic outline should be parallel, that is, use the same grammatical form. If one heading is a noun, all headings on the same level should take the form of a noun or a noun phrase.

Sentence outline:

I. Some types of television programs consist of a combination of existing forms.

    A. News programs use techniques of news gathering and presentation already existing in the fields of radio broadcasting and newspaper publishing.

    B. Variety shows include the kind of entertainment found in the circus, vaudeville, and the music hall.

II. Other types of television programs are new forms, which have developed as a result of the nature of the medium of television.

    A. The drama documentary is a factual report presented dramatically and graphically.

    B. The talk show is a new form of discussion.

The sentence outline indicates the actual content of the paper more completely than the topic outline. Because the writing of sentences forces the writer to be specific about the division of ideas in the paper, a sentence outline often brings the writer closer to a final organization of the paper than a topic outline.

Your instructor probably will have a preference or requirement concerning the type of outline you use. You might be asked to develop either a topic outline or a sentence outline, or you might be asked to begin with a topic outline and write a sentence outline from it. You should ask about the form required at each stage. The topic outline will be used in the discussion of outlining in this chapter.

THE PATTERN OF ORGANIZATION

Before you begin to outline, you should write out your controlling idea for the rough draft of your paper. Then you can decide on a pattern of organization appropriate for the development and support of this controlling idea. The major points in your paper might be arranged according to one of the following principles: chronology (past, present, future); spatial or geographical order (city, state, nation, world; or West, Midwest, South, East); or logical relationships (cause and effect; comparison and contrast; or arguments for and against).

You should choose the pattern of organization most appropriate to your subject. For example, if your research on pay television led you to the conclusion that there are both advantages and disadvantages to the system, you would probably organize your discussion with arguments for and against pay television. If, however, you concluded that pay television is superior to commercial television, you might write a paper of comparison and contrast.

The decision you make about the overall logical pattern of your paper will likely produce two or three major divisions for the body of the paper. These should be recorded beside capitalized roman numerals. The writer of the paper on soap operas decided that the organizing principle of the paper should be cause and effect and recorded the two major divisions of the paper as:

I. The nature of soap operas (Cause)

II. Effect of soap operas on viewers (Effect)

Another writer might organize a paper on soap operas completely differently. A person who chose to discuss the evolution of radio soap operas into television soap operas might divide the paper chronologically:

I. Radio soap operas (1930–1960)

II. Television soap operas (1946–1979)

A writer who chose to compare and contrast radio soap operas and their television offspring might choose a pattern of analysis, dividing soap operas (on both media) into parts:

I. Plots

II. Characters

Remember that your headings must demonstrate a logical pattern of organization and division of your paper. The following outline does not represent a logical division of the subject because the elements do not correspond in scope, importance, or category of ideas.

> I.   Television soap operas
>
> II. <u>Days of Our Lives</u>
>
> III. Effects on viewers

EXERCISE 4.2

Circle any heading in each of the following outlines that violates principles of logical division or ordering of ideas.

Outline 1

> I.   Talk shows
>
> II. Daytime television programming
>
> III. Game shows

Outline 2

> A. Advertising time
>
> B. Nielsen ratings
>
> C. Programming time

Outline 3

> I.   Japan
>
> II. United States
>
> III. Great Britain
>
> IV. Development of television technology

Outline 4

> A. Effects of television on children
>
> B. Rise in reading scores
>
> C. Decrease in ability to concentrate

Once you have the major divisions that result from the pattern you select, you can begin to flesh out each section by using the same process. The writer of the sample paper employed the method of analysis to divide the section on effects of soap operas into three parts.

II. Effect of soap operas on viewers

    A. Emotional strength

    B. Moral support

    C. Educational resources

The writer determined that the cause of these effects lay in the nature of soap operas and divided the first section of the outline into three subdivisions to define and explain this nature.

I. The nature of soap operas

    A. Definition of the kind of program

    B. Content (plot, character)

    C. Form (structure)

Each of these subdivisions can also be divided, as section I-C of the outline for the sample paper illustrates.

    C. Form

        1. Daily serial

        2. Primacy of character over actor

        3. Near-realism

        4. Aural nature

This process of subdivision can be repeated as often as necessary. For a paper of 2,500 to 5,000 words an outline including three levels of subdivision usually provides enough detail. Your instructor may ask that you submit a topic outline or a sentence outline before you write your rough draft; and you should find out how much detail is required in the outline.

ELIMINATION OF INFORMATION

Excluding information that does not logically support your controlling idea is just as essential to good outlining as including information that does. You probably will not be able to use every category on your note cards in your outline. When you began your research you were working with a broad controlling question, which means that you probably took notes on a wide range of aspects of your subject. When the writer of the sample paper reached the conclusion that the appeal of soap operas lies in their unique treatment of the family, those notes that did not deal with soap opera's relationship to the family had to be discarded. A category of cards dealing with stage and screen actors who began their careers on soap operas, which could have been used in a paper about the artistic merits of soap operas, had to be omitted from the outline of a paper about soap operas and the family. Any note cards that do not fit logically into your outline should be put aside; but you should not throw them away. You may discover as you work that you can use the information in a footnote or that a change you make in the outline will allow you to use the idea.

Writing the Rough Draft

Before you begin to write, you should have a complete outline and note cards separated into bundles for each division or subdivision of the outline. The cards should be arranged in the order in which you plan to use them.

THE WRITING PROCESS

At the draft stage you should not worry too much about style, word choice, or sentence structure. During the revisions of your draft you will be able to polish the language. As you write and review, you should ask yourself the following questions about the content:

1. Does everything in the paper contribute to the support of the controlling idea?
2. Are the paragraphs arranged in a logical sequence?
3. Do any sections overlap or repeat others?

The physical appearance of the draft should not concern you either as long as you can read it. The rough draft will not and should not look like a final copy. You should allow yourself room on the paper to revise by skipping lines if you write in longhand or by triple-spacing if you type. This space will permit you to rewrite, add, or eliminate phrases and sentences without recopying the whole draft.

Body Paragraphs

You should formulate a clear topic sentence for each body paragraph. This topic sentence serves two purposes. First, it expresses your conclusion about the materials and information you intend to present in the paragraph. Second, it tells your reader how the paragraph will contribute to the support of your controlling idea and how it relates to material you have previously presented. The topic sentence should generally be in your own words and should not include quotations. In developing the paragraph you will proceed by integrating the ideas on your note cards with your own ideas.

To provide variety and interest you should think about using the several methods of paragraph development you have learned: illustration, supporting details, comparison and contrast, definition, and analysis. Before you begin each paragraph, you should ask yourself which of these methods is most suitable for the material. If you find that you are developing every paragraph in one way, you should attempt to vary the method. You may want to review the discussion of the methods of paragraph development presented in Chapter 1.

Introduction and Conclusion

It is often easier to write the introduction to the paper last rather than first. Your controlling idea can serve as an introduction for the rough draft, and you can concentrate on developing the body paragraphs to support your controlling idea. If you do write the introduction first, you should revise it after drafting the body of the paper; also, you should not labor over the conclusion until you are certain that the paper supports your controlling idea.

SELECTION OF SOURCES

Your purpose in using sources is to support your own conclusions. Therefore, you should use the ideas on your note cards to support your points rather than to repeat what others have said. While you do have the responsibility for noting the points at which other writers agree or disagree with your ideas, a research paper reflects your own conclusion developed from your own research.

You may find that you cannot use all of the ideas you have on note cards without overloading your paragraphs; and you will have to make some selections. In cases where two or more authors have said approximately the same thing, you will have to choose the one you want to cite or quote in the body of the paper, leaving the other for mention in a bibliographical note. In the case of a controversial or disputable point, you should choose the writer with the most authority or competence in the field. If you have two authors with equal expertise, you probably will want to choose one you have not previously cited in order to give wider support to your views. Where authority is not as essential, you may choose the writer who phrased the idea in the most distinctive or dramatic form. In each case, you would then refer to the other writer in the text or in a bibliographical note.

FORMS FOR INCLUDING IDEAS FROM SOURCES

You may present ideas from your sources in two basic forms: direct quotation or summary. Your decision about which of these to use should be based on the nature of the material and the purpose it is to serve in your paper. In either case, you must give credit to your sources (page 122) in the form of a note.

Direct Quotation

Direct quotation, the inclusion of sentences or phrases in the source's words, is appropriate when you wish to retain the effect of the original wording or when you want to add force to your own conclusion by citing an authority. You should use direct quotation discriminatingly and sparingly, however, for the words of others should complement and strengthen your writing, not replace or overshadow it. In the final version of your paper you will indicate a note by placing a number raised one-half space above the line, called a *superscript,* after the quotation or summary. The number refers the reader to a numbered note either at the back of the paper or at the bottom of the page that provides information about the source. The superscript should be placed at the end of any sentence in which an idea from a source appears or at the end of a phrase when ideas from more than one source are present in a sentence. (See pages 122–27 for further information about indicating your use of someone else's ideas.)

You may incorporate a direct quotation in your paper in several ways. When you use a complete sentence from your source, you can precede it with a phrase or sentence indicating the name and/or the professional identity of the person being quoted.

Bud Kloss, producer of <u>All My Children</u>, states, "If we

feel a subject we haven't done fits into our story, we

back it up; we go to the network and fight for it."[45]

The identifying information may also come at the conclusion of the direct quotation, and the superscript follows the entire sentence.

"The prospect of the mystery is one of forbidden excitement, and the detective allows us to experience it without being dirtied," Horace Newcomb explains.[2]

When direct quotations run more than four lines in your text, they are indented and single spaced. (See typing instructions on page 142). In this case, the indented material is *not* placed in quotation marks, as in the following excerpt from paragraph 15 of the sample paper.

Dr. John R. Lion, a psychiatrist who also believes that soap operas can be therapeutic, points out the value of the form:

In the end, I think the most realistic programs on TV are the soap operas. They portray life with all its complexities and insolubilities. Many of my patients are helped by watching them, and I often suggest . . .

Because this indentation tends to interrupt the flow of the paper and to distract the reader, long direct quotations should be used only when you are certain they are necessary.

The punctuation of direct quotations, whether they are double or single spaced, follows the grammatical rules for the use of punctuation. If the quotation is introduced preceding or following a word like "says," the sentence is punctuated with a comma and quotation marks in the same way that a direct quotation is inserted into an essay or a story.

"According to our research," Gerald S. Lesser concludes, "beyond responding to puppets and animated figures, children generally prefer watching and listening to other children rather than to adults."[5]

When the introduction to a quotation is a complete sentence and the succeeding quotation demonstrates or illustrates a point made in that introductory sentence, a colon is used.

Richard K. Doan points out another of the fallacies in rating systems: "Horrendous stories have been told of ratings being influenced by homes leaving a set on at a stretch with nobody watching, or turned on to 'amuse' a pet dog, or to keep the family cat warm."[16]

In either case, the quotation is considered part of the same sentence which introduces it, and the entire sentence should be punctuated according to rules for correct usage.

Partial quotation, the direct quotation of a phrase or portion of a sentence, allows you to use the exact words of your source without including material irrelevant to your purpose. In partial quotation, you integrate the direct quotation into your own sentence, as the writer of the sample paper did in the following sentence.

Ideal television actors are a "blur of countenance and outline," McLuhan believes.[33]

In Chapter 2 you learned to use brackets to indicate additions or changes within direct quotations and ellipses to indicate any deletions. You should also use these symbols in your paper whenever you change a direct quotation in any way. Remember that your changes must not distort the meaning of the original. When you use only a phrase from your source, you do not need to use ellipses on either side, since it is obvious that the portion was not a complete sentence in the original source.

The authors of Presidential Television maintain that "television influences public opinion."[5]

The following sentence employs partial quotation, utilizing ellipses to indicate material omitted.

In a speech to the House Subcommittee on Communications,

Dr. Thomas Elmendorf stated that "the accumulation of

evidence suggests . . . that children will copy TV

violence. . . ."[5]

| Three of the ellipsis points show that although the word *violence* completes a grammatical sentence, it was not the end of the original sentence. | The fourth point serves as a period marking the end of the sentence in the research paper. | Ellipsis shows that a phrase has been omitted. |

Including Ideas from Sources through Partial Quotation

Summary

Summary or indirect quotation, the statement in your own words of ideas contained in the source, should be used whenever you have no reason to retain the language of the source through direct quotation. A superscript at the end of a sentence refers the reader to the origin of the material you summarize. With this form you should be particularly careful about your presentation of the source, being certain that you have not misunderstood or misstated the ideas.

Your introduction to a summary may include the name of the source, as in the following example from the sample paper.

After using soap operas in therapy groups, psychiatric

social worker Anne Kilguss concluded that the motiva-

tion for watching them was an attempt to deal with

problems rather than to escape from them.[34]

If the name of the source is not of significance to the point you are making, you can identify the source as part of the note.

When punishments for actions against the family are not

supplied by the script, viewers often demand them in

angry letters.[41]

EXERCISE 4.3

Turn to selection 13, by William Melody, in the Sourcebook. Use paragraph 2 to complete the following assignments.

1. Write a paragraph in which you introduce a complete sentence of direct quotation of Melody.
2. Write a paragraph in which you use a partial quotation of Melody.
3. Write a paragraph in which you summarize Melody's ideas in your own words.
4. Write a paragraph in which you use the ellipsis to delete material from a direct quotation of Melody.

PRINCIPLES OF DOCUMENTATION

As you incorporate ideas from the note cards into your paper, you should keep in mind the principles of documentation in order to avoid plagiarism. You should cite the source of every idea you have learned or formulated from your reading for the research paper, whether you express the idea in your own words or quote the author directly.

The use of two or more consecutive words from a source, when those words express the essence of a writer's idea or involve distinctive phrasing, is considered direct quotation and requires the use of quotation marks. Suppose a writer were to have on a note card the following sentence by Edward Jay Epstein: "If correspondents cannot find plausible balancing views, producers generally prefer that they present the story ironically, rather than as a one-sided polemic." The use of the common words *rather than* or *as a* would not require quotation marks in a research paper, but phrases of even two words such as "balancing views" and "one-sided polemic" must be quoted directly because they represent the expression of an original idea of the source.

The only ideas you need not document are items that are common knowledge ("July 4 is Independence Day in the United States"; or, "Walter Cronkite was anchorman on CBS's evening news during Watergate") and opinions that you have held or facts that you have known for so long that you do not remember their source. Although you might already know a fact, if you come across a statement of it in your reading or if your research indicates that others share your opinions, you should note this in your documentation, both because it strengthens your own conclusions or judgments and because you want to acknowledge another's expression of the same idea. Plagiarism generally results from carelessness with these principles of documentation.

EXERCISE 4.4

Read carefully the following sentence from selection 12 in the Sourcebook (paragraph 27).

The advent of multi-channel cable television and of pay television will reinforce this trend, already apparent at the margins of broadcast television (i.e., UHF stations, morning and late-evening programs, etc.), toward a more selective utilization of the medium.

Determine which of the uses of the ideas in this sentence in the following direct and indirect quotations constitute plagiarism and which are correct citation of the source. Write a *P* in the space to indicate plagiarism and a *C* to indicate correct documentation.

_____ 1. Development and diversification in television technology will result in more selective utilization of television.
_____ 2. The development of new forms of television technology will result in more selective viewing of television.[1]
_____ 3. Viewing of programs on UHF stations tends to be more selective than viewing of programs on VHF stations.
_____ 4. Kas Kalba believes that "selective utilization" of television will increase with "the advent of multi-channel cable television and of pay television."[1]

The following annotated paragraph from a research paper on the ways in which television has transformed modern life provides a review of the criteria for selection of sources and the forms for including ideas from sources, and the principles of documentation. The names of the authors and the paragraph numbers given in the annotations refer to articles in the Sourcebook. By examining the original sources (Newcomb, selection 15, paragraphs 11 and 12; Boorstin, selection 1, paragraphs 9 and 12; Kalba, selection 12, paragraphs 1 and 4) you can see how this writer used them to support the topic sentence.

Television has also transformed our lives by separating us from one another. Families who once had lively discussion of the events of the day at the dinner table now sit in silence watching the evening news. Often they do not even share their reactions with each other. People who might have joined their neighbors for an evening of conversation or music now more often spend their time sitting silently in front of their own private television sets. Daniel J. Boorstin points out that even other people who once shared public events such as drama or sports have now been replaced by simulated audience response.[1] Commentators and directors intercede between viewers and athletes to shape our responses to sports events.[2] Television has also separated us from our elected representatives in government. Indeed, Boorstin maintains that the segregating effect of television has altered our view of our democratic system: "Newly isolated from his government . . . the citizen felt a frustrating new disproportion between how often and how vividly political leaders could get their messages to him and how often and how vividly he could get his message to them."[3] And if Kas Kalba's predictions about "tomorrow's electronic community" are correct, we will also be separated from other officials and professionals in our society, since activities such as education and banking will take place at home through the television set.[4]

CITATION AT THE DRAFT STAGE

The citation of your sources in your final draft will take the form of notes on a separate page at the end of your paper, as the note pages of the sample research paper demonstrate. When you are writing your rough draft, however, you can avoid interrupting your work with the writing of a separate notes page by inserting within the text the information necessary to write notes. There are three different types of notes—source notes, bibliographical notes, and informational notes—and you can prepare for writing them on a separate note page later by placing a minimal amount of material in brackets in your rough draft.

Source Notes

Source notes provide the information necessary to locate the material cited; that is, they provide the author's name, the title, and the facts of publication. In the rough draft, the author's last name, part of the title if you have more than one work by the same author, and the appropriate page number or numbers are enough to enable you to write the full source note later, using your bibliography cards to supply the rest of the needed information.

A week-long monitoring of soap opera conversations in a 1970 study found that the subject discussed most frequently was the family. /Katzman, p. 212/

The abbreviated source note should be placed as close as possible to the sentence or phrase containing the quoted, paraphrased, or summarized material so that you will know precisely which words and/or ideas were derived from the source.

The soap opera, which Horace Newcomb has called "a world of words" /Newcomb, p. 168/ on a visual medium of television, is suited to viewers whose attention is partially distracted by their own family situations.

Your purpose in noting sources at the draft stage is to help yourself remember when you have taken an idea from one of your sources. You may change the exact placement of the notes at the final stage to streamline your paper, but now you must be extremely careful to note your sources accurately.

Bibliographical Notes

Bibliographical notes indicate materials the reader could use to explore a particular issue or facet of the subject in greater depth or to locate a useful discussion of a particular point. The information the writer will need to write such a bibliographical note (note 8 of the sample paper, for example) is included within brackets in the draft.

Thurber's definition contains truth as well as humor and

is a useful analysis of television as well as radio soap

operas, since many of the essential elements of the con-

tent and form of both have remained the same. /Edmond-

son and Rounds; Stedman contains histories of radio soap

operas/

Informational notes

Material that will help your reader to understand the subject, but that is either so long or so peripheral that it disrupts the flow of your writing, should be placed in an informational note. Informational notes may appear in the text of a rough draft in two forms. If you know when you are writing that you want to include an informational note at a particular point, you can simply place the information necessary in abbreviated form within brackets, as the writer did with the material developed in note 12 of the sample paper.

The name "soap opera," in fact, probably derives from

the sponsorship of the radio daytime serials by the man-

ufacturers of soap. /Wakefield, p. 13; Wakefield also

points out that "soap" means light or fluffy; Denison

gives other possibilities for the origin of the name/

In addition, if you discuss some facet of your subject that you later find does not fit smoothly or logically into the paper, yet you feel the material is interesting or important, you can present it in an informational note. In this case, you can place brackets around the appropriate sentences of the rough draft to reserve them for a note.

Turn to the note page of the sample research paper. For each of the first fifteen notes write whether the note is (a) source, (b) bibliographical, (c) informational, or (d) a combination of these.

1. _____   6. _____   11. _____

2. _____   7. _____   12. _____

3. _____   8. _____   13. _____

4. _____   9. _____   14. _____

5. _____   10. _____   15. _____

Testing the Reasoning

Throughout the writing of your rough draft you should examine the reasoning rigorously and objectively to be certain that you support your controlling idea with facts and opinions that provide solid and sufficient evidence. This process involves applying to your own writing the same criteria you learned to apply to the writing of others in Chapter 2.

EFFECTIVE USE OF FACTS AND OPINIONS

When you reason from facts, you must ask yourself whether you are presenting the facts necessary to sustain your conclusion. For example, to prove the assertion that the principal content of soap operas is the family, a single example of a program with a family central to its content would not be effective. To demonstrate this point in the sample research paper the writer presented the statistic that eleven of the fourteen currently running soap operas focus on one or two families as central to their content and cited as examples three of the leading programs (paragraph 3). If you use statistical facts, you must be certain that you interpret and present them accurately and provide any information, such as context, necessary for completeness and precision.

When you reason from opinions, you should check them for expertise and the presence of bias. To substantiate the conclusion that soap operas can benefit viewers emotionally, the writer used the opinions of a psychiatric social worker and a psychiatrist, both of whom qualify as experts, since they are professionals who have used soap operas as part of therapy programs (paragraph 15). While writers and producers of soap operas have very likely made similar statements, the writer did not use them because a reader could question the objectivity of their opinions. As you select opinions to support your controlling idea, you should constantly be evaluating their reliability.

SUFFICIENT EVIDENCE

If you find that you do not have enough evidence to develop and support your controlling idea, you may have to return to the library for more information. No matter how conscientious you have been in taking notes or how thoroughly you have traced sources on your topic, it is quite possible that you will have to search for additional materials. Even the most experienced researchers find that they want to reread an article to verify the accuracy of their note cards or to look for information that they recall reading but did not think necessary to record at the time. Any reworking of your controlling idea or reorganization of your outline could mean that you have to add a subject you might have previously thought inappropriate for your paper. In this case, you might have to locate new materials. All changes and additions of this kind should be made while the paper is still at the rough draft stage. The next step is polishing the paper into its final draft form.

5
Writing the final draft

How do I finish my paper?

Ideally, you should complete your rough draft early enough to put it away for at least several days before you begin the process of producing a final draft. Time away from your draft will enable you to be more objective about it than is possible when you are in the midst of writing. Revising the rough draft may involve shifting paragraphs or sentences, writing new sections, or eliminating sentences or whole paragraphs. The quality of your research paper, however, depends on your willingness to rework your rough draft, several times if necessary, until you are completely satisfied that everything in it is right.

Polishing the Writing

The writing in your research paper should allow your reader to concentrate on the ideas you present and to understand how the ideas relate to one another. A reader who has to stumble over awkward phrases, grammatical errors, and misspellings or who cannot see a logical plan of development is likely to misunderstand the paper or to lose interest in it. The most brilliant insights can be obscured by poor writing. Therefore, correcting and polishing the writing in the paper is a step crucial to the entire process of writing a research paper.

COHERENCE

As you learned in Chapter 1, coherence is the logical arrangement and development of ideas, sentences, and paragraphs. When you are certain that your ideas are arranged logically, you may need to supply your reader with transitions, or links, between them. Remember that your reader is likely to be much less familiar with your subject than you are and will need assistance in understanding how your sentences and paragraphs relate to each other and to the controlling idea. Transitions help the reader understand your paper by explaining such connections.

Transitions can be provided in several ways. You can make connections between the major sections of a paper with transitional paragraphs (see paragraph 12 of the sample research paper). A method of supplying a transition between sentences or paragraphs is the repetition of key words or their synonyms. Pronouns referring to key words also serve as transitions. In addition, certain words and expressions function as transitional devices; *on the other hand, similarly,* and *consequently* are a few of these. Your choice of transitional expression should accurately reflect the logical relationship of the ideas you connect. If, for example, you wish to indicate that you are adding more evidence similar to the kind that has preceded, you would not choose the expression *however,* which indicates the introduction of a different kind of idea. Rather, you would choose an expression such as *in addition* or *furthermore.* Any kind of transition you use should help your reader to follow your paper, but should not call attention to itself.

EXERCISE 5.1

Write down the transitional devices you find in paragraph 5 of the sample research paper, page 153. Your list should include repetition of key words, pronouns referring to key words, and transitional expressions.

_____   _____

_____   _____

FLUENCY

Fluency is the quality of smoothness in writing. Awkward sentences, stilted or pompous phrasing, and wordiness can break the smooth flow of ideas. You should rewrite your sentences until they read smoothly. A good way to test the fluency of your paper is to read it out loud or have someone else read it to you. If the reader hesitates in reading a sentence, it probably needs revision.

Assignment

Turn back to Chapter 1, page 29, and write down the controlling idea for your final draft.

WORD CHOICE

In writing your rough draft you may have used a few words repeatedly rather than taking the time to look up synonyms or more precise words. Such repetition produces monotonous prose and also may be a sign you have settled for approximate, rather than exact, meanings. During the process of revision you will have time to look for the best words for each idea, thereby providing variation and accuracy of expression.

Word choice is particularly important in the introductions to the sources you quote directly or indirectly. These introductory phrases should reflect the tone, nature, or strength of the idea as well as your own attitude toward it. In the basic phrase "John Doe says . . .," you might substitute one of the following words for *says: explains, continues, adds, postulates, states, declares, claims, mentions, advises, argues, notes, reasons, believes, demonstrates, emphasizes, insists, points out, contends, theorizes,* or any of a number of other synonyms for *says.* Each of these words conveys a slightly different meaning. If you write "John Doe claims that television news coverage is inadequate," you suggest that you may disagree with him. With the statement "John Doe explains that television news coverage is inadequate," you indicate that this statement is part of an extended explanation of the scope of television news coverage. With "Jane Doe demonstrates that television news coverage is inadequate," you imply that her presentation of evidence is convincing. The word you select to introduce either direct or indirect quotation, then, should accurately reflect your stance toward it, the context of the idea in the source, and its relation to other ideas on the same point.

The paragraph on page 132 demonstrates the revisions made in the rough draft to achieve correctness of grammar, coherence, fluency, variety of word choice, and accuracy in the introduction of a source.

receptive *controversial subjects*

Viewers seem particularly ~~open~~ to ~~information~~ pre-

for a variety of reasons

sented on soap operas. People do not have to be embar-

rassed by asking a neighbor for advice. (Watching a soap

opera can be a very private experience.) Knowledge is

imparted

~~given~~ in an impersonal way without the viewer ~~having to~~ *revealing*

a need for it. *has theorized*

~~say she needs it.~~ Daniel Boorstin ~~says~~ that televi-

sion has replaced gossip as a source of information

/Boorstin, <u>The Americans</u>, p. 487, and the fact that soap

are *a*

operas ~~have~~ educational ~~material in them~~ substantiates

opinion *embody*

that ~~view.~~ Soap operas, which ~~show~~ a problem in a ~~rea-~~

who seems real

~~listic~~ person, and allow viewers to watch that person

are often

resolve the problem over a long period of time, ~~can be~~

more convincing

~~more effective~~ than news programs or documentaries.

~~When an issue is dramatized as an individual's problem,~~

~~an audience can grasp its relationship to its own life~~

~~and is less likely to see it as an abstraction.~~

Handling the Technical Aspects

When you have a well-organized and well-written draft, you have completed the most difficult part of writing a research paper. The remainder of the process, however, is important and requires both time and care. The final stages include the preparation of notes, bibliography page or pages, and title page.

NOTES

Notes are indicated in the final draft by a raised number, or superscript, as you learned in Chapter 4 and as you can see in the sample paper and the Sourcebook. The notes themselves appear on a separate page or pages following the body of the research paper. See pages 181–91 for sample note pages. The purpose of notes is to give your reader information necessary to locate the materials you cite, to provide additional bibliographical information, or to amplify the text through further explanation.

To prepare notes you will need information from both your working bibliography cards and your rough draft. You should first number each bracketed note in your rough draft consecutively, checking carefully to be sure that you have not omitted any note in your numbering. This is also the time to check your bracketed notes against the note cards for accuracy of information, such as page numbers, and to make certain that the information on your working bibliography cards is complete.

First Reference

The first time you cite a source in a note, you include the author's name in first name, last name order; the name of the work; and the facts of publication, including the page number or numbers on which the material you have used appears. With the exception of the specific pages in question, which you have on your note cards and in your draft, the information you need to write such a note is on your bibliography card. The format this information takes in a note is different, however, as the illustrations demonstrate.

BIBLIOGRAPHY CARD

First reference to a book, basic form

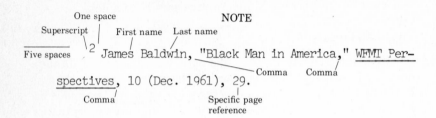

Baldwin, James. "Black Man in America." WFMT Perspectives. 10 (Dec. 1961), 25-30.

First reference to an article, basic form

NOTE

One space

Superscript | First name   Last name

Five spaces ^{2} James Baldwin, "Black Man in America," WFMT Per-
                                              Comma   Comma
spectives, 10 (Dec. 1961), 29.
        Comma   Specific page
                                 reference

This comparison of the form you used on your bibliography cards and the form for the first reference in your notes demonstrates the different principles involved.

Bibliography Card Form	First-Reference Form for Notes
1. Author's name appears last name first.	1. Author's name in first name, last name order, preceded by a superscript.
2. Title includes any subtitle present on the title page of a book or in the title of an article.	2. Subtitle may be omitted, and should be if it is long.
3. Book: Facts of publication *do not* appear in parentheses.	3. Book: Facts of publication *do* appear in parentheses.
4. Book: No page number is given; the reference is to the entire book.	4. Book: The abbreviation for page(s), *p.* or *pp.,* is followed by number(s) indicating the page(s) of the material used.
Article: Inclusive page numbers for the entire article are given.	Article: Only the page number(s) of the material used is entered.
5. Periods separate parts of the entry.	5. Commas separate parts of the entry.

Subsequent Reference

After you have presented complete information in the first reference to a work, you need not repeat all of it when you refer to the same work again. If you have used only one work by an author, the author's last name and the page(s) are sufficient to identify the work.

[22] Vogel, p. 35.

[23] Smith, Jones, and Pierce, pp. 96-98.

When you have more than one work by the same author, you should add the title for clarity.

[24] Arlen, "Griefspeak," p. 224.

[25] Arlen, "Wednesday Evening in Chicago,"

    pp. 236-37.

If you refer to more than one volume of a work by the same author, you should enter the volume number as identification.

[26] Ruskin, V, p. 21.

In your reading you may find the abbreviated Latin terms *ibid.*, *op. cit.*, and *loc. cit.* used for subsequent reference. These abbreviations are no longer recommended since they are unnecessarily confusing, and they have been replaced by the forms shown above. For the meaning of these and other abbreviations currently or formerly in use in articles and research papers, consult Appendix C.

Reference to More than One Work

When you cite two or more sources in one note, semicolons separate the individual notes. In the following example of a note with multiple reference, the first and third sources are cited as subsequent references, and the second source is cited as a first reference.

[27] Rivers and Slater, p. 21; Carnegie Commission

on Educational Television, Public Television (New York:

n.p., 1967), p. 37; Schramm, Lyle, and Parker, pp. 127–31.

Bibliographical Notes

The information in a bibliographical note takes the appropriate note form, *not* bibliography form, and it is presented within a sentence that explains the nature of the material cited. Bibliographical notes may refer to an entire work or to specific pages within a work.

[28] For a thorough discussion of the early years of radio, consult Erik Barnouw, A Tower in Babel (New York: Oxford Univ. Press, 1966).

[29] Thomas E. Patterson and Robert D. McClure present another view of the power of television to shape national elections in The Unseeing Eye: The Myth of Television Power in National Elections (New York: Putnam, 1976), particularly pp. 123–56.

Informational Notes

The source of the material is cited in note form either within or at the end of the informational note.

[12] Wakefield, p. 13. Wakefield points out that soap also connotes light or fluffy content. On the origin of the name see also Merrill Denison, "Soap Opera," Harper's, 180 (Apr. 1940), 408–505. Denison states that another name for radio soap operas was "strips show," perhaps a mispronunciation of "script show" or a reference to the comic strips, a form to which soap operas have been compared.

Source notes, bibliographical notes, and informational notes may be combined, but regardless of the combination, the note form appropriate for each is used.

BIBLIOGRAPHY

Your bibliography cards contain all the information you will need to write your bibliography pages, the final pages of your paper. You should be aware of three types of bibliographies: a complete bibliography, an annotated bibliography, and a bibliography of works cited.

Complete Bibliography

A complete bibliography lists all works the writer consulted while doing research, even works not cited in the paper. If a complete bibliography is long, it may be divided into sections for different types of works, such as books, journals, and newspapers.

Annotated Bibliography

An annotated bibliography includes a sentence or two for each work listed to give an evaluation of the work and/or a brief statement about its approach or content.

Newcomb, Horace. TV: The Most Popular Art. Garden
City, New York: Anchor Books, 1974. This work,
which the author labels "a study of television as
a popular art," is insightful, interesting, and
well written. The chapters are divided by program
type, such as Westerns, mysteries, and adventure
shows; and useful observations about the social and
cultural effects of television are made in the final chapter.

Bibliography of Works Cited

For most college papers instructors require a bibliography of works cited, works to which you refer in the text of your paper and in your notes. If you used a work only for background reading or if you decided that you could not use the notes from some of the works you consulted, you should not enter those works in this type of bibliography.

To prepare a bibliography of works cited you should remove from your working bibliography file all the cards for works you do not cite in your research paper. You should again check bracketed information in your rough draft to be sure you do not omit the card for any work mentioned in your notes.

Format

Regardless of the type of bibliography you prepare, on your bibliography pages you should list works in alphabetical order (by the last names of the authors). When no author is given for a work, you should alphabetize by the title (omitting *a, an,* and *the*) along with the authors' names for other works. If you cite more than one work by an author, a line approximately 1 inch long is substituted for the author's name after the first entry. See pages 193–197 for sample bibliography pages.

Before you begin your bibliography, you should once again check your bibliography cards to be certain that they are in alphabetical order. The form you will use is the same one you used to write your bibliography cards, with differences only in spacing and indentation, as the illustrations show.

BIBLIOGRAPHY CARD

Basic form for a book

BIBLIOGRAPHY PAGE

> Baldwin, James. "Black man in America."
> *WFMT Perspectives*, 10 (Dec. 1961),
> 25-30.

Basic form for Articles in periodicals

BIBLIOGRAPHY PAGE

Baldwin, James. "Black Man in America." WFMT Perspec-

tives, 10 (Dec. 1961), 25-30.

These basic note and bibliography forms demonstrate the principles involved in all note and bibliography forms. For variations of the basic book and article forms and for other sources, you should consult Appendix A. For example, if you want to cite a television program, you should look up the heading "Television program" in Appendix A, where you will find the appropriate note and bibliography forms.

EXERCISE 5.2

A. By referring to Appendix A and to the preceding section on note and bibliography forms, decide (1) whether each example is a note form or a bibliographical form and (2) whether the entry is for a book, periodical, or other source. Write your answers in the blanks below each entry.

1. Dizark, Wilson P. Television: A World View. Syracuse:

Syracuse Univ. Press, 1966.

Form: _____ Type of Source: _____

2. [4] "The Real Issue," editorial, Broadcasting,

13 Mar. 1972, p. 74.

Form: _____ Type of Source: _____

3.   [21] U.S. Cong., Senate, Committee on Interstate and Foreign Commerce, <u>Television Inquiry</u>, <u>Television Network Practices</u>, Report, 85th Cong., 1st sess., 1957, p. 8.

Form: _____   Type of Source: _____

4.   [27] William D. Wells, "Children as Consumers," <u>On Knowing the Consumer</u>, ed. Joseph D. Newman (New York: John Wiley, 1966), p. 140.

Form: _____   Type of Source: _____

5. Vogel, A. J. "The Changing Face of the Children's Market," <u>Sales Management</u>, 93 (18 Dec. 1964), 35-36.

Form: _____   Type of Source: _____

    B. Identify each of the following items (taken from the preceding examples) as the (1) author, (2) title, or (3) fact of publication.

_____ 1. Syracuse:

_____ 2. "The Real Issue,"

_____ 3. 85th Cong., 1st sess., 1957

_____ 4. William D. Wells

_____ 5. 93 (18 Dec. 1964), 35-36.

_____ 6. ed. Joseph D. Newman

    C. Write a note of first reference for each of the following:

1. Gattegno, Caleb. <u>Towards a Visual Culture: Educating Through Television</u>. New York: Discus Books, 1971.

    (Your note refers to pages 143 through 148.)

2. White, Stephen. "Television: Culture in the Wee Hours." _Horizon_, 4 (Sept. 1961), 113–14.

3. Lelyveld, Joseph. "TV Debates: The Record Is Not Very Promising." _New York Times_, 9 June 1977, p. E-1, col. 3.

4. Connell, D. D., and E. L. Palmer. "_Sesame Street—A_ Case Study." In _Broadcaster/Researcher Cooperation in Mass Communication Research_, ed. J. D. Halloran and M. Gurevitch. Leeds, England: Kavanagh and Sons, 1971.

(Your reference is to pages 48 and 49.)

TITLE

The title you select for your paper should be brief and descriptive of the content of your paper. You may encounter catchy titles in your reading, but they are not appropriate for a college research paper.

Producing the Final Draft

Creating the final draft for submission to your instructor involves typing or writing a neat, clean copy and proofreading it carefully for errors.

MATERIALS

Most instructors will accept either a handwritten or a typed research paper. A typed paper is preferable, however, since the idiosyncrasies of handwriting are eliminated and the reader is free to concentrate on the content.

For typed papers, use 8½ × 11 inch, white, unlined paper of a quality grade. Type on one side of a sheet only and leave 1½ inch margins on all sides. Be sure to have correction fluid or correction tape at hand to correct errors.

For handwritten papers, use 8½ × 11 inch, lined paper. Write in blue or black ink, skip every other line, and leave 1½ inch margins on all sides.

FORMAT

Your final draft should include the following parts arranged in this order: title page, outline, the body of the paper, note page, bibliography page.

Numbering begins after the title page. Any material following the title page and preceding the body of the paper, such as the outline, should be numbered consecutively in small roman numerals. You should use arabic numerals for the body of the paper, numbering consecutively from the introduction through the bibliography page.

Title Page

The title should be centered about halfway down the page. Capitalize the first letter of the first word and all words except articles, conjunctions, and prepositions. The title of a research paper should not be underlined, placed in quotation marks, or capitalized in full. Center the word *by* 2 spaces under the title and your name 2 spaces below that. Information identifying the instructor, the course, and the date should be placed below the title and to the right. Artwork and decoration are not appropriate for a college paper. (See page 145).

Outline

Place the controlling idea at the top of the outline page. Double-space the outline. A period and 2 spaces follow each numeral or letter. Indent each level of heading in the outline 4 spaces and be sure that equivalent headings are aligned. (See page 147.)

Body

The first line of each paragraph should be indented 5 spaces. Double-space the entire body of the text with the exception of quotations running more than 4 lines of typescript (approximately 10 words to a line). These should be single spaced and indented 10 spaces from the left margin. When quotations are single spaced, they do not require quotation marks. Double quotation marks are used when a quotation appears within an indented, single-spaced quotation.

Note Page

The word *Notes* serves as a title. Indicate each note with a superscript number placed 5 spaces from the left margin. Skip 1 space and begin the note. Double-space all lines. (See page 181.)

Bibliography Page

The word *Bibliography* serves as a title. Alphabetize entries by the author's last name or by the title of the work when no author is given. When you have two or more works by the same author, a line of approximately 1 inch (8 to 10 spaces with the underlining key) followed by a period is substituted for the name. Each entry begins at the margin, and subsequent lines in an entry are indented 5 spaces. Double-space all lines. (See page 193.)

PROOFREADING

Be certain that you allow yourself time to proofread your paper before you turn it in. You must check everything in the paper, particularly quotations and numbers, to be certain that it is accurate. You should refer to your final draft, note cards, and bibliography for this process.

Proofreading is extremely important for typed copy. When you type material yourself, errors are very hard to see. By reading carefully you may find that you have transposed letters or numbers or omitted letters, words, or entire lines. Even if a professional types your work, you have to proofread carefully. It is your responsibility to find errors and have the typist make corrections.

Fasten the pages of your research paper together in the upper left corner with a paperclip. Enclosing the paper in a folder or plastic page makes it difficult for the instructor to read or to write comments on your paper.

Sample Research Paper

Soap Operas: An Explanation of Their Popularity

by

Susan Carmichael

English 13, Section 177

Dr. Williams

May 12, 1979

Controlling Idea: The unique form of soap operas and their concentration on family themes provide viewers with emotional, moral, and educational resources for dealing with their own family lives.

I. The nature of soap operas

    A. Definition of the program type

    B. Content

        1. Focus on the family

        2. Centrality of women characters

    C. Form

        1. Daily serial

        2. Primacy of character over actor

        3. Near-realism

        4. Aural nature

II. Effect of soap operas on viewers

    A. Emotional strength

        1. Experience of a range of emotions

        2. Confrontation with problems

    B. Moral support

        1. Family as source of happiness

        2. Punishment of actions against family

    C. Educational resources

        1. Models of behavior

        2. Information on controversial subjects

Waugh, p. 1458   2, 7, 48

[Waugh concludes his article on
the attraction of soap operas and
the reality of the characters with
the statement that when he lifts his
glass on New Year's Eve, he will be
thinking of his soap opera friends,
among others.]

Note 1

Thurber, p. 191
"A soap opera is a kind of sandwich
whose recipe is simple enough, although it took years to compound.
Between thick slices of advertising,
spread twelve minutes of dialogue,
add predicament, villainy, and female suffering in equal measure,
throw in a dash of nobility, sprinkle
with tears, season with organ

Thurber, p. 191 (cont.)
music, cover with a rich announcer
sauce, and serve five times a week."

Note 7

1   British novelist Alec Waugh toasts the health of — Series of
examples for
soap opera characters on New Year's Eve,[1] Supreme Court   illustration

Justice Thurgood Marshall follows his favorite soap op=

era when court sessions permit,[2] universities offer

courses on soap operas,[3] and college students pack into

campus lounges every afternoon to watch soap operas com-

munally.[4] Soap operas, once the sole province of house-

wives, many of whom dared not admit they watched them,

are now legitimate and even fashionable. Soap operas,   Use of
summary
in fact, consistently have larger audiences than any

other type of television program.[5] The A. C. Nielsen —— Statistics used
as evidence
Company estimates that the average audience for a soap

opera is 7,430,000 people.[6] This popularity may be ex-

plained in large part by their focus on the family, a

source of universal concern and fascination. The   Controlling
idea, the
unique form of soap operas and their concentration on   writer's formulation of an
family themes provide viewers with emotional, moral,   explanation of
the popularity
and educational resources for dealing with their own   of soap operas

family lives.

                                                           Brief histori-
2   Soap operas have been in existence since the late cal back-
                                                           ground and
1920's when the form originated on radio. Writing in   definition

1948, James Thurber defined radio soap operas, from   Complete sentence ending
which television soap operas were spawned in 1951, as   with a colon
introduces the
follows: indented
quotation

        A soap opera is a kind of sandwich. . . .   Direct quota-
     Between thick slices of advertising, spread   tion to pre-
     twelve minutes of dialogue, add predicament, vil-   serve style and
     lainy, and female suffering in equal measure, throw   humor of
     in a dash of nobility, sprinkle with tears, season   source
     with organ music, cover with a rich announcer
     sauce, and serve five times a week.7   Phrase omit-
                                                           ted after
                                                           sandwich is
                                                           indicated by
                                                           an ellipsis

                                                           Single-spacing
                                                           and indention
                                                           because the
                                                           quotation runs
                                                           more than 4
                                                           lines in the
                                                           text

Barthel, p. 144

    direct quotation from Lyle Hill,
producer of As the World Turns:
"The success of the show is related to the fact that we return
to these two recurring families,
which gives us good identification."

Note 9

Thurber's definition contains truth as well as humor and ———————— is also a useful analysis of television soap operas, since many of the essential elements of content and form have remained the same.[8]

3   The principal content of the soap opera sandwich—— the object of the "predicament, villainy, and female suffering"——is the family. Eleven of the fourteen current soap operas focus on the lives of one or two central families. The most popular soap opera, As the World Turns, revolves around the lives of the Lowell and Hughes families; and it is to the organizing device of centering on these families that producer Lyle Hill attributes the size and fidelity of the show's audience: "The success of the show is related to the fact that we return to these two recurring families. . . ."[9] Simi- larly, All My Children, a favorite of college students, centers around the Tyler and Martin families; and second-ranked The Guiding Light chronicles events in the Bauer family. The three soap operas that are not organ- ized around families revolve around the personal and family lives of the members of professional teams or small communities: The Edge of Night involves the attempts of two law partners to fight crime in the city of Monticello; and The Doctors and General Hospital por- tray hospital staffs, which must in effect function as family units to perform their professional responsibili- ties. Even on these programs family problems and re- lationships of the characters predominate.[10]

Line not indented because it is part of the paragraph in which the quotation was introduced

Refers to a bibliographical note

Demonstration, primarily with examples, that the content of soap operas is the family

Ellipsis to indicate that the word *families* does not mark the end of a sentence in the original even though it ends the sentence in the paper

Note placed at the end of the paragraph to give appropriate credit for the source of many details while not distracting the reader with excessive notation within the paragraph

KATZMAN, p. 210

" The high frequency of conversations about health and romance is not surprising in light of the main problems, and events of soap operas. On the other hand, the fact that there were many more conversations about family relationships (kin other than spouses) than about marriage indicates that in the world of the

KATZMAN, p. 210 (cont.)

soap opera the family unit, and its problems, was a center of attention.

Note 11

4   A week-long monitoring of soap opera conversations
in a 1970 study found that the subject discussed most
frequently was the family. The researcher concluded
that "the fact that there were many more conversations
about family relationships (kin other than spouses) than
about marriage indicates that in the world of soap opera
the family unit, and its problems, was a center of
attention."[11] Health and romantic relationships fol- ———————

Reference to the source of the monitoring study mentioned in the first sentence and to the conclusions cited in the second; since both sentences refer to the same study, one note suffices for both

lowed closely as frequent topics of conversation. Such
conversations, and even those about matters such as
crime and business, generally take place on soap operas
within the context of the family. For example, discussion of the influenza meningitis, which the young
teen-ager Laura suffered on <u>General Hospital</u>, revealed
that the attack was a psychosomatic reaction to the excessive attention paid her by Leslie, whom Laura does
not know to be her real mother. A possible appointment
to a job in Tokyo for Johnny Collins on <u>Days of Our
Lives</u> is discussed for the effect it may have on his
wife's child by a previous marriage. Nearly all sub- ——————

Topic sentence serves as the conclusion to the paragraph

ject matter of soap opera conversations, then, relates
to the family.

5   The family focus of the soap opera is also revealed
by an examination of soap opera advertising, which is so ————— Development
by analysis
intimately bound up with this type of program that it
can almost be considered part of the subject matter, as
Thurber's definition indicates. The name "soap opera,"

WAKEFIELD, p. 13

" The soap opera got its name of course
because the sponsors of the programs
were mostly manufacturers of different
brands of soap that they hoped to sell
to the audience of mostly housewives
who listened to the program; and, ironically, 'soap' had another connotation
of sudsy, fluffy, and insubstantial,
characterizing the kind of 'operas'
these were supposed to be. ... "

Note 12

LaPota, p. 560

" twenty-two minutes of ... plot
time during a half-hour show. "

Note 13

GUTCHEON, p. 79

" The question of content on soaps
depends on ratings first, with morals,
taste, audience response, and responsibility running a distant third. Content
is proposed by head writers, then
approved, abridged or vetoed by the
network or sponsors, or both. "

Note 14

in fact, probably derives from the sponsorship of the
radio daytime serials by the manufacturers of soap.[12]
Advertising occupies a relatively large proportion of
the air time, six to eight of every thirty minutes in
comparison with about five minutes per thirty on prime-
time serials.[13] Also, advertising for household products for family use predominates, and it is geared to
the woman's role as purchaser of goods to please her
family. Furthermore, since soap operas bring in more
advertising dollars than they cost to produce, and
since the profits subsidize evening programming, advertisers have the final say on soap opera content, often
discouraging or vetoing material that might alienate
viewers.[14] Advertisers seem to find the family a safe
and appealing subject. Thus, the focus on the family
of soap operas is reinforced by the advertising content
and the viewpoints of the sponsors.

6   The central figure in soap opera families is frequently a woman, a suffering woman as Thurber pointed

Reference to
Thurber's def-
inition to pro-
vide unity

out; she endures and overcomes both predicament and villainy when they threaten the security of her family. On
soap operas, men are active and aggressive in the business or professional world; but in the realm of emotional problems and personal relationships, they often
depend on women for guidance and support. On television

Notes are not
needed since
the source of
the general in-
formation on
soap opera
plots has been
given in note
10 and some of
these observa-
tions result
from the
writer's view-
ing of soap
operas

the nature of the predicaments has extended in range beyond the stock radio soap opera plots of thwarted romance and marital conflicts to include problems ranging

BEHANNA, letter to author

"Adult women (18+) made up 70.2% of the viewing audience. Women 18-49, 41.2%. Women 55+, 24.6%."

Note 16

"Love of Soap Opera" CBS 9 June 1977

Young woman (20's) explained to a reporter what she liked about soap operas:

"... the female stars make an impression on me..."

Note 17

from drug addiction to incest. The villains on television soap operas, however, are, as they were on radio, those characters who interfere in marriages or who attempt to undermine family life.

7   When either predicament or villainy leaves these women without husbands, the women gain opportunities to demonstrate personal strength independent of men, to take jobs to support their families, or to become romantically involved again. Perhaps the most notable example of this matriarchal figure is Bertha Bauer on The Guiding Light, a widow with two grown sons, who provides guidance and emotional support for a large extended family. Joanne Tate Vicente of Search for Tomorrow exemplifies self-sacrifice, taking a job to avoid losing custody of her daughter after her first husband died and giving generous help to friends and relatives.[15] The prominence of women characters is one of the major attractions of soap operas for their audience, approximately 70 percent of which is female.[16] A typical reaction is that of a young woman interviewed at a soap opera festival who said she watched them because "the female stars make an impression on me."[17]

8   The form of the soap opera is well suited to a powerful, effective treatment of family life. As a serial it can mirror the development and charge of familial relationships on a daily basis over long periods of time. The daily serial form allows situations to develop slowly

Continuation of the development of the idea about the centrality of women characters (paragraph 6); material too long for one paragraph is divided at a logical point

Source of specific information about plot and character is given, since this conclusion about it was not original with the writer

Transition from a discussion of content to a section on form

Topic sentence

Introduction to an analysis of the form of soap operas continuing through paragraph 11

PORTER, p. 783-84

"Unlike all traditionally end-
oriented fiction and drama, soap
opera offers process without progres-
sion, not a climax and a resolution,
but mini-climaxes and [784] provi-
sional denouements that must never
be presented in such a way as to
eclipse the suspense experienced
for associated plot lines."

Note 18

FACTER, p. 59

"Charita Bauer, GL's [The Guiding
Light] 'living legend,' joined the
cast in 1950, a year after the role
of Bertha Bauer (Bert to her friends)
had been created."

Note 19

over months, even years, in the same way and at the
same pace that family problems often grow and change.

Development
by supporting
details

Because continuity is part of soap opera form, situations are rarely settled as are the plots of traditional dramas in which the action leads toward a climax or crisis, a resolution, and an ending.[18] Soap
opera characters, like family members, carry with them
a history of successes and failures that occasionally re-
surface to affect new situations. Continuity is strength-
ened by the tendency of soap operas to have very long
runs. The Guiding Light debuted over forty years ago on
radio, and the central character has been played by the
same actress for twenty-seven years.[19] Also, soap opera
life runs parallel to the life of its audience in the
sense that holidays and celebrations are marked at appropriate times: Christmas is celebrated by soap opera
families on the show aired on December 25; and on the
Memorial Day telecast soap opera families raise flags to
commemorate their dead. This kind of timeliness is possible because a new program is filmed for each week day
of the year and soap operas are never rerun.[20] The
frequency and duration in the soap opera format enable
soap operas to deal with family life in a way that allows
viewers to build strong associations with the soap opera families.

9   Another aspect of the form of soap operas that
suits them to portraying families is the primacy characters have over actors. An actor may leave a soap opera series, and the character can survive, the part
simply being taken by another actor, without the same
kind of dislocation to the audience that would occur if

Transition and
context for the
paragraph

"Karen Horney," p. 42

Karen Horney dismissed from her part as Tara Brent on _All My Children_

her press agent reported that AMC producer Bud Kloss "informed Karen that he felt she had outgrown the role of Tara and was in essence too strong an actress for the part."

Note 21

ASTRACHAN, p. 13

"Paul Rauch, once a vice-president at CBS and now producer of 'Another World' at NBC, refuses to admit that the classical soap opera is fantasy, however.... 'Its characters are realistic, believable, do things that a lot of the viewing public do.'"

Note 22

RUBIN, p. 43

"Soap operas are, at best, a pale imitation of real life and literature. They are oversimplified stories written to accommodate scheduled commercial breaks."

Note 24

a different actor played each act of a drama. In fact,
when actors develop too much individual style or a
star personality, they are sometimes replaced. Karen
Gorney, who played Tara Brent on All My Children was
replaced because the producer considered her "too
strong an actress for the part."[21] Actors on soap operas often become known to the audience as members of a
soap opera family rather than as actors with independent identities.

The soap opera is also a powerful form for presenting family life because of its nearly realistic style.
That is, writers of soap operas strive to show life as
it is and to provide an illusion of reality rather than
to create a fantasy world. Paul Rauch, producer of
Another World, declares, "Its characters are realistic,
believable. . . ."[22] Lyle Hill, producer of As the World
Turns, regards soap operas as "the true mirroring of
life."[23] (Some commentators do regard soap operas as presenting an idealized or fantasy world, which is distant from reality. Dr. Theodore L. Rubin, a psycho-
analyst, sees soap operas as "a pale imitation of real
life" and "oversimplified.")[24] Many viewers concur with
the description of the programs as realistic. When a
soap opera character threw her engagement ring into an
ashtray on a Chicago-bound train, viewers rushed out to
search for the ring on actual trains going to Chicago.[25]
Even sophisticated viewers find themselves beginning to
regard soap opera characters as real, as novelist Dan
Wakefield admits in All Her Children. Perhaps the best
description of soap opera's realism is Professor Natan
Katzman's designation of them as "almost-realism."[26]

Direct quotation used to reinforce the fact that the producer made this statement and to give strength to the argument

Topic sentence presents another aspect of the form of soap operas

Connective to the two preceding paragraphs for fluency

Direct quotation to communicate the spirit of these statements and to preserve distinctive wording

Mention of an opposing point of view to fulfill the researcher's obligation to point out areas of disagreement

Citation of Wakefield's book by title within the sentence is sufficient, since the book has already been cited in note 3

Use of quotation marks for two consecutive words from a source because they express an original idea

Adler, p. 80

"It is not necessary technically to watch. Since most of the characters address each other incessantly by name, one can catch it all from another room, like radio."

Note 27

Newcomb, p. 165

"As subject matter begins to vary in the series, we may be admitted to the 'pad' of a hippy or even the hovel-like room of the drug addict. Again, definition is minimal, representational, symbolic."

Note 28

NEWCOMB, pp. 168-69

"There is, then, no action in soap opera, nothing of the sort we are used to in prime-time programming.... (169) This is a world of words."

Note 29

8

11   Finally, the soap opera form allows it to fit com-

fortably into the viewers' own family and domestic lives.

Perhaps because of its radio origins, soap opera is pri-

marily an aural, rather than a visual, form. Producers

assume that the audience will be engaged in some house-

hold activity at least part of the time and design soap

operas so that they can be understood without continu-

ous viewing. Conversations between two, and rarely

more than three, characters constitute the bulk of soap

opera activity, and the names of the speakers are in-

serted frequently to identify them for a listening audi-

ence.[27] Very little action occurs on camera. The or-

gan music Thurber mentions, one of the most parodied as-

pects of soap opera, signals changes in scene and trans-

itions in mood for a partially distracted audience. The

emphasis on the aural nature of soap operas is also re-

vealed by the use of simple low-budget sets that serve

only to suggest particular places rather than to con-

tribute to the meaning of the story.[28] Also, because

the audience may miss portions of a program or an en-

tire show due to domestic or other responsibilities, the

narrative situation is reviewed often within the drama

to ensure that the audience can follow the story. The

soap opera, which Horace Newcomb has called "a world of

words" on a visual medium of television,[29] is suited to

viewers whose attention is partially distracted by

their own family situations.

Transition in the topic sentence prepares for the end of the discussion of form

Notation follows the clause to indicate that the entire sentence should not be attributed to the source

ASTRACHAN, p. 62

Susan Lucci, who plays Erica on _all_ _my_ _Children_, went to Princeton for a session of Prof. George Forgie's seminar.

She called soap opera "a way of going home again without the pettiness and pressure of really going home."

Note 31

LaGUARDIA, p. 189

Eileen Fulton (plays Lisa Shea) received vicious, threatening letters and was assaulted physically." At that point Ellen had a guard escort her from her apartment at Lincoln Towers to the show, and then back again."

Note 32

9

2   The form of the soap opera, then, treats family
life, soap operas' principal subject, in a nearly realistic way. Soap operas in turn have an impact on the
family lives of their viewers. Soap operas function to
strengthen viewers' emotional ability to cope with family life by providing them with opportunities to experience a wide range of emotions and with resources for
solving family problems.

3   Soap operas allow their audience to experience human relations and a wide range of emotions without the
pain of the actual experiences. Professor George
Forgie, who conducted a seminar on popular culture at
Princeton University in which he included the soap opera All My Children, found that one motive for the students' watching it was "the desire to get involved with
the lives and emotions of people close to their own age
and outlook--without having the responsibility for
them."[30] Susan Lucci, the actress who plays Erica on
the show, observed after visiting a session of the seminar that for the students soap operas constituted "a
way of going home without the pettiness and pressure of
really going home."[31] Also, viewers are able to vent
their hostilities through soap opera characters. Some
soap opera fans, in fact, develop tremendous hatred for
the villains on the shows. The scheming Lisa Shea of
As the World Turns was attacked several times by irate
viewers and received so much threatening mail that she
hired a bodyguard to accompany her to the studio.[32]

Transition word signaling conclusion indicates that the entire paragraph is a transition between the two major sections of the paper

Summary of the first section

Introduction to the second section

Transition supplied by the repetition of key words from the preceding paragraph

Direct quotations used to preserve the original wording

McLUHAN, p. 288

"[T]he hot movie medium needs people who look very definitely a _type_ of some kind. The cool TV medium cannot abide the typical because it leaves the viewer frustrated of his job of closure or completion of image. President Kennedy could have been anything from a grocer or a professor to a football

---

McLUHAN, p. 288 (Cont.)

coach. He was not too precise or too ready of speech in such a way as to spoil his pleasantly tweedy blur of countenance and outline."

Note 33

KILGUSS, p. 530

"There is much controversy as to whether soap operas are escapist fantasy. I tend to agree with the view that says they are not. The constant, unresolvable isolation and loneliness are not escapist, but more of a depressive, repetitious attempt to master the pain and impulses of life."

Note 34

10

Viewers can express at these characters anger they might
have to suppress were "real" people involved.

14   It is largely the primacy of characters over actors
on soap opera that produces this intense emotional experience on the part of viewers according to Marshall
McLuhan's theory of television. McLuhan described television as a "cool" medium, which means that it is low in
visual detail, requiring the viewer to complete the
image. Therefore, McLuhan speculates, personalities
most compatible to television are not highly defined:
"The cool TV medium cannot abide the typical /a person
who can be closely identified with one profession or
type7 because it leaves the viewer frustrated of his job
of 'closure.'" Ideal television actors are a "blur of
countenance and outline," McLuhan believes.[33] Thus, the
fact that actors on soap operas often are not as highly
defined as movie stars allows viewers to supply the material to fashion the character to their own image of a
mother, neighbor, or friend, thereby increasing viewers' emotional participation with the soap opera family.

15   Soap operas also provide emotional resources for
the members of their audience by helping them to confront and solve the problems of their own families.
After using soap operas in therapy groups, psychiatric
social worker Anne Kilguss concluded that the motivation for watching them was an attempt to deal with problems rather than to escape from them.[34] Because soap

Brackets en-
close the
writer's expla-
nation of a
term McLuhan
uses

Single quota-
tion marks
used within
double quotes
to indicate
that the word
appears in
quotation
marks in the
original source

Expert
opinion used
to support the
topic sentence

Newcomb, p. 180

[Quoting Dr. John R. Lion, a psychiatrist at the Univ. of Maryland Medical School] "In the end, I think that the most realistic programs on TV are the soap operas. They portray life with all its complexities and insolubilities. Many of my patients are helped by watching them, and I often suggest to patients who have an overly glamorized view of the world that they view these

Newcomb, p. 180 (cont.)

programs in order to see, in admittedly caricatured form, what life is like. I suggest more soap operas showing the lives, say, of criminals and their inner torment. I suggest showing the inner workings of the mind of a wealthy executive, and I suggest that we are shown by the media how empty the life of the Godfather really is." [Baltimore Sun, 18 Feb. 1973]

Note 35

opera characters usually do resolve their problems successfully, viewers are given the courage and confidence
that they will be able to master similar situations.
Also, they see that everyone, even a person they might
have regarded as invulnerable because of wealth or fame,
has problems. Dr. John R. Lion, a psychiatrist who also
believes that soap operas can be therapeutic, points
out the value of the form:

> In the end, I think the most realistic programs on
> TV are the soap operas. They portray life with
> all its complexities and insolubilities. Many of
> my patients are helped by watching them, and I of-
> ten suggest to patients who have an overly glamor-
> ized view of the world that they view these pro-
> grams in order to see, in admittedly caricatured
> form, what life is like. I suggest more soap op-
> era, showing the lives, say, of criminals and their
> inner torment. I suggest showing the inner work-
> ings of the mind of a wealthy executive, and I sug-
> gest that we are shown by the media how empty the
> life of the Godfather really is.[35]

And since the dilemmas of soap opera characters are often exaggerated and concentrated, almost realistic but
not quite, viewers can reconcile themselves to their own
problems, which are likely to be of less magnitude and
fewer in number. Winifred Wolfe, head writer for As the
World Turns, notes, "Whenever things go badly for characters on our show, our ratings go way up."[36] Since, as
the saying goes, "misery loves company," soap operas
provide the comfort of fellow sufferers for their audience.

Interesting de-
tail in long
quotation jus-
tifies inclusion
in its entirety

Common ex-
pression that
needs no
documentation;
quotation
marks indicate
the words are
not original
with this
writer

Efron, p. 159

"... Only 'bad' people in soap operas are anti-baby. The fastest bit of characterization ever accomplished in the history of drama was achieved on _Secret Storm_, when Kip's father arrived on the scene. He said: 'I can't stand all this talk about babies.' This instantly established him as a black-hearted villain."

Note 37

Astrachan, p. 54

"Erica Kane ... of ABC's _All my Children_, had television's first legal abortion in May, 1971, so that her pregnancy would not interfere with her plans to work as a model... Erica was duly punished by getting septicemia from the abortion." [Mail from the audience showed both approval and disapproval.]

Note 38

12

16   In addition to benefiting viewers by providing emotional resources, soap operas present a moral stance that
upholds traditional values, a moral stance that apparently satisfies viewers and provides support for their
own beliefs. In spite of the fact that many soap operas now break the once rigid rule that no happy woman
works, it is still traditional marriage and the traditional family that bring happiness and satisfaction to
most characters in soap operas. As Edith Efron has
pointed out, a character can instantly be established as
a villain by making an "anti-baby" remark.[37] Furthermore, those characters who take actions that threaten the
family are nearly always duly punished. A single act of
intercourse outside of marriage often brings pregnancy,
as in the case of Trish on Days of Our Lives; and characters who have or even contemplate having abortions are
often punished. Erica Kane of All My Children, who had
the first legal television abortion in May, 1971, to be
able to pursue a modelling career, was punished by con-
tracting septicemia as a result of the procedure.[38]
When Susan Martin contemplated having an abortion on Days
of Our Lives, she was informed by her doctor that cancer of the uterus would prevent her from having a child
other than the one she was carrying. She decided to
keep the baby even though the pregnancy had resulted
from a casual encounter with a stranger.[39] And although extramarital affairs are legion on soap operas,
they generally meet with disapproval, and the parties
are punished. "If a man has an affair," says Nick

Transition to
presentation of
another effect
on viewers

Source not
cited since the
writer viewed
the episode

Source is an
article, which
must be
documented

"The Code of Sudsville," p. 94

Sudsville — usually a small, vaguely midwestern town - is a highly structured social community and a highly ordered moral universe. Evil is eventually punished there, even if it takes years, and good finally emerges triumphant after a prolonged purgatory. "If a man has an affair," says Nick Nicholson, producer of <u>The Edge of Night</u> on CBS, "he has to have a good rea-

"The Code of Sudsville," p. 94 (cont.)

son for it. Then he should feel guilty and suffer so that we can salvage him. Finally, he has to do something noble; then the audience will feel better about him. The bonds of marriage are still sacred.'"

Note 40

KILGUSS, p. 529

"Entertainment tells our mobile population what they can and should expect of each other; thus, [David] Riesman assumes media have a far greater role in character formation than in earlier times. He states that for traditional societies folk tales acted as socializing agents." [in <u>The Lonely Crowd</u>]

Note 42

13

Nicholson, producer of The Edge of Night, "he has to
have a good reason for it. Then he should feel guilty
and suffer so that we can salvage him. Finally he has
to do something noble; then the audience will feel better about him. The bonds of marriage are still sacred."[40]

17   When punishments for actions against the family
are not supplied by the script, viewers often demand
them in angry letters.[41] The punishments seem to reassure viewers that their own family lives cannot be undermined by similar actions. The increasingly frequent
breakup and separation of family groups perhaps do not
indicate a devaluation of family life, for the audience
seems to want to see united families. In their emphasis on the integrity and interrelatedness of the family unit, soap operas convey the message that an individual's decisions and actions are significant because they
affect his or her family.

18   Along with the emotional and moral support, soap operas provide education on matters important to family
life. Indeed, as sociologist David Riesman theorizes in
The Lonely Crowd, the media serve as a modern substitute
for the folktales that previously instructed people on
how to act and live.[42] Soap operas accomplish this
educational function by presenting models of behavior
and by supplying information about family issues. As
models of action in family matters, soap operas provide what Madeleine Edmondson and David Rounds call
"education in intimacy." "Where else," they ask, "can

Elaboration of
ideas in previ-
ous paragraph
with focus on
audience's
reaction

Summary and
conclusion to
this section of
two para-
graphs

Introduction of
third major ef-
fect preceded
by allusion to
the two effects
already dis-
cussed

Use of expert
opinion to sub-
stantiate the
topic sentence

Quotation di-
vided with
"they ask" for
variety in
direct quota-
tion

EDMONDSON & ROUNDS, p. 249

"Soaps show their audience how young lovers talk to each other after a long separation, how a wife reacts to the discovery of her husband's infidelity, how a couple quarrel and then forgive. Where else can the audience learn how other parents advise their children about marriage, how deeply one friend questions another

---

EDMONDSON & ROUNDS, p. 249 (cont.)

about his wife's alcoholism, how much a father tells his daughter about his divorce."

Authors label this "education in intimacy"

Note 43

WAKEFIELD, p. 61

Quoting Bud Kloss. "We've had story lines on abortion, on the Vietnam war, or male sterility. ... If we feel a subject we haven't done before fits into our story, we back it up; we go to the network and fight for it."

Note 45

the audience learn how other parents advise their children about marriage, how deeply one friend questions another about his wife's alcoholism, how much a father tells his daughter about his divorce?"[43] Viewers can watch characters react to situations in various ways and then select a mode of action that suits them. By overhearing conversations between family members viewers can learn to communicate with their own families.

.9   Some writers and producers of soap operas make deliberate attempts to educate their audience by providing information on controversial issues that affect the family. Abortion, rape, incest, miscegenation, and drug addiction, as well as problems of sterility, frigidity, menopause, and cervical cancer, have all been presented on soap operas in recent years, often before these subjects were acceptable on evening television.[44] The educational function of soap operas is important to at least some writers and producers. Bud Kloss, producer of All My Children, states, "If we feel a subject we haven't done fits into our story we back it up; we go to the network and fight for it."[45] The writer of that serial, Agnes Eckhardt Nixon, is said to be the person most responsible for pushing soap operas into new and controversial areas. She arranged for the actress who plays her character Cathy Craig to participate in a program for drug addicts at Odyssey House in New York so that film of her experience there could be integrated into episodes of several weeks of the show.[46] She had a

Development
by supporting
details

Wakefield, p. 167

A reporter on <u>All</u> My Children wrote a booklet on venereal disease. When a similar booklet entitled "Venereal Disease: A Fact We Must Face and Fight" was actually published, ABC received 10,000 Requests for copies.

Note 47

BOORSTIN, p. 393

"This was again the familiar consequence of having a centralized and enlarged source [of news, entertainment, experience], now not merely for running water or running electricity! Just as Rebecca no longer needed to go to the village well to gather her water (and her gossip), so now, too, in her eighth-floor kitchenette she received the current of hot and cold running images."

Note 48

journalist character on the same program supposedly
write a pamphlet on venereal disease, which was offered
to the audience free.[47] The response to both of these
presentations was thousands of requests for additional
information on the subjects.

Viewers seem particularly receptive to the presentation of controversial subjects on soap operas for a
variety of reasons. Watching a soap opera can be a very
private experience. Knowledge is imparted in an impersonal way without the viewer's revealing a need for
it. People need not risk the embarrassment of asking
a neighbor or friend for advice. Daniel Boorstin has
theorized that television has replaced gossip as a
source of information,[48] and the educational aspect of
soap operas seems to substantiate that opinion. Soap
operas, which embody a problem in a person who seems
real and allow viewers to watch that person resolve the
problem over a long period of time, are often more convincing than news programs or documentaries.

The power of the soap opera treatment of family
life can be demonstrated by comparing it to another
type of television drama that deals with family groups,
the situation or domestic comedy. Many characteristics
of situation comedies serve to deflect the viewers'
attention from the problems of family life. First, the
audience knows that any problem on a situation comedy
will be resolved within the half-hour time slot, while
problems on soap operas develop over long periods of
time and sometimes are never resolved. On situation

Indirect quota-
tion

Writer's con-
clusion de-
rived from
Boorstin's
theory

Beginning of
the conclusion

Development
by comparison
and contrast

Series of con-
trasts provide
a summary of
the paper

NEWCOMB, pp. 25-58

    Chapter on situation and domestic comedies

26 "Television's own form of comedy"

28 "strong sense of the 'unreal'"

31 next week's episode is not dependent on tonight's

33 complications take form of "human error" and confusion

36 "set of regular characters"

38 supporting characters closer to the

NEWCOMB, pp. 25-58 (cont.)

    audience than the central character

41 "No one intends to cause pain ... no one intends evil."

Note 49

Adler, p. 83

    "This is not the evening's entertainment, which one watches presumably with members of the family; not the shared family-situation comedies, which (with the important exception of All In The Family) are comfortable distortions of what family life is like."

Note 50

comedies a new situation is presented each week, and unlike soap opera characters, situation comedy characters
do not live with the consequences of their decisions and
mistakes from the previous week. Also, the humor in
situation comedies serves to provide distance. The
principal characters must remain intact through any crisis; they cannot be killed or destroyed, for the character and situation that produce the humor must be main-
tained. Situation comedy characters rarely grapple with
serious problems. Their stress causes amusing confusion
rather than genuine sorrow, while soap opera characters
confront the most brutal facts of life and death.[49]
Situation comedies, which have been called "comfortable
distortions of what family life is like,"[50] can be
shared with other family members as evening entertainment because they are shown at a time when many families
can be together and because they do not produce much
emotion or conflict. Soap operas, however, raise dis-
tressing issues and emotions concerning family life, and
perhaps as a result, many viewers watch soap operas
alone.

Transition to emphasize contrast

22   Although soap operas provide diversion and compan-
ionship, they are not exclusively entertainment. The
unique form and content of soap operas combine to produce a portrayal of family life that is at once disturbing and satisfying. But whether people watch soap operas for emotional release, moral support, information,
or simply for enjoyment, they do watch them, and in
steadily increasing numbers.

Final section of the conclusion

Links to the major points of the paper: form and content—effects on viewers

Reference to the introduction where the popularity of soap operas is presented as the impetus for the research leading to this paper

17

Notes

First reference
note for arti-
cle, basic form,
Appendix A,
number 20

[1] Alec Waugh, "The Secret Storm," National Review, 19 (26 Dec. 1967), 1438.

First reference
note for un-
signed article,
Appendix A,
number 23

[2] "Sex and Suffering in the Afternoon," Time, 107 (12 Jan. 1976), 46.

First reference
note for book,
basic form,
Appendix A,
number 1

[3] Dan Wakefield, All Her Children (New York: Avon, 1976), pp. 150-57.

[4] Wakefield, pp. 148-49.

Subsequent
reference note
for unsigned
article: In-
cludes title
and page
number

[5] "Sex and Suffering in the Afternoon," p. 46.

Form for per-
sonal letter,
Appendix A,
number 34

[6] Personal letter from William R. Behanna, A. C. Nielsen Company, 21 June 1977.

[7] James Thurber, The Beast in Me and Other Animals (New York: Harcourt Brace, 1948), p. 191.

[8] For a history of radio soap operas see Madeleine Edmondson and David Rounds, The Soaps (New York: Stein and Day, 1973) and Raymond Stedman, The Serials (Norman: Univ. of Oklahoma Press, 1971).

[9] Joan Barthel, "The World Has Turned More Than 3,200 Times . . . and 8 Million People Keep Watching," New York Times Magazine, 8 Sept. 1968, p. 144.

18

[10] Bryna Laub, <u>The Official Soap Opera Annual</u> (New York: Ballantine Books, 1877), pp. 156-234. Laub describes the basic situations and 1976 action for the fourteen soap operas currently on the air. Many of the general observations about plots and characters in this paper are derived from this source.

[11] Natan Katzman, "Television Soap Operas," <u>Public Opinion Quarterly</u>, 36 (Summer 1972), 210.

ond refer-
e and in-
national
e: This ma-
ial is anec-
al rather
n central to
develop-
nt of the
er

[12] Wakefield, p. 13. Wakefield points out that <u>soap</u> also connotes light or fluffy content. On the origin of the name see also Merrill Denison, "Soap Opera," <u>Harper's</u>, 180 (Apr. 1940), 408-505. Denison states that another name for radio soap operas was "strips show," perhaps a mispronunciation of "script show" or a reference to the comic strips a form to which soap operas have been compared.

e writer
es her own
ervations
mary re-
rch) not as
dence in the
er, but to
port the
lings of the
rce

[13] Margherite LaPota and Bruce LaPota, "The Soap Opera," <u>English Journal</u>, 62 (Apr. 1973), 560. The authors estimate that twenty-two minutes of each half-hour are devoted to the story. This researcher found that advertising on soap operas consumed between six and eight minutes of each half-hour, often six in the first part of an hour program and eight in the final half-hour, and that the evening situation comedy <u>All in the Family</u> includes approximately five minutes of advertising per half-hour.

19

[14] Beth Gutcheon, "There Isn't Anything Wishy-Washy about Soaps," _Ms._, 3 (Aug. 1974), 79. Some commentators have speculated that advertisers encourage material designed to keep viewers, women in particular, at home, where viewers watch soap operas and consume the products advertised and that thus soap operas include just enough contemporary content to give viewers the illusion that they are keeping up with the times when in fact nothing disturbing enough to jolt them out of their living rooms is presented. Marya Mannes maintains that advertisers consider it "essential that the image of the full-time housewife be enthroned as the single highest good--and the greatest consumer of our society." Marya Mannes, "Everything's Up to Date in Soap Operas," _TV Guide_ (15 Mar. 1969); rpt. in _Television_, ed. Barry G. Cole (New York: The Free Press, 1970), p. 165.

[15] Robert LaGuardia, _The Wonderful World of TV Soap Operas_ (New York: Ballantine Books, 1974), p. 304.

[16] Behanna.

[17] "Love of Soap Opera," _June Magazine_, prod. David Lowe, Jr., narr. Sylvia Chase, CBS, 9 June 1977.

[18] Dennis Porter, "Soap Time," _College English_, 38 (Apr. 1977), 783.

[19] Sue Facter, "40 Years of Broadcasting--_The Guiding Light_," _Soap Opera Digest_, 2 (June 1977), 59.

ormational e: The ter wishes resent an ect of the ject of the ationship of ertising to content of p operas, ich is not tral to the er. Form reprint in a ection, Appdix A, nber 11. e writer d the ret, not the ginal.

rst reference te to a tele- sion pro- am, Appen- x A, number

[20] Wakefield, p. 176.

[21] Karen Gorney, <u>Soap Opera Digest</u>, 2 (May 1977), 42.

[22] Anthony Astrachan, "Life Can Be Beautiful/ Relevant," <u>New York Times Magazine</u>, 23 March 1977, p. 13.

[23] Barthel, p. 147.

[24] Theodore I. Rubin, "Psychiatrist's Notebook," <u>Ladies' Home Journal</u>, 93 (Jan. 1976), 43.

[25] Louis Botto, "That Family Sure Has Its Share of Problems," <u>Look</u>, 35 (7 Sept. 1971), 64.

[26] Katzman, p. 212.

Subsequent
reference note,
followed by
first reference
note. The two
are separated
by a semico-
lon.

[27] Katzman, p. 209; Renata Adler, "Afternoon Tele- vision," <u>The New Yorker</u>, 45 (12 Feb. 1972), 80.

[28] Horace Newcomb, <u>TV: The Most Popular Art</u> (Garden City, N.Y.: Anchor Press, 1974), pp. 164-66.

[29] Newcomb, p. 168.

[30] Astrachan, p. 62.

[31] Astrachan, p. 62

[32] LaGuardia, p. 189.

21

[33] Marshall McLuhan, <u>Understanding Media</u> (New York: New American Library, 1964), p. 288.

[34] Anne F. Kilguss, "Using Soap Operas as a Therapeutic Tool," <u>Social Casework</u>, 55 (Nov. 1974), 530. Commentators disagree about whether soap operas represent escape from or confrontation with reality. Adler also believes that they are not escapist fantasy, while Porter argues that they present an idealized world that provides escape. Boorstin perceives an interaction of fantasy and reality in television portraits of families, which he has written are a "shadowy mirror reflection" of American families, who in turn try to imitate the image of themselves. Daniel Boorstin, <u>The Image</u>, 1962; rpt. (New York: Harper and Row, 1964), p. 258.

[35] Baltimore <u>Sun</u>, 18 Feb. 1973, cited in Newcomb, p. 180.

[36] Botto, p. 64.

[37] Edith Efron, "The Soaps—Anything but 99 44/100 Percent Pure," <u>TV Guide</u> (13 Mar. 1965); rpt. in <u>Television</u>, ed. Barry G. Cole (New York: The Free Press, 1970). p. 159.

[38] Astrachan, p. 54.

[39] LaGuardia, p. 250.

[40] "The Code of Sudsville," <u>Time</u>, 99 (20 Mar. 1972), 94.

st reference e for arti- basic form, pendix A, nber 20. e writer s on to pre- t several nts of view the subject how that source's clusion is univer- ly accepted. e last name he source rter, Adler) fices when ir works ve already n cited in notes. The first refer- e is neces- y for orstin, to om the ter has not referred.

e writer nd the quo- ion in New- mb, not in e original wspaper ar- le (Appen- A, num- rs 22, 23). th sources ust be cited.

22

[41] Gutcheon, p. 79.

e writer
ed Riesman's
eories as
ey were pre-
ated in
other
arce,
guss.

[42] Cited in Kilguss, p. 529. The educational nature of soap operas was evident even in their radio form. During the Presidential election of 1936 the Republicans adapted soap operas in programs called "Liberty at the Crossroads" to demonstrate the flaws of the New Deal. Daniel Boorstin, The Americans (New York: Random House, 1973), p. 477.

[43] Edmondson and Rounds, p. 249.

bsequent
erence note:
cludes the
le because
re than one
rk by the
thor has
en cited (see
es 34 and
.

[44] LaPota, p. 559.

[45] Wakefield, p. 61.

[46] Gutcheon, p. 45.

[47] Wakefield, p. 167.

[48] Boorstin, The Americans, p. 393.

[49] Newcomb, pp. 27-58.

[50] Adler, p. 83.

Behanna, William R. Letter to
the author. 21 June 1977

Boorstin, Daniel. *The Americans: The
Democratic Experience*. New York:
Random House, 1973.

Boorstin, Daniel. *The Image: A
Guide to Pseudo-Events in
America*. 1962; rpt. New York:
Harper and Row, 1964

23

Bibliography

Adler, Renata. "Afternoon Television: Unhappiness Enough
  and Time." The New Yorker, 45 (12 Feb. 1972), 74-83.

Astrachan, Anthony. "Life Can Be Beautiful/Relevant."
  New York Times Magazine, 23 Mar. 1975, pp. 12-13ff.

Barthel, Joan. "The World Has Turned More Than 3,200
  Times . . . and 8 Million People Keep Watching."
  New York Times Magazine, 8 Sept. 1968, pp. 66-67ff.

Behanna, William R. Letter to author. 21 June 1977.

Boorstin, Daniel. The Americans: The Democratic Experience. New York: Random House, 1973.

_____. The Image: A Guide to Pseudo-Events in
  America. 1962; rpt. New York: Harper and Row,
  1964.

Botto, Louis. "That Family Sure Has Its Share of Problems." Look, 35 (7 Sept. 1971), 64-65.

"The Code of Sudsville." Time, 99 (20 Mar. 1972), 93-94.

Denison, Merrill. "Soap Opera." Harper's, 180 (Apr.
  1940), 408-505.

Edmondson, Madeleine, and David Rounds. The Soaps: Daytime Serials of Radio and TV. New York: Stein and
  Day, 1973.

Efron, Edith. "The Soaps--Anything but 99 44/100 Percent Pure." TV Guide, 13 Mar. 1965. Rpt. in Television: A Selection of Readings from TV Guide Magazine. Ed. Barry G. Cole. New York: The Free Press,
  1970, pp. 156-62.

Facter, Sue. "40 Years of Broadcasting-- The Guiding
  Light. " Soap Opera Digest, 2 (June 1977), 59-71.

LaPota, Margherite, and Bruce LaPota. "The Soap Opera: Literature To Be Seen and Not Read." *English* Journal. 62 (Apr. 1973), 556-63.

"Love of Soap Opera." June Magazine. Prod. David Lowe, Jr. and narr. Sylvia Chase. CBS. 9 June 1977.

Newcomb, Horace. *TV: The Most Popular Art.* Garden City, N.Y.: *Anchor Press,* 1974.

24

Gutcheon, Beth. "There Isn't Anything Wishy-Washy about
⛛   Soaps." Ms., 3 (Aug. 1974), 42-43ff.

"Karen Gorney," Soap Opera Digest, 2 (May 1977), 42.

Katzman, Natan. "Television Soap Operas: What's Been
     Going on Anyway?" Public Opinion Quarterly, 36
     (Summer 1972), 200-12.

Kilguss, Anne F. "Using Soap Operas as a Therapeutic
     Tool." Social Casework, 55 (Nov. 1974), 525-30.

LaGuardia, Robert. The Wonderful World of TV Soap
     Operas. New York: Ballantine Books, 1974.

LaPota, Margherite, and Bruce LaPota. "The Soap Opera:
     Literature to Be Seen and Not Read." English
     Journal, 62 (Apr. 1973), 556-63.

Laub, Bryna. The Official Soap Opera Annual. New
     York: Ballantine Books, 1977.

"Love of Soap Opera." June Magazine. Prod. David
     Lowe, Jr., and narr. Sylvia Chase. CBS. 9 June
     1977.

McLuhan, Marshall. Understanding Media: The Extensions
     of Man. New York: New American Library, 1964.

Mannes, Marya. "Everything's Up to Date in Soap Operas."
     TV Guide, 15 Mar. 1969. Rpt. in Television: A Sel-
     ection of Readings from TV Guide Magazine. Ed. Barry
     G. Cole. New York: The Free Press, 1970, pp. 163-
     68.

Newcomb, Horace. TV: The Most Popular Art. Garden
     City, N.Y.: Anchor Press, 1974.

Rubin, Theodore J. "Psychiatrist's Notebook." _Ladies' Home Journal_, 93 (Jan. 1976), 43.

Thurber, James. _The Beast in Me and Other Animals_. New York: Harcourt Brace, 1948.

25

Porter, Dennis. "Soap Time: Thoughts on a Commodity Art
    Form." <u>College English</u>, 38 (Apr. 1977), 782–88.

Rubin, Theodore I. "Psychiatrist's Notebook." <u>Ladies'</u>
    <u>Home Journal</u>, 93 (Jan. 1976), 43.

"Sex and Suffering in the Afternoon." <u>Time</u>. 107 (12
    Jan. 1976), 46–53.

Stedman, Raymond. <u>The Serials: Suspense and Drama by</u>
    <u>Installment</u>. Norman: Univ. of Oklahoma, 1971.

Thurber, James. <u>The Beast in Me and Other Animals</u>. New
    York: Harcourt Brace, 1948.

Wakefield, Dan. <u>All Her Children</u>. New York: Avon, 1976.

Waugh, Alec. "The Secret Storm." <u>National Review</u>, 19
    (26 Dec. 1967), 1438.

Two

Sourcebook for a Paper

1

Daniel Boorstin, former professor of American history at the University of Chicago, won the Pulitzer Prize for The Americans. *He is currently the Librarian of Congress.*

This book was published by Random House in New York in 1973.

From The Americans: The Democratic Experience
DANIEL BOORSTIN

1   ÉMILE ZOLA'S OBSERVATION that "you cannot say you have   *390* thoroughly seen anything until you have got a photograph of it," now applied a hundredfold in the world of television. By the late twentieth century the man on the spot, the viewer of the experience where it actually happened, began to feel confined and limited. The full flavor of the experience seemed to come only to the "viewer," the man in the television audience. Suddenly, from feeling remote and away the televiewer was painlessly and instantaneously transported *into* the experience. Television cameras made him a ubiquitous viewer. The man there in person was spacebound, crowd-confined, while the TV viewer was free to see from all points of view, above the heads of others, and behind the scenes. Was it he who was *really* there?

2   Making copies of experience, sights and sounds, for *later* use was one thing. Conquering space and time for instantaneous viewing was quite another, and even more revolutionary.

. . .

3   Television was a revolution, or more precisely, a cata-   *391* clysm. For nobody "wanted" television, and it would create its own market as it transformed everyday life. It extended simultaneous experience, created anonymous audiences even vaster and more universal than those of radio, and incidentally created a new segregation.

. . .

4   Radio had remained primarily an "entertainment" and "news" medium, allowing people to enjoy the melodrama of "soap serials," the jokes of Jack Benny, Fred Allen, and Bob Hope, the songs of Bing Crosby, the breathless sportscasting of Grantland Rice. The newscaster himself—H. V. Kaltenborn or Lowell Thomas—was a kind of "performer" who told the radio listener in solemn or lively tones what it was really like to be there.

5   TELEVISION OPENED another world. It did not simply multiply the sources of news and entertainment, it actually multiplied experience. At the TV set the viewer could see and hear what was going on with a rounded immediacy. Simultaneity was of the essence. When you took a picture you had to wait to have it developed; when you bought a phonograph record you knew in advance how it would sound. But now on TV you could share the suspense of the event itself. This new category of experience-at-a-distance would transform American life more radically than any other modern invention except the automobile.

6   On the surface, television seemed simply to combine the *393* techniques of the motion picture and the phonograph with those of the radio, but it added up to something more. Here was a new way of mass-producing the moment for instant consumption by a "broadcast" (i.e., undefinable and potentially universal) community of witnesses. Just as the printing press five centuries before had begun to democratize learning, now the television set would democratize experience, incidentally changing the very nature of what was newly shared.

7   Before, the desire to share experience had brought people out of their homes gathering them together (physically as well as spiritually), but television would somehow separate them in the very act of sharing. While TV-democratized experience would be more equal than ever before, it would also be more separate. TV segregation confined Americans by the same means that widened their experience. Here was a kind of segregation that no Supreme Court ruling could correct, nor could it be policed by any federal commission. For it was built into the TV set.

8   This was again the familiar consequence of having a centralized and enlarged source, now not merely for running water or running electricity. Just as Rebecca no longer needed to go to the village well to gather her water (and her gossip), so now, too, in her eighth-floor kitch-

enette she received the current of hot and cold running 393
images. Before 1970, more than 95 percent of American
households had television sets. Now the normal way to
enjoy a community experience was at home in your living
room at your TV set.

9   In earlier times, to see a performance was to become
part of a visible audience. At a concert, in a church, at a
ball game or a political rally, the audience was half the
fun. What and whom you saw in the audience was at least
as interesting as and often humanly more important than
what you saw on the stage. While she watched her TV set,
the lonely Rebecca was thrust back on herself. She could
exclaim or applaud or hiss, but nobody heard her except
the children in the kitchen or the family in the living
room, who probably already knew her sentiments too well.
The others at the performance took the invisible form of
"canned" laughter and applause. The mystery of the listening audience which had already enshrouded radio now
became the mystery of the viewing audience. The once
warmly enveloping community of those physically present
was displaced by a world of unseen fellow TV watchers.
Who else was there? Who else was watching? And even if
they had their sets turned on, were they *really* watching?

10   Each of the millions of watching Americans was now 394
newly segregated from those who put on the program and
who, presumably, were aiming to please him. Television
was a one-way window. The viewer could see whatever
they offered, but nobody except the family in the living
room could know for sure how the viewer reacted to what
he saw. Tiny island audiences gathered nightly around
their twinkling sets, much as cave-dwelling ancestors had
clustered around their fires for warmth and safety, and for
a feeling of togetherness. In these new tribal groups, each
child's television tastes were as intimate a part of family
lore as whether he preferred ketchup or mustard on his
hamburger. With more and more two-TV families (even
before 1970 these were one third of all American households) it became common for a member of the family to
withdraw and watch in lonely privacy. Of course, broadcasters made valiant and ingenious efforts to fathom these
secrets, to find out what each watcher really watched,
what he really liked and what he really wanted. But the
broadcasters' knowledge was necessarily based on samples, on the extrapolation of a relatively few cases, on estimates and guesses—all merely circumstantial evidence.

11   There was a new penumbra between watching and   *394*
not-watching. "Attending" a ball game, a symphony concert, a theatrical performance or a motion picture became
so casual that children did it while they wrote out their
homework, adults while they played cards or read a magazine, or worked in the kitchen or in the basement. The TV
watcher himself became unsure whether he was really
watching, or only had the set on. Experience was newly be-
fogged. The most elaborate and costly performances ceased
to be special occasions that required planning and tickets;
they became part of the air conditioning. Radio, too, had
become something heard but not necessarily listened to,
and its programing was directed to people assumed to be
doing something else: driving the car, working at a hobby,
washing the dishes. Car radios, which numbered 15 million in 1950, exceeded 40 million by 1960. With the rise of
the transistor, miniaturized radio sets were carried about
on the person like a fountain pen or a purse, to assuage
loneliness wherever the wearer might be.

12   Newly isolated from his government, from those who
collected his taxes, who provided public services, and who
made the crucial decisions of peace or war, the citizen felt
a frustrating new disproportion between how often and
how vividly political leaders could get their messages to
him and how often and how vividly he could get *his* message to them. Except indirectly, through the opinion polls,
Americans were offered no new avenue comparable to
television by which they could get their message back.
Private telegrams began to become obsolete. The citizen
was left to rely on the telephone (which might respond to
his call with a "recorded message") or on a venerable
nineteenth-century institution, the post office.

13   By enabling him to be anywhere instantly, by filling his   *395*
present moment with experiences engrossing and overwhelming, television dulled the American's sense of his
past, and even somehow separated him from the longer
past. If Americans had not been able to accompany the as-
tronauts to the moon they would have had to read about it
the next morning in some printed account that was engrossing in retrospect. But on television, Americans
witnessed historic events as vivid items of the present. In
these ways, then, television created a time myopia, focusing interest on the exciting, disturbing, inspiring, or
catastrophic instantaneous *now*.

14   The high cost of network time and the need to offer
something for everybody produced a discontinuity of programing, a constant shifting from one sort of thing to
another. Experience became staccato and motley. And
every act of dissent acquired new dramatic appeal, especially if it was violent or disruptive. For this lost feeling of
continuity with the past, the ineffective TV antidote was
Old Movies.

15   TELEVISION, THEN, BROUGHT a new vagueness to everyday experience: the TV watcher became accustomed to
seeing something-or-other happening somewhere-or-other
at sometime-or-other, but all in Living Color. The
common-sense hallmarks of authentic firsthand experience (those ordinary facts which a jury expected from a
witness to prove that he had actually experienced what he
said) now began to be absent, or only ambiguously present, in television experience. For his TV experience, the
American did not need to go out to see anything in particular: he just turned the knob, and then wondered while he
watched. Was this program live or was it taped? Was it
merely an animation or a simulation? Was it a rerun?
Where did it originate? When, if ever, did it really occur?
Was it happening to actors or to real people? Was that a
commercial?—a spoof of a commercial—a documentary?
—or pure fiction?

16   Almost never did the viewer see a TV event from a single individual's point of view. For TV was many-eyed,
alert to avoid the monotony of any one person's limited vision. While each camera gave an image bigger and clearer
than life, nobody got in the way. As the close-up dominated the screen, the middle distance dissolved. The
living-room watcher saw the player in left field, the batter
at the plate, or rowdies in a remote bleacher more sharply
than did the man wearing sunglasses in the stands. Any
casual kook or momentary celebrity filled the screen, just
like Humphrey Bogart or President Nixon. All TV experience had become theater, in which any actor, or even a
spectator, might hold center stage. The new TV perspective made the American understandably reluctant to go
back to his seat on the side and in the rear. Shakespeare's
metaphors became grim reality when the whole world had
become a TV stage.

17   In this supermarket of surrogate experience, the old   396
compartments were dissolved. Going to a church or to a
lecture was no different from going to a play or a movie or
a ball game, from going to a political rally or stopping to
hear a patent-medicine salesman's pitch. Almost anything
could be watched in shirt sleeves, with beer can in hand.
The experience which flowed through the television channels was a mix of entertainment, instruction, news, uplift,
exhortation and guess what. Successful programing offered entertainment (under the guise of instruction),
instruction (under the guise of entertainment), political
persuasion (with the appeal of advertising) and advertising (with the charm of drama). The new miasma, which no
machine before could emit, and which enshrouded the TV
world, reached out to befog the "real" world. Americans
began to be so accustomed to the fog, so at home and sol-
aced and comforted by the blur, that reality itself became
slightly irritating because of its sharp edges and its clear
distinctions of person, place, time, and weather.

18   As broadcasting techniques improved, they tended to
make the viewer's experience more indirect, more controlled by unseen producers and technicians. Before, the
spectator attending a national political convention would,
simply by turning his head, decide for himself *where* he
would look, but the TV watcher in the living room lacked
the power to decide. Cameramen, directors, and commentators decided for him, focusing on this view of a brutal
policeman or that view of a pretty delegate. As these conventions became guided tours by TV camera, the commentators themselves acquired a new power over the citizen's
political experience, which was most vividly demonstrated
at the Democratic National Convention in Chicago in
1968. Even as the American's secondhand experience
came to seem more real and more authentic, it was more
than ever shaped by invisible hands and by guides who
themselves upstaged the leading performers and became
celebrities.

19   Television watching became an addiction comparable
only to life itself. If the set was not on, Americans began to
feel that they had missed what was "really happening."
And just as it was axiomatic that it was better to be alive
than to be dead, so it became axiomatic that it was better
to be watching *something* than to be watching nothing at
all. When there was "nothing on TV tonight," there was a
painful void. No wonder, then, that Americans revised

their criteria for experience. Even if a firsthand experi- *396*
ence was not worth having, putting it on TV might make *397*
it so.

20

Of all the wonders of TV, none was more remarkable
than the speed with which it came. Television conquered
America in less than a generation, leaving the nation
more bewildered than it dared admit. Five hundred years
were required for the printing press to democratize learning. And when the people could know as much as their
"betters," they demanded the power to govern themselves.
As late as 1671, the governor of Virginia, Sir William
Berkeley, thanked God that the printing press (breeder of
heresy and disobedience!) had not yet arrived in his col-
ony, and he prayed that printing would never come to Virginia. By the early nineteenth century, aristocrats and
men of letters could record, with Thomas Carlyle, that
movable type had disbanded hired armies and cashiered
kings, and somehow created "a whole new democratic
world." Now with dizzying speed, television had de-
mocratized experience. It was no wonder that like the
printing press before it, television met a cool reception
from intellectuals and academics and the other custodians
of traditional avenues of experience.

QUESTIONS FOR STUDY AND DISCUSSION

1. What does Boorstin mean when he says that television "multiplied experience"?
2. What other inventions in the history of mankind does Boorstin
consider of equal importance to television? Do you agree or can
you think of other inventions you regard as equally, or more,
important?
3. What kind of proof does Boorstin offer for his assertion that
television has segregated Americans? Do you agree with him
on this point?
4. Boorstin states, "Television, then, brought a new vagueness to
everyday experience. . . ." What does he mean? Do you agree?
5. Boorstin believes that "television created a time myopia." Does
he convince you with his reasons for this statement?
6. What are the implications of Boorstin's description of television as "many-eyed, alert to avoid the monotony of any one person's limited vision"?

7. Have you ever felt that as a television viewer you had an advantage over people actually attending an event? If so, when and why?
8. Do you think that television gives us a "one-way window"? Do you feel that this one-sidedness is an inevitable quality of the medium of television or that it is caused by the way entertainers, politicians, and viewers use television?

2

Thomas Elmendorf, past president of the California Medical Association, delivered this speech to the United States House of Representatives Subcommittee on Communications.

The article was published in Vital Speeches of the Day *in volume 42 dated October 1, 1976.*

Violence on TV: The Effect on Children
THOMAS ELMENDORF

1   Suppose you sent your child off to the movies for three   *764* hours next Sunday. And three hours on Monday and the same number of hours Tuesday, Wednesday, Thursday, Friday and Saturday. That is essentially what is happening to the average child in America today, except it is not the screen in the movie house down the street he sits in front of, it is instead, the television set right in your own home.

2   According to the Nielson Index figures for TV viewing, it is estimated that by the time a child graduates from high school he has had 11,000 hours of schooling, as opposed to 15,000 hours of television. I would like to repeat that. By the time a child is 18 years old, he has spent more hours in front of the television set than he has in school. Over TV he will have witnessed by that time some 18,000 murders and countless highly detailed incidents of robbery, arson, bombings, shootings, beatings, forgery, smuggling and torture—averaging approximately one per minute in the standard television cartoon for children under the age of ten. In general, seventy-five percent of all network dramatic programs contain violence with over seven violent episodes per program hour.

3   Concurrent with this massive daily dose of violence over our television screens has been a dramatic rise in violence in our society. In 1973, 18,000 young Americans from 15 to 24 years of age, died in motor-vehicle accidents, with one of every six of these fatalities estimated to be due to

From *Vital Speeches of the Day*, 42, no. 24 (1 Oct. 1976), 764–66. Reprinted with permission.

suicide. In 1973, more than 5,000 were murdered, and an *764* additional 4,000 committed suicide. The death rate for this age group was 19 percent higher in 1973 than in 1960, due entirely to deaths by violence.

4   The largest rise in deaths by homicide during the past two decades was at the ages of one to four. More than a million American children suffer physical abuse or neglect each year, and at least one in five dies from mistreatment. It is a social problem of epidemic proportions.

5   In fact, murder is the fastest growing cause of death in the United States. The annual rate of increase exceeded 100 percent between 1960 and 1974. Our homicide rate is 10 times greater than in the Scandinavian countries. More murders are committed yearly in Manhattan, with a population of one-and-a-half-million, than in the entire United Kingdom, with a population of 60-million.

6   The age group most involved, with the greatest number of both victims and arrests, is 20 to 24. In 1972, 17 percent of all homicide victims and 24 percent of all arrests were in this age group. Teenagers from 15 to 19 account for another nine percent of all murder victims and nearly 19 percent of the arrests. In commenting about such crimes by youths, one author said, "It is as though our society had bred a new genetic strain, the child-murderer, who feels no remorse and is scarcely conscious of his acts."

7   What is to blame for these heinous statistics? What are the chances that this trend of rising violence can be controlled and reversed? The probabilities are small unless something is done about the moral and socioeconomic environment in which our young people are growing up today in America. One thing is certain. For a considerable proportion of American children and youth, the "culture of violence" is now both a major health threat and a way of life.

8   We of the medical profession believe that one of the factors behind this violence is televised violence. Television has become a school of violence and a college for crime.

9   Let us take a look at some of the evidence. The Surgeon *765* General of the United States has said, based on a six-volume study of the problem, that "there is a causative relationship between televised violence and subsequent antisocial behavior, and that the evidence is strong enough that it requires some action on the part of responsible authorities, the TV industry, the government, the citizens."

10   This report was a twin to the Surgeon General's report on smoking. This report on TV violence, in effect implied, "Warning: The Surgeon General Has Determined That Viewing of TV Violence is Dangerous to Your Health."

11   Much of the report has been clouded in dispute, so that its full impact has not reached society as effectively as it could. Let me point out just one of the disputes. The committee responsible for summing up the evidence gathered said that the 23 studies of the report, done by renowned scientists, provide "suggestive evidence in favor of the interpretation that viewing violence on television is conducive to an increase in aggressive behavior, although it must be emphasized that the causal sequence is very likely applicable only to some children who are predisposed in this direction." This has led critics to downgrade the report and say that violence on TV really only affects those already aggressive individuals, anyway. I would like to say to that, so what? If it makes aggression-prone people more aggressive, that is enough to make me say something should be done about violence on TV. But what is even more alarming is what the Surgeon General said about those predisposed to violence. He said that television can *cause* the predisposition. This point has been overlooked. So, televised violence can increase a child's aggressive behavior, especially if he has a predisposition for aggression. And, in addition to this, the predisposition itself can be caused by the viewing of TV.

12   Dr. Robert M. Liebert, associate professor of psychology, at the State University of New York at Stony Brook, concluded in an overview of several studies of the report that "at least under some circumstances, exposure to television aggression can lead children to accept what they have seen as a partial guide for their own actions. As a result, the present entertainment offerings of the television medium may be contributing, in some measure, to the aggressive behavior of many normal children. Such an effect has been shown in a wide variety of situations."

13   And earlier in the report he said, "Experimental studies preponderantly support the hypothesis that there is a directional, causal link between exposure to television violence and an observer's subsequent aggressive behavior."

14   Let us go beyond the report to other findings. Dr. Albert Bandura of Stanford University set out to determine what happens to a child who watches as aggressive personalities on television slug, stomp, shoot and stab one

another. His research team reached two conclusions about aggression on TV: 1, that it tends to reduce the child's inhibitions against acting in a violent, aggressive manner, and, 2, that children will copy what they see. Dr. Bandura points out that a child won't necessarily run out and attack the first person he sees after watching violence on the screen, but that, if provoked later on, evidence suggests that then he may very well put what he has learned into action. The reasons that children do not indiscriminately copy their TV characters is that parents suppress any such learning that they don't consider desirable—that is, the children get punished—and children rarely have access to weapons necessary for showing off what they have learned. "If," says Dr. Bandura, "they were provided with switchblade knives, blackjacks, explosives, six-shooters and nooses, it is safe to predict that the incidence of tragic imitative aggression connected with television viewing would rise sharply."

15   One of the lessons of television is that violence works. If you have a problem with someone, the school of TV says to slap him in the face, stab him in the back. By aggressive acts, the bad guy, for example, may gain control of grazing land, gold mines, nightclubs, and perhaps the whole town. Not until the very end is he usually punished. And, as in the case of the "Godfather," parts one and two, punishment may never really occur. Because most of the program has shown how well violence has paid off, punishment at the end tends not to have much of an inhibitory effect.

16   "From these findings," Dr. Bandura says, "we can conclude that if children see the bad guy punished, they are *not* likely to imitate spontaneously his behavior. But they do acquire—and retain—concrete information about how to behave aggressively, and punishment of the bad guy does not make them forget what they have learned. They may put into practice this knowledge on future occasions if they are given adequate instigation, access to the necessary weapons and the prospect of sufficiently attractive rewards for the successful execution of the behavior."

17   Other studies have shown that viewing violence blunts a child's sensitivity to it. They become jaded to violence on the screen. They condition themselves to avoid being upset by the gougings, smashings and stompings they see on TV. If they *did* get involved, their emotions could be shattered.

18   What about the long-term effects of violence on TV? Researcher D. J. Hicks found that even eight months after

viewing a violent episode only once, almost half of all the *765*
children could act out again what they had seen so long
ago. In 1955, Dr. Leonard Eron, head of research for the
Rip Van Winkle Foundation, looked into the long-range
correlations between a child's favorite television program,
the program's violence content and the aggressiveness of
the child as reported by his classmates. The project, which
covered a span of about 10 years, from age eight to 18, was
later picked up by the Surgeon General's study on TV
violence. The investigators found a strong correlation between the early viewing of television violence and aggressive behavior in the teenage years. In fact, according to
the study, a child's television habits at age eight were
more likely to be a predictor of his aggressiveness at eigh-
teen than either his family's socioeconomic status, his relationships with his parents, his IQ or any other single
factor in his environment. The report concluded that a
preference for violent television at a young age leads to
the building of aggressive habits.

19   As equally alarming as these studies are the findings of
researcher George Gerbner, dean of the Annenberg School
of Communications at the University of Pennsylvania. He
said, "Anyone who watches evening network TV receives
a heavy diet of violence. More than half of all characters
on prime-time TV are involved in some violence, about
one-tenth in killing." Because of this, TV breeds suspicion
and fear. The report said, "People who watch a lot of TV
see the real world as more dangerous and frightening than
those who watch very little. Heavy viewers are less trustful of their fellow citizens."

20   To cope with this fear the heavy watcher also gets a *766*
thick skin. He becomes conditioned to being a victim. He
becomes apathetic to violence. Gerbner concludes with the
observation that "acceptance of violence and passivity
in the face of injustice may be consequences of far greater
social concern than occasional displays of individual
aggression."

21   So, we have a two-edged sword. Television violence
tends to make some people more violent, and others it
makes more willing to accept violence as a way of life.

22   All in all, 146 articles in behavioral science journals and
related reports, representing 50 studies involving 10,000
children and adolescents from every conceivable background, all showed that viewing violence produces increased aggressive behavior in the young.

23   The accumulation of evidence suggests, as you have   *766*
heard, that children will copy TV violence, that they often
do *not* do so because of parental control and lack of access
to weapons, that TV teaches a child that often violence
succeeds and that problems can be solved by violence, that
viewing TV violence blunts sensitivity to violence in the
real world, that children remember specific acts of TV violence, and that preferring violent television at an early
age leads to more aggressive teenage behavior. . . .

24   That is why the American Medical Association at its recent annual meeting, acting on a resolution introduced by
the California delegation, has declared violence on TV an
environmental health risk and has asked doctors, their
families and their patients to actively oppose programs
containing violence, as well as products and services of the
sponsors of such programs.

25   In other words, if you, as a parent, see something on TV
that you feel is too violent for your child to watch, turn
the TV off or change the channel, and don't buy the products of the firms that support the program through their
advertising.

26   As a representative of the California Medical Association, I want to thank you for allowing me to explain our
position, and why we have taken this stand.

QUESTIONS FOR STUDY AND DISCUSSION

1. What studies does Elmendorf use to argue his case? Does he
   mention any authors whose names you recognize from the
   Sourcebook?
2. Which of the statistics or information Elmendorf presents do
   you find most forceful or effective in building his argument?
3. Do any of the statistics cited have a questionable relationship
   to violence on television?
4. Does the fact that this material was prepared for oral presentation affect its style? In what way?
5. If children learn violence from television, why, in the author's
   opinion, don't they commit violent actions more often?
6. What solutions to the problem does the author suggest? Can
   you think of others?

3

Edward Jay Epstein, who has a Ph.D. from Harvard University, is a free-lance writer. He is a frequent contributor to The New Yorker *and has written several other books on social and political problems. His latest book is on Lee Harvey Oswald.*

This book was published by Random House in New York in 1973.

From News from Nowhere: Television and the News

EDWARD JAY EPSTEIN

1   More than fifty years ago Walter Lippmann suggested   *164*
that newspaper reporting was in large part a process of
filling out an established "repertory of stereotypes" with
current news. In a similar way, network news is involved
with illustrating a limited repertory of story lines with
appropriate pictures. One NBC commentator, Sander
Vanocur, observed that "network news is a continuous
loop: there are only a limited number of plots—'Black versus White,' 'War is Hell,' 'America is falling apart,' 'Man
against the elements,' 'The Generation Gap,' etc.—which
we seem to be constantly redoing with different casts of   *165*
characters." Many of the correspondents interviewed complained about the need to fit news developments into developed molds or formulas, and to order stories along
predetermined lines; at the same time, most accepted it as
a practical necessity. Again, the fact that a film story requires the coordinated efforts of a large number of
individuals—reporters, cameramen, sound men, writers,
producer, editor and commentator—working on the product at different times, makes it necessary that there be a
stable set of expectations of what constitutes a proper
story. Moreover, producers generally assume that a given
audience will have certain preferences in terms of both the
form and the content of news stories. "Every program has

certain requirements and guidelines for its filmed re-   *165*
ports," an ABC executive explained. "Eventually these
might harden into formulas and clichéd plots, but when
they fail to hold the audiences' attention, the producer or
the program is usually changed.

. . .

2 NBC and CBS news programs have similar requisites   *168*
for film stories, which specify the desired length, format
and particular focus for news.

3 In terms of content, however, the producers' unwritten
but generally known preferences for certain types of
stories are of much more importance to correspondents,
who generally find it necessary to "sell themselves" to
producers of the news programs by the kind of stories they
do. These preferences, in turn, are predicated on certain
assumptions about what types of news stories are most
likely to interest, and least likely to disconcert, the special
audiences that producers are most concerned about: network executives, affiliate managers and news directors,
other newsmen, and in a general way, the home viewing
audience.

4 *The Dialectical Model.* A prime concern of network executives, as perceived by the producers interviewed, is
that news stories appear to be balanced and nonpolitical so
as not to conflict with the FCC's Fairness Doctrine.
"Executives simply don't want the headaches of answering
complaints about one-sided news or news that advocates a
definite position," one NBC producer explained. To avoid   *169*
such headaches, producers order correspondents, field producers and writers to include in their story lines opposing
views as a matter of policy. Not surprisingly, then, story
lines tend to follow a point-counterpoint format, with correspondents providing some sort of synthesis of, though
not necessarily an answer to, the opposing views in a final
comment. Most correspondents assume that they are expected by executives to take a completely neutral position,
and to identify with the audiences as far as possible. "In
this country play it down the middle," William S. Paley,
chairman of the board of CBS, is quoted as saying.

5 *The Ironic Model.* If correspondents cannot find plausible balancing views, producers generally prefer that they
present the story ironically, rather than as a one-sided

polemic. This involves a straight exposition of some unex-   *169*
pected turn of events.

· · ·

6   The joking news story, which uses zany photography,   *170*
nostalgic music and commentators' wry smiles as its cues
to the audience, have increasingly become the only viable
alternative for producers faced with stories that do not fit
into the point-counterpoint model. One NBC producer
said, "The president of this company wants us to end with
a light piece and leave the audience smiling, which means
there is always a demand for a news joke." . . .

7   *The National News Package.* A second audience that must
be taken into consideration by network producers is the affiliate managers, who determine when and if network
news will be shown on their station. As mentioned earlier,
one main demand of affiliate managers is that network   *171*
news stories concern "national" rather than local events.
As one CBS affiliate manager put it: "We don't expect the
network news to be simply a replay of various local stories;
it must be something different."

8   While there are always stories on such national institutions as Congress, the Presidency and the Supreme Court,
as well as international events, which easily qualify as
"national news," it is more difficult to fit stories that occur
outside Washington, D.C. (and which are likely to be reported by some affiliates as local stories) into a network
news program. Yet such local happenings might hold substantial interest for a national audience, or be needed to
give the program geographic balance. Hence, a key problem for network news producers is to transform news
stories about local events into a national story.

9   A commonly used solution is "nationalizing news stories"
by fusing together two or more local stories into a "package" which purports to show a national trend. The process
involves shooting parallel stories in different cities related
to some essentially local story which for one reason or
another the producer wants to use. Then a commentator
will do an introduction which describes the national trend,
which the film stories are presented, in sequence, as illustrations of. For example, to illustrate the problems of
blacks in the cities in February 1969, five separate stories
on this theme were commissioned in the five cities in
which NBC owns television stations. As described in the
evaluation report, they were "Lem Tucker on slums and
welfare in New York; Valeriana with crime, using

Washington as an example; Bill Matney in Chicago with   *171*
urban blight and Negro discontent over housing; Mark
Landsman in Cleveland on black politics; also Perkins [in
Los Angeles] on Negro job opportunites; . . . and Tucker
wrap-up. Each segment had appropriate illustrative footage." None of these reports involved a news happening
that day; all were commissioned in advance so that the   *172*
package could be presented as a report on a national trend
on the first anniversary of the National Commission on
the Causes and Prevention of Violence on February 27.
(The same sort of "nationalization" can be accomplished
without commissioning or finding a second similar story
by having the reporter simply comment on the national
significance of the event in his on-camera remarks.)

10   No matter how this imperative is achieved, according to
Reuven Frank, ideally network news subjects should be
microcosms of national problems. The format for a network news story must therefore provide a way of linking a
local (or even unique) happening with a more general
trend. Many of the trend stories—transportation, urban
decay, national crime problems and so on—derive from the
need to nationalize local stories.

11   *The Action Story.* A third critical, though less well defined audience is the home viewers that determine the
Nielsen ratings of news programs. While it is presumed
that network news does not *attract* an audience, it can reduce the already existing audience. To satisfy this requisite, the producers interviewed generally assumed that
the home audience is more likely to be engrossed by visual
action than a filmed discussion of issues, or "talking
heads," and so they placed a high value on action film.
Each producer has his own style for an action story. Some
prefer to begin with a "news bite," or dramatic film, continue with the correspondent's comments, and then go on
to the unfolding drama; others prefer to build a story, beginning with the correspondent's introduction, followed by
the rising drama leading to some climax of action. However, virtually all the stories given high marks for action
at NBC involved violence toward humans: "head-busting"
(i.e., police charging groups of demonstrators), "bang-bang
stuff" (i.e., shoot-outs or combat) and "rioting" were the
terms in which such action pieces were favorably described to the executive producers. Terms which denoted a
dearth of action included "talking heads" (i.e., conversa-   *173*
tion), "nothing happened," or a "quiet walk" (i.e., an unop-
posed demonstration).

12   The one ingredient most producers interviewed claimed *173*
was necessary for a good action story was visually identifiable opponents clashing violently. This, in turn, requires some form of stereotype: military troops, fighting
civilians, black versus white students, workers wearing
hardhats manhandling bearded peace demonstrators were
cited by producers as examples of the components for such
stories. Demonstrations or violence involving less clearly
identifiable groups make less effective stories, since, as
one CBS producer put it, "it would be hard to tell the good
guys from the bad guys."

13   The scenarios for action stories are thus organized on
the principle of stressing the presumed claims and differences of opposed groups. Interviews and narration that
define these distinctions and prepare the audience for the
ensuing action are preferred over discussions that point to
a more complex relationship between and within the
groups. In the case of the student strike at Harvard in
1968, for example, interviews with student leaders which
suggested the existence of numerous factions, with objectives that were not always consistent, were not used in the
network reports. Instead, students were shown as a more
or less united and monolithic group. "We tried to show
what the students had in common," an NBC producer explained to me, "not what the petty differences were."

14   *The Nostalgia Model....* Special audiences must be *174*
reached through a treatment of the news that is general
enough to interest *all* members of the audience. To reach
the rural audiences (which for technical reasons are dis-
proportionately important in maintaining good Nielsen
ratings) ... requires an approach which is still of general
interest to urban viewers. One device, used at all three
networks for satisfying these audience demands, is the
"nostalgia" format, which in its most elemental form focuses on a traditional value threatened or replaced by a
modern value. The chief requisite of this type of story, according to correspondents interviewed, is "pretty pictures," as one put it. By either narration, interviews or
juxtaposition of images, the story is told in terms of the
conflicting values. ...

15   To be sure, all network news stories do not fit neatly in
the various pigeonholes described above. Some momen-
tous events fit no preconceived story line; some more specialized subjects fit in less well defined models; and still
others require elements from more than one model.
Moreover, the repertory itself changes from time to time

and network to network. Nevertheless, at any given time, *174* the requisites of network news make it necessary to have some preformed story lines for containing the chaotic flow of news.

16   Editing involves selecting certain fragments of a film of a given subject and arranging them in an order which appears to represent a coherent view of the event. The same set of pictures can, however, yield different coherent views, depending on how they are edited. "Given at random, say, half a dozen shots of different nature and subject, there are any number of possible combinations of the six that, with the right twist of commentary, could make film sense," a leading film editor suggested. In network *175* news, the meaning is prescribed by the story line. Film editors in network news typically defined their role as being noncreative: "Our job is simply to put together the story ordered by the producer in a professional way," one chief film editor for NBC observed.

17   In editing a news story with sound, the film editor usually works closely with a field producer or correspondent, who at times literally stands over his shoulder. First the footage is viewed in its entirety, and the producer or correspondent designates which of the newsmakers' sentences are to be pulled out and used in the final piece. Whatever sound portions are chosen are transferred to magnetic tape and "laid out" according to the sequence dictated by the story line. Historical continuity is not required; on the contrary, often a sentence used toward the end of a news conference will be used as the beginning of the film, and vice versa. Then the film editor chooses cutaways of the correspondents and suitable establishing shots, and uses them to create the illusion that there was continuity to the sound portions.

18   In the case of silent footage, film editors have considerably more discretion. Usually the story line calls for some general effect, such as "crowds milling" or "street fighting," and it is left to the editor to achieve this scene.

19   Producers have definite expectations as to what constitutes a visually effective editing job. First of all, according to the editors interviewed, they are supposed to eliminate all technically inferior film footage (unless otherwise instructed by a producer) and reduce visual noise or disconcerting elements. The CBS News Manual states, for example:

A convincing realism demands that only the best-quality scenes *175* should be selected. Avoid using scenes that are poorly exposed. . . . Be sure the sound quality is distinct and easily grasped. Distorted sound or low-level audio will most certainly destroy the realism of the news story.

Paradoxically, carefully prepared or even rehearsed news scenes are far more likely to satisfy these criteria for a "convincing reality" than spontaneous news scenes which, by their very nature, have unpredictable lighting and sound conditions.

20   A second editing norm, which all the editors interviewed accepted without qualification, is the desirability of concentrating scenes of action so as to heighten the visual effect. "Our job is to cut out all the deadwood and dull moments," one NBC editor commented. The procedure involves routinely eliminating the intervals in which little of visual interest occurs, and compressing the remaining fragments into one continuous montage of unceasing visual action. For instance, an attempt by the SDS faction at Columbia University to block the registration of students in September of 1968 involved, according to my observations, a few speeches by SDS leaders, hours of milling about, in which the protest more or less dissipated for lack of interest, and about one minute of violence when five SDS leaders attempted to push their way past two campus patrolmen at the registration hall. The half-hour of film taken that day by an NBC camera crew recorded various views of the crowd from 9 A.M. until the violence at about 2 P.M., and the minute or so of violent confrontation. However, when the happening was reduced to a two-minute news story for the NBC Evening News, the editors routinely retained the violent scenes, building up to them with quick cuts of speeches and crowd scenes. The correspondent, who was not himself present at the demonstration that day, simply narrated the scenes of concentrated violence in the accepted formula used for campus violence at the time—which juxtaposed the demands and violence of the students with the enlightened negotiating efforts of the university administration. The process of distilling action from preponderantly inactive scenes was not perceived as any sort of distortion by any of the editors interviewed. On the contrary, most of them considered it to be the accepted function of editing; as one chief editor observed, it was "what we are really paid for." *176*

21   A third value accepted without question by film editors *176* is that only the portions of film that fulfill the agreed-upon story should be used; film that contradicts or even appears to undercut any point in the story should be omitted. The CBS News Manual states that "the film editor should cut the pictures with a story line or general script in mind. . . . The scenes should tell the story—beginning, middle, and end—with the accompanying narration adding the related facts."

22   If, for example, a story concerns the integration of a school, the editor is supposed to choose footage showing black and white students together, even if the vast preponderance of footage shows either all black or all white students congregating together—a situation which often occurs, since integration is frequently token rather than real, and "integrated" schools often maintain a de facto segregation by using "track" systems. NBC producers in New York, for example, criticized the editing of a story about the integration of the Shaker Heights (Ohio) schools, since the establishing shots failed to show Negro and white students mixing. One New York producer told the field producer in Cleveland, "You need a recut to get some Negroes in there . . . You never see any signs of integration. You definitely need some Negroes in the opening scene. I'm hoping you can drop some in." The Cleveland producer replied over the telephone that there was in fact very little mixing, since "integration is just beginning here," but that he would have the film editors "put in whatever we have." However, the field editors were unable to find such footage, and the producers in New York expressed a great deal of dissatisfaction with the piece.

23   Further, from the total film footage available, editors presume that their job is to ferret out the shots which most exactly illustrate the script. This may call for shots of bearded students in a peace march, militant Afro-style *177* black leaders in an urban riot, or clean-cut college students in a political campaign, depending on the story line. (Editors also are expected to select the appropriate background sounds from a library of tape recordings, which include such titles as "Washington Gallery Hubbub," "Arab Mumbles," "Crowd Cheering," "Crowd Chanting," "Pickets Yelling," "Noisy Riot," "Gunfire" and "Black Demonstrators.") In a very real sense, editing practices tend to reinforce existing stereotypes as well as the established stories.

24　　Film editing can also be used to enforce the policies of 　*177*
producers and executives. Unlike correspondents, who at
least claim some autonomy in interpreting news occurring
in their presence, film editors think of themselves as working directly for the producer of a program, and their function as complying with his instructions (except where it
violates the technical norms of editing). As one NBC producer said, "My final control is in the editing room."
Robert MacNeil describes graphically in his book how the
more gruesome shots of battle casualties in the Vietnam
war were deleted in the editing room. This was an unwritten policy of the Evening News because, as one person
commented, "We go on the air at suppertime." The fear
among network executives was that such grisly footage
would cause home viewers to switch the program off, an
NBC vice-president subsequently explained to me. Film
editors were thus instructed to edit out all "upsetting
shots" of casualties. Similarly, profanity and obscene references, no matter how germane they may be to a story
about provocation and reaction, are also cut out in the
editing room.

25　　Finally, when the edited picture track is merged with
the sound track, and narration and special effects added,
the process of reconstructing reality is completed. The fact
that stories are reconstructed routinely according to certain established guidelines, practices and policies, tends to
preform, if not determine, the resulting images of reality
in a number of ways. First, since cameramen, corre- 　*178*
spondents, producers and editors all tend to favor articulate and prepared scenes over confused and spontaneous
happenings—deleting inarticulate statements and any
sort of distraction—viewpoints are presented as highly resolved and crisply articulated issues, and the news makers
become cogent advocates of a cause. By seeking or induc-
ing opposing viewpoints—and editing them in a point-
counterpoint format—network news further adds a di-
mension of logic and order that often is lacking in the
realm of spontaneous news.

26　　Second, network news tends to favor pictures of action
over inaction. As one NBC producer pointed out, "There is
a three-stage distillation of news footage": that is, producers seek out stories with a high potential for action
footage; within these stories, cameramen seek out the
most "action-packed moments"; and editors then further
concentrate the action. Even when an event is charac-

terized by an unexpected low degree of activity, television *179*
can create the illusion of great activity. The relatively un-
enthusiastic reception General MacArthur received in
Chicago during his homecoming welcome in 1951, thus
appeared to be a massive and frenetic reception on television because all the moments of action were concentrated
together, according to the previously cited study by Kurt
and Gladys Lang. In collapsing the time frame of events
and concentrating the action into a continuous flow, television news tends to heighten the excitement of any group
or other phenomena it pictures, to the neglect of the more
vapid and humdrum elements.

27   Third, since news stories tend to be constructed from
those aspects of a happening that can be easily filmed and
recorded, and not from the more poorly lit, softly spoken or
otherwise inaccessible moments, events tend to be explained in terms of what one producer called "visual
facts." One correspondent pointed out, for example, that
television coverage of riots or protests at night tends to
focus on fires, even if they are insignificant "trash-can
fires," since they provide adequate light for filming.
Hence, urban riots tend to be defined in terms of the "vis- *180*
ual facts" of fires, rather than more complicated factors.
Visual facts, of course, cover only one range of phenomena,
and thus tend to limit the power of networks to explain
complex events.

28   Finally, the entire process of reconstructing stories
tends to fulfill preconceived expectations about how various events occur. Rather than recording the actual flow of
events, network news follows predetermined lines, from
the developing of a story line to the photographing of
selected aspects of the happening to the final editing.
Since each of the participants in the process—the cameraman, sound recorder, correspondent, editor and
producer—has relatively fixed ideas of what material
is wanted for each type of story, the "reality" produced
tends to be shaped, if not predetermined, by this web of
expectations.

QUESTIONS FOR STUDY AND DISCUSSION

1. What are the possible effects on television news of the use of
   the models or formulas that Epstein describes?

2. To whom do correspondents gear their news stories? What audiences do producers try to please?
3. Can you think of an example of a news story you have seen that you would place in the category of the "Ironic Model"?
4. What kinds of distortion of the news might result from the process of nationalizing news stories?
5. What requirements do producers impose on film editors?
6. Does Epstein believe that the editing process changes television news? How does he convey this belief? (Direct statement? Examples? Quotations?)

4

George Gerbner, Dean of the Annenberg School of Communication at the University of Pennsylvania, served on the Surgeon General's Scientific Advisory Committee on Television and Social Behavior. Larry Gross is an associate professor at the Annenberg School of Communication. The article is based on research conducted under a grant from the National Institute of Mental Health.

This article originally appeared in the volume 9 issue of April, 1976, of Psychology Today *on pages 41–45, 89.*

The Scary World of TV's Heavy Viewer
GEORGE GERBNER AND LARRY GROSS

1   MANY CRITICS WORRY about violence on television, most out   *41* of fear that it stimulates viewers to violent or aggressive acts. Our research, however, indicates that the consequences of experiencing TV's symbolic world of violence may be much more far-reaching.

2   We feel that television dramatically demonstrates the power of authority in our society, and the risks involved in breaking society's rules. Violence-filled programs show who gets away with what, and against whom. It teaches the role of victim, and the acceptance of violence as a social reality we must learn to live with—or flee from.

3   We have found that people who watch a lot of TV see the real world as more dangerous and frightening than those who watch very little. Heavy viewers are less trustful of their fellow citizens, and more fearful of the real world.

4   Since most TV "action-adventure" dramas occur in urban settings, the fear they inspire may contribute to the current flight of the middle class from our cities. The fear may also bring increasing demands for police protection, and election of law-and-order politicians.

5   Those who doubt TV's influence might consider the impact of the automobile on American society. When the automobile burst upon the dusty highways about the turn of the century, most Americans saw it as a horseless carriage, not as a prime mover of a new way of life. Similarly,

those of us who grew up before television tend to think of it 41
as just another medium in a series of 20th-century mass-
communications systems, such as movies and radio. But
television is not just another medium.

6   If you were born before 1950, television came into your
life after your formative years. Even if you are now a TV 42
addict, it will be difficult for you to comprehend the trans-
formations it has wrought. For example, imagine spend-
ing six hours a day at the local movie house when you
were 12 years old. No parent would have permitted it. Yet,
in our sample of children, nearly half the 12-year-olds
watch an average of six or more hours of television per
day. For many of them the habit continues into adulthood.
On the basis of our surveys, we estimate that about one
third of all American adults watch an average of four or
more hours of television per day.

7   Television is different from all other media. From cradle
to grave it penetrates nearly every home in the land. Unlike newspapers and magazines, television does not require literacy. Unlike the movies, it runs continuously,
and once purchased, costs almost nothing. Unlike radio, it
can show as well as tell. Unlike the theater or movies, it
does not require leaving your home. With virtually unlimited access, television both precedes literacy and, increasingly, preempts it.

8   Never before have such large and varied publics—from
the nursery to the nursing home, from ghetto tenement to
penthouse—shared so much of the same cultural system of
messages and images, and the assumptions embedded
in them. Television offers a universal curriculum that
everyone can learn.

9   Imagine a hermit who lives in a cave linked to the outside world by a television set that functioned only during
prime time. His knowledge of the world would be built exclusively out of the images and facts he could glean from
the fictional events, persons, objects and places that appear on TV. His expectations and judgments about the
ways of the world would follow the conventions of TV programs, with their predictable plots and outcomes. His
view of human nature would be shaped by the shallow
psychology of TV characters.

10   While none of us is solely dependent upon television for
our view of the world, neither have many of us had the opportunity to observe the reality of police stations, court-
rooms, corporate board rooms, or hospital operating 44

rooms. Although critics complain about the stereotyped *44*
characters and plots of TV dramas, many viewers look on
them as representative of the real world. Anyone who
questions that assertion should read the 250,000 letters,
most containing requests for medical advice, sent by viewers to "Marcus Welby, M.D." during the first five years of
his practice on TV.

11   If adults can be so accepting of the reality of television,
imagine its effect on children. By the time the average
American child reaches public school, he has already
spent several years in an electronic nursery school. At the
age of 10 the average youngster spends more hours a week
in front of the TV screen than in the classroom. Given continuous exposure to the world of TV, it's not surprising
that the children we tested seemed to be more strongly
influenced by TV than were the adults.

12   At the other end of the life cycle, television becomes the
steady and often the only companion of the elderly. As failing eyesight makes reading difficult, and getting around
becomes a problem, the inhabitants at many nursing
homes and retirement communities pass much of the day
in the TV room, where the action of fictional drama helps
make up for the inaction of their lives.

13   To learn what they and other Americans have been
watching we have been studying the facts of life in the
world of evening network television drama—what that
world looks like, what happens in it, who lives in it, and
who does what to whom in it. We have explored this world
by analyzing the content of the situation comedies, dramatic series, and movies that appear in prime time, between eight and 11 P.M.

14   Night after night, week after week, stock characters and
dramatic patterns convey supposed truths about people,
power and issues. About three fourths of all leading
characters on prime-time network TV are male, mostly
single, middle and upper-class white Americans in their
20s or 30s. Most of the women represent romantic or family interests. While only one out of every three male leads
intends to or has ever been married, two out of every three
female leads are either married, expected to marry, or involved in some romantic relationship.

15   Unlike the real world, where personalities are complex,
motives unclear, and outcomes ambiguous, television presents a world of clarity and simplicity. In show after show,
rewards and punishments follow quickly and logically.

Crises are resolved, problems are solved, and justice, or at   *44*
least authority, always triumphs. The central characters
in these dramas are clearly defined: dedicated or corrupt;
selfless or ambitious; efficient or ineffectual. To insure the
widest acceptability, (or greatest potential profitability)
the plot lines follow the most commonly accepted notions
of morality and justice, whether or not those notions bear
much resemblance to reality.

16   In order to complete a story entertainingly in only an
hour or even a half hour, conflicts on TV are usually personal and solved by action. Since violence is dramatic, and
relatively simple to produce, much of the action tends to be
violent. As a result, the stars of prime-time network TV
have for years been cowboys, detectives, and others whose
lives permit unrestrained action. Except in comic roles,
one rarely sees a leading man burdened by real-life constraints, such as family, that inhibit freewheeling activity.

17   For the past four years, we have been conducting surveys to discover how people are affected by watching the
world of television. We ask them questions about aspects   *45*
of real life that are portrayed very differently on TV from
the way they exist in the real world. We then compare the
responses of light and heavy viewers, controlling for sex,
education, and other factors.

18   Anyone trying to isolate the effects of television viewing
has the problem of separating it from other cultural
influences. In fact, it is difficult to find a sufficiently large
sample of nonviewers for comparison. For this article we
have compared the responses of light viewers, who watch
an average of two hours or less per day, and heavy viewers, who watch an average of four or more hours per day.
We also surveyed 300 teenagers in the 6th, 7th, and 8th
grades, among whom the heavy viewers watched six hours
or more per day.

19   Since the leading characters in American television
programs are nearly always American, we asked our respondents: "About what percent of the world's population
live in the United States?" The correct answer is six percent. The respondents were given a choice of three percent
or nine percent, which obliged them either to underestimate or overestimate the correct percentage. Heavy viewers were 19 percent more likely to pick the higher figure
than were the light viewers.

20   We next took up the subject of occupations, since the occupational census in prime time bears little resemblance

to the real economy. Professional and managerial roles make up about twice as large a proportion of the labor force on TV as they do in the real world. To find out if this distortion had any effect on viewers, we asked: "About what percent of Americans who have jobs are either professionals or managers—like doctors, lawyers, teachers, proprietors, or other executives?" When forced to make a choice between either 10 or 30 percent (the correct figure is 20 percent), the heavy viewers were 36 percent more likely to overestimate.

21　　One might argue, correctly, that heavy viewing of television tends to be associated with lower education and other socioeconomic factors that limit or distort one's knowledge about the real world. But when we controlled for such alternative sources of information as education and newspaper reading, we found that although they did have some influence, heavy television viewing still showed a significant effect. For example, while adult respondents who had some college education were less influenced by television than those who had never attended college, heavy viewers within both categories still showed the influence of television. We obtained similar results when we compared regular newspaper readers with occasional readers or nonreaders.

22　　The only factor that seemed to have an independent effect on the responses was age. Regardless of newspaper reading, education, or even viewing habits, respondents under 30 consistently indicated by their responses that they were more influenced by TV than those over 30. This response difference seems especially noteworthy in that the under-30 group on the whole is better educated than its elders. But the under-30 group constitutes the first TV generation. Many of them grew up with it as teacher and babysitter, and have had lifelong exposure to its influence.

23　　Anyone who watches evening network TV receives a heavy diet of violence. More than half of all characters on prime-time TV are involved in some violence, about one tenth in killing. To control this mayhem, the forces of law and order dominate prime time. Among those TV males with identifiable occupations, about 20 percent are engaged in law enforcement. In the real world, the proportion runs less than one percent. Heavy viewers of television were 18 percent more likely than light viewers to overestimate the number of males employed in law enforcement, regardless of age, sex, education, or reading habits.

Violence on television leads viewers to perceive the real *45* world as more dangerous than it really is, which must also influence the way people behave. When asked, "Can most people be trusted?" the heavy viewers were 35 percent more likely to check "Can't be too careful."

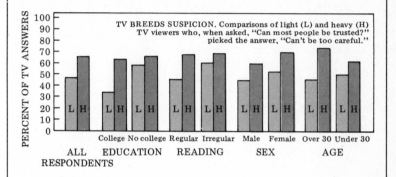

TV BREEDS SUSPICION. Comparisons of light (L) and heavy (H) TV viewers who, when asked, "Can most people be trusted?" picked the answer, "Can't be too careful."

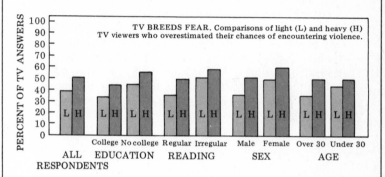

TV BREEDS FEAR. Comparisons of light (L) and heavy (H) TV viewers who overestimated their chances of encountering violence.

25   When we asked viewers to estimate their own chances of being involved in some type of violence during any given week, they provided further evidence that television can induce fear. The heavy viewers were 33 percent more likely than light viewers to pick such fearful estimates as 50-50 or one in 10, instead of a more plausible one in 100.

26   While television may not directly cause the results that have turned up in our studies, it certainly can confirm or encourage certain views of the world. The effect of TV should be measured not just in terms of immediate change in behavior, but also by the extent to which it cultivates certain views of life. The very repetitive and predictable nature of most TV drama programs helps to reinforce these notions.

27   Victims, like criminals, must learn their proper roles,   *45*
and televised violence may perform the teaching function
all too well [see "A Nation of Willing Victims," *pt,* April
1975]. Instead of worrying only about whether television
violence causes individual displays of aggression in the   *89*
real world, we should also be concerned about the way
such symbolic violence influences our assumptions about
social reality. Acceptance of violence and passivity in the
face of injustice may be consequences of far greater social
concern than occasional displays of individual aggression.

28   Throughout history, once a ruling class has established
its rule, the primary function of its cultural media has
been the legitimization and maintenance of its authority.
Folk tales and other traditional dramatic stories have always reinforced established authority, teaching that when
society's rules are broken retribution is visited upon the
violators. The importance of the existing social order is
always explicit in such stories.

29   We have found that violence on prime-time network TV
cultivates exaggerated assumptions about the threat of
danger in the real world. Fear is a universal emotion, and
easy to exploit. The exaggerated sense of risk and insecu-
rity may lead to increasing demands for protection, and to
increasing pressure for the use of force by established authority. Instead of threatening the social order, television
may have become our chief instrument of social control.

QUESTIONS FOR STUDY AND DISCUSSION

1. Why do the authors refer to television as the "universal curriculum"?
2. What reasons do the authors give for the large amount of violence on television?
3. How do television plots contrast with real-life situations according to the authors?
4. What views or attitudes did the authors find that heavy television viewers, regardless of education and economic level, hold
about society? Was there a single factor that made a difference
in attitudes?
5. What information led the authors to conclude that the
influence of television is more far-reaching than had been
thought?
6. Why didn't the authors use nonviewers rather than light viewers for comparison with heavy television viewers?

5

Gerald Lesser, a professor of Education and Developmental Psychology at Harvard University, was Chairman of the Board of Advisors of the Children's Television Workshop.

This book was published by Random House, Incorporated, in New York in 1974.

From Children and Television: Lessons From Sesame Street
GERALD LESSER

1   Television is not an isolated experience in a child's life. *244* Each child uses it in his own way. What a child learns from television is only one element in a complex balancing act of simultaneous influences—peers, siblings, parents and people in his neighborhood as well as television. One example is the simple finding from the Educational Testing Service's evaluation of *Sesame Street:* Among the disadvantaged children who watched at home, those who gained most had mothers who often watched *Sesame Street* with them and talked with them about it. Although Joan Cooney set out to make *Sesame Street* an effective experiment in the use of television, she acknowledged early that it is only one influence among many, saying, "Television has a very important role to play in education. Still, it's just a big cold box, and just can't replace a loving teacher or parent who cares about a child." (*Time,* November 23, 1970)

2   Children are simply too complex, and the influences upon them too diverse, to expect that a single influence—like television—will have a uniform effect upon their lives. Nevertheless, there are some minimum guarantees that must be assured, the most obvious being that television must avoid damaging any child. Richard H. Granger, a Yale professor of clinical pediatrics,[1] applied to television the basic principle of medical practice: "First do no harm!"

[1]Granger, 1973.

That television do no harm is little enough to ask. But can it   *244*
bring any distinctive benefits to children?

3   The simplest benefit we can expect for our children from
television is the one that it seems to have been supplying
throughout its history and the one that many people attack
as exactly what is wrong with television: It gives children   *245*
an important source of present enjoyment. To describe this
as a benefit seems to share in television's traditional defense of itself, that it only provides what the public wants.
Haven't we had enough "entertainment" from television? I
think it depends upon what we mean by entertainment.
Writing about children's movies in the New York *Times*,
Benjamin DeMott, an essayist and astute social commentator, gives us his definition:

> The purpose of children's shows is to entertain, and the key to
> entertainment is involvement: steady, sympathetic, deep-
> breathing identification with the cares, troubles, and feelings of
> somebody not myself. . . . Implicit in it is a conviction that in-
> volvement isn't a game or holiday—not when experienced by a kid
> worried about the fate of the hero, and not when assessed by any
> developmental psychologist with a humane sense of the stages by
> which a sane, sensitive and effective grownup comes into being.

> The act of imaginatively participating in a hero's life, the process of
> worrying intensely and lovingly about a vulnerable danger-
> courting small animal—these have moral consequences, they
> nourish a kid's awareness of other lives and his power of going
> beyond himself. [September 12, 1971]

4   Enjoyment in this sense need not be frivolous and empty.
The idea even has been applied to the analysis of what
happens in schools, long the bastions of earnest nonfrivol-
ity. Failing to find clear evidence that performance in
school affects a child's later achievement or income,
Christopher Jencks and his colleagues[2] concluded that the
only unequivocal basis for evaluating a school should be
whether the students and teachers find it a satisfying place
to be. Making a child's education useful to his future is
important, of course. But making his life more pleasant
now is not offered as an excuse for either the schools' or
television's inability to do more. It is no small achievement
in itself.

[2]Jencks et al., 1972.

5 Television does not hover over children with demands and expectations. They can watch without being tested, graded, reprimanded or even observed by others. They are safe from the threat of humiliation or ridicule for not living up to what is expected of them.

6 There is little doubt that we all need retreats, some sanctuary from forces that correct and direct us. But we have not made up our collective mind about whether they should exist. We fear that they may engulf us in escape and illusion, and that the indulgence may become addictive. Yet periodic escape from surveillance and exacting expectations need not be equivalent to escape from reality. For those children who need it, television used in moderation can provide a temporary refuge.

7 Television differs from traditional teaching in some major ways. Traditional teaching depends primarily upon oral language; television combines the visual as well as auditory means. Television moves, in contrast to the more static techniques in schools and classrooms. Traditional teaching tries to control the level and pace of the materials presented to children, giving them what we believe they need, organized and sequenced into progressive steps, followed by appropriate reinforcements. Television does not meet these standard criteria, usually being more helter-skelter and richer in surplus meanings. Some children learn very well from traditional techniques; others need an alternative like television.

8 Using this alternative, what can children learn? From our experience with *Sesame Street,* we know that they can learn certain language skills and number concepts, and that the symbols of words, numbers, shapes and forms are used in thinking. We do not yet know if children can use television to learn how to learn, but there is evidence that it can help children move from "knowing that" to "knowing how," as psychologist Jerome Bruner puts it.[3] First, *Sesame Street* had some success in teaching mental processes that aid learning, such as classifying and ordering objects and events by size, form, function or class; making inferences; generating and testing predictions. Also, other studies seem promising. For example, in a series of reports,[4] Jerome Kagan and his colleagues at Harvard have

[3]Bruner, 1972.

[4]For example, Kagan, Pearson, and Welch, 1966. Also: Debus, 1970; Ridberg, Parke, and Hetherington, 1971.

shown that watching models can "modify an impulsive tempo"—that is, models can teach children to stop to think instead of acting upon the first idea that occurs to them. Gavriel Salomon, a psychologist working at the Hebrew University in Israel,[5] has shown that zoom-in camera techniques can help children learn to pick out the important details in a problem-solving situation, discriminating them from those details to be ignored as irrelevant to the problem being solved. Douglas and Nancy Denney, psychologists now at the University of Kansas,[6] have found that "information-processing strategies" can be taught to young children by televised models. Working with a "Twenty Questions" procedure, the Denneys found that six-year-olds could model constraint-seeking questions—that is, they would learn to ask fewer random, shotgun questions ("Is it the car?" "Is it the dogs?") and ask more questions that narrowed down the choice by eliminating more than one alternative from the array ("Is it a tool?" "Does it fly?" "Is it red?"). Thus, children can not only learn simple intellectual skills from television, but they also may be helped to learn how to think and solve problems systematically.

Through television, we also may be able to portray for children socially valued behavior. Television's ability to teach antisocial behavior is regrettably evident, but our *Sesame Street* experience suggests that we also can teach children to take another person's point of view; to cooperate by combining resources, taking turns or dividing labor; to understand certain rules that ensure justice and fair play, such as sharing and reciprocity. Other studies have shown that televised models can teach altruism and kindness, self-control, affection, the initiation of social contacts, and the inhibition of deviant behavior.[7] These observations led us to think about additional experimentation that the Children's Television Workshop might conduct with preschoolers or children in the early elementary grades, and we outlined some of our ideas as follows:

A new experiment by the Children's Television Workshop will be designed to study whether television can be used to increase a

---

[5]Salomon, 1972, 1973, and 1974.
[6]Denney, Denney, and Ziobrowski, 1973.
[7]Some of these studies are noted in Chapter 2.

child's psychological awareness of his own thoughts and feelings   *248*
as well as his understanding of the thoughts and feelings of
others. In this process, can the child learn that his thoughts
and feelings are not unique to him but are shared by others—that
he is not alone either in what he enjoys or in what causes him
anxiety?

Our expectation is that, if television can help the child to better
understand himself, he will:

1. feel better about himself.
2. rely with more confidence on his own resources.
3. find constructive outlets for his emotions.
4. be more likely to face failure without collapsing.

With a better understanding of others, he will:

1. be able to take another person's point of view, to understand
   that person's perspective, thoughts, and feelings.
2. anticipate how others will react to his actions, to reflect upon
   the possible consequences of his actions.
3. communicate effectively with others.
4. enter groups constructively and work comfortably within
   them.
5. understand the value of sharing, helping, and reciprocity.

With a better sense of shared experience, he will: *249*

1. appreciate both the similarities and differences between
   himself and others.
2. discriminate when to accept and when to reject peer-group
   influences.
3. discriminate when aggression is appropriate and inappropriate.
4. find alternative forms of resolving conflict with others,
   without resort to violence.

> Extract from a document prepared by staff of
> Children's Television Workshop, July 1972.

10   Any new experiment in teaching socially valued behavior through television would need to involve the whole
family. Whereas the teaching of intellectual skills by television benefits from the direct involvement of parents and
older siblings, the teaching of socially valued behavior
almost demands it. We were proposing, therefore, to design television for family viewing, and there are no precedents for how to achieve this successfully. Clearly, the

televised situations used must be familiar to young chil- 249
dren yet universal enough to interest all members of the 250
family.

11   Perhaps television's most useful mission for young children is to show them interesting things about the world
that they haven't seen before and probably will not see
without the benefit of television. It can show children
things they have never seen, sounds they have never
heard, people and ideas they have not yet imagined. It can
show them how things work, how other people use them,
what goes on in the world and how to think about it. The
events need not be dramatic or exotic. Children are still
trying to unravel and understand the ordinary, commonplace world as it is.

12   Television has always tried for the dramatic, escalating
into more and more extreme violence, sex, catastrophe and
political encounters. The more extreme, the better. This
search for the exotic is shared by films, books, theater, advertising and journalism, which all assume that only new
instances of extraordinary human behavior can stimulate
our jaded interests. Perhaps adults who are over-familiar
with the ordinary do need this escalation of the unusual
(although even for them, it quickly seems to reach the
point of diminishing returns). And even adults take trips
just to see people and places they have never seen before,
not because they expect dramas to unfold before their eyes
but just to be there, to see what it's like.

13   For children, television can do more than supply drama.
It can show them that there are other people out there in
the world, going about their lives, sharing this exact moment in history with them, all having no meaning in
terms of drama whatever. It is when the ordinary escapes
from the dramatic that television seems to come alive. We
saw numerous examples of this on *Sesame Street.*

14   Some of these we planned. Others just happened. In de-
vising our curriculum, we deliberately included the category of "natural environment." We showed a boy learning
to ride a bike. We showed what happens on a fishing ship, 251
in the back room of a bakery, on a farm, on a bus ride
around the city. We showed where mail goes, what happens to junk and garbage when it is discarded, what goes
on under a manhole cover in the street.

15   Other unplanned, life-sized events happened on *Sesame
Street* to emphasize the power of the ordinary. Kermit the

Frog and a little girl are talking about the words "near *251* and far." As they demonstrate being "near" to each other, on impulse they exchange kisses. The girl catches a bit of the puppet Kermit's fuzz on her lips, becomes intrigued by Kermit's fuzziness, and begins to explore it by gently rubbing his head and body. Kermit understands her curiosity and holds patiently, as does the camera. The girl's sense of wonder has been shared by viewing children who encounter other wonderful imponderables in their own lives.

Another example of the ordinary on *Sesame Street* involves an adult cast member, children and puppets discussing the fact that objects have different-sounding names in different languages. One small girl in the group knows both Spanish and English, and as the group relies more and more upon her to supply the names in these languages, her face shines with joy and a modest smile. Her message to the viewer: What pleasure there is in knowing *two* languages, *two* ways to speak!

A final example from *Sesame Street:* John-John, a small, black three-year-old, is counting to twenty with one of the Muppet Monsters. John-John is brimming with confidence, throwing back his head and bellowing each number in turn. Suddenly, reaching fourteen, he falters and realizes he does not know how to proceed. Confusion covers his face, his sublime confidence crumbles. The monster encourages him, telling him that he knows he can do it. And suddenly he does; "Fourteen!!" exclaims John-John. His face clears, his confidence returns, and he bellows the remaining numbers triumphantly. We have seen how one little boy handles an ordinary event, not knowing or remembering something, with strength and poise.

The children's program, *Zoom,* introduced in 1972 over public-broadcasting stations, uses familiar, commonplace activities in children's lives effectively. Episodes include a *252* boy building a raft from the beginning stages to its completion, a group of children laying out a playing field in a vacant lot and then proceeding to play an improvised version of field hockey, and a country girl going about her chores in her home in Virginia. Such episodes of everyday life attracted great attention among viewers.[8]

Even for adults, we probably underestimate the interest of unexceptional televised events. One of the most popular series on the commercial networks during the 1972–73

[8]Hines, 1973.

season was *The Waltons,* a low-keyed collection of stories   *252*
involving a rural family living during the Depression decades ago. The events were ordinary and unsensational.
No one expected the show's great popularity.

20   If television did begin to balance the ordinary against
the dramatic, it would bring a further change with it. Most
of what television displays in its search for the dramatic is
catastrophic, unhappy, sick or disrupted—at least slightly
out of its mind. Perhaps this reflects the actual daily experience of people in this country, but I doubt that most
people are usually in the state of sustained hysteria that
television presents. Including some ordinary experience in
television may bring it closer to our lives, if we are not too
glutted from our overdose of the dramatic to accept it.

21   Another value in television's showing the world as it is
would be to display to children how people actually go
about trying to solve the typical problems they encounter
and the consequences of these attempts. William Kessen,
a child psychologist at Yale University,[9] summarized the
limited ways in which television currently shows how
problems are solved, with almost the only problems ever
shown on television stemming from differences in power
among people. Solutions are restricted to magic, guile or
what Kessen calls "automatic virtue:" somehow it all
works out, often because of the stupidity of the authority
figure.

22   We know almost nothing about how our youngest chil-   *253*
dren, those younger than three, respond to television, although some of them are surrounded by it from the time
they are born. Yet we can expect that television's greatest
impact of all, for better or worse, is precisely upon these
youngest children. Samuel Gibbon, the original studio
producer of *Sesame Street* who perennially frets over the
mysteries of television's effects upon children, speculates[10]
that television is one of the earliest organizers of the
young child's experience, a resource for learning how to
sort, classify, predict and otherwise process the reality
surrounding him, including that portion of the reality,
mixed with fantasy, that is provided by television itself.
He claims that as soon as the child is able to make some
predictions about the reality that surrounds him, it must
occur to him that televised reality is easier to predict than

[9]Kessen, 1973.
[10] Gibbon, 1973.

most of his other experiences. The recurring formats, the *253* redundancy, the regular schedules, the characters who are never out of character—all present ideal conditions for learning rules about behavior. Joyce Maynard, the Yale undergraduate who at age nineteen reflected upon her childhood,[11] also observed that when she was young, television seemed to her to be one of the most accessible ways to learn about the rules and regularities in life. She says that she found it marvelously comforting to find that at least something in life could be predictable. If these speculations are correct (and it would be a critical experiment to test them), the regularities of television that may be for adults a retreat from the unpredictability in their lives may be for our youngest children a source of help in making life understandable.

23   However, even this simple function of television—to show young children the world as it is—is not without detractors. Marya Mannes, an incisive journalist, writes under the headline "Has Childhood Been Raped?" that television deprives children of their rightful period of innocence; exposure to mass communications propels them *254* into an adult world for which they are not ready. Television's presentation of the ever-more-exotic may justify this view. But surely there is no harm in showing children the persons, places and things of this world and what is basic in human life.

24   Presenting the world as it is does not mean that television cannot help to lead children to a vision of the world as it might be. Michael J. Arlen, who for a time was television critic for *The New Yorker*,[12] describes the importance of television in creating the myths for children to live by:

All of us, whether we are aware of it or not, whether we wish it or not, live in relation to myths. In the past, the myths our people lived by were largely religious and literary—myths of Christian love, of family, of conquest, of bravery in combat . . . People, one imagines, have never—or have very, very rarely—done arduous things (such as living) just for the thing itself; and the same is no less true today.

There is a difference nowadays, though, or so it seems to me. First, the myths we Americans have lived by are not working . . .

[11]Maynard, 1972.
[12]Arlen, 1971.

and we have no new myths to put in their place. The second dif-   *254*
ference is that the source of mythmaking in our society has
changed . . . Increasingly, the sources of our myths are movies,
and journalism, and, most pervasive of all, television.

25   These "myths" need not be modern resurrections of
valor in combat, romantic love or religious zeal. Myths for
children can be simple presentations of simple goodness.
We hear that children are now so worldly wise, so gorged
by a wide range of visual experiences, that they avoid sen-
timentality at all costs. I doubt it. It surely is true that
children do not like to be preached at, but television can
show simple instances of caring, examples of good people   *255*
in this world who are doing good things for others and for
themselves. Perhaps seeing such people at home, on television or wherever is all children need to build their own
myths.

26   Of course, there are other myths that we are providing
now. Through them, we provide training in irony and
cynicism, rearing what Benjamin DeMott has called "a
generation of toddler-ironists." We teach them that the
appearance of simple goodness is usually a cover-up for
personal selfishness, and they must learn how to see
through this. We teach them that caring about another
person's life exposes you to disappointment and rejection,
and they must learn to remain detached to escape this. We
teach them that life is full of tension and deprivation, and
they must learn to accept this. Television has helped to
create these myths for children. Surely it can create others
that help them toward a more humane vision of life.

27   This history of *Sesame Street* ends where it must:
money. Television is not going to go away. There simply is
too much money in it.[13] The problem is that a dispropor-
tionately small share of it is invested in children.

28   Commercial networks will continue to spend only the
minimum investment necessary to keep the Federal
Communications Commission at bay, and since the FCC
does not press them too hard, that minimum of dollars and
talent will be small indeed. Commercial broadcasters
know what works in the ratings, which means they know
how to make money, and they are not going to give that
up. The recent record of public-broadcasting support is

[13]Detailed descriptions appear in Brown, 1971; Pearce, 1972.

equally disheartening. Foundations regard their proper 255 role as helping to start new, experimental projects, but not to provide funds to sustain them over time. Government funding of public broadcasting is whimsical, totally at the 256 mercy of political forces.

29   There are no easy solutions, of course, but Joan Cooney suggests the direction for change when she says that the provision of good programs for children must be removed from the free enterprise system and made a public service. For the commercial networks, this would mean that they "half-nationalize themselves,"[14] with television for adults remaining free enterprise but television for children becoming public interest. But this means that commercial broadcasters will have to decide by themselves to do this. Not likely.

30   For public broadcasting, children's programs would have to be removed from the political pressures that determine funding. Some precedents do exist. We have special school taxes in this country, and the British Broadcasting Corporation levies a special tax on television sets to run its system; both are at least somewhat insulated from politics.

31   Having ended this record of one episode in children's programs on the topic of money, I am no longer certain that I have been writing about television at all. Perhaps I have really been writing about our society as a whole: its sense of futility, its elation when even small signs of progress appear, its desperate hope that all is not lost even when all seems truly lost, its persisting faith that individual genius still can make everything all right. I do not say this to make this book seem more important than it is. But the state of children's television seems so accurately to reflect our exasperation at what we are doing to ourselves, along with our unwillingness to abandon the dream that somehow our individual genius will magically rescue us from our corporate stupidity.

32   Television can inform children and create visions of what their lives can be. It also can inter them endlessly in Plato's Cave, watching removed images of life passing them by. Interment is what television has given them so far, with only a rare glimpse of what they need to see and to hear. Maybe we can change that. Edward R. Mur-

[14] Geoghegan, 1972.

row, one of few who can claim a lasting contribution to   *257*
television broadcasting in this country, encouraged us to
try:

This instrument can teach, it can illuminate: Yes, and it
can even inspire. But it can do so only to the extent that
humans are determined to use it to those ends. Otherwise, it is merely lights and wires in a box.

6

Eric Barnouw, Professor Emeritus of Dramatic Arts of Columbia University, has written numerous books on broadcasting and film. He has been a director, writer, and editor for both CBS and NBC and is currently with the Smithsonian Institute. Gayle Gibbons and Larry Kirkman are on the staff of Televisions *Magazine.*

This interview was originally published in the Autumn 1976 issue of Televisions *Magazine, pages 8–9.*

Blue Sky Blues: Monopolies, Sponsorship and New Technologies

AN INTERVIEW WITH ERIC BARNOUW BY
GAYLE GIBBONS AND LARRY KIRKMAN

1 . . . Historically the sponsor and the advertising agency 8 own the program. They produce/conceive, very often for a specific merchandising purpose.

2 Now, however, the relation of the sponsor to the program is much more indirect. He's buying just minutes and the network execs say he has no influence whatsoever over programming. That I doubt because he isn't buying minutes the way he buys them in England or Italy. He's always buying a specific minute in a program. The value of the minute or half minute he buys is subject to continuous negotiation so that there is a constant auction going on.

3 It is more or less like the stock market. The value of a spot on a certain program goes up or down from week to week. If the series is a success, the price immediately goes up. If it is slipping, the price goes down. So on any one program—let's say there are 5 spots on a program—they may all have been bought at different prices.

4 More and more Nielsen has reported not only households listening to a program but has given the sponsor a demographic breakdown. More and more the sponsor is in a position where he doesn't need to watch programs. He just gets from Nielsen the demographic breakdown of this or this program. He can then match those to the

From *Televisions* Magazine, Autumn 1976, 8. Reprinted with permission.

same demographic breakdown of the people who buy his *8* product.

5   Then he can say to the producer: I don't want to pay for men and children. I am just interested in women between the ages of 18–24, and that's all I'm going to pay for. What assurance can you give me?

6   Actually, the larger advertisers are getting an assurance that they will not have paid more than so much per 1000 women in the category they're interested in. If, after the period of 3 months according to the Nielsen statistics, they have paid more than that they get some bonus spots to make up the difference. That means the sponsor is constantly turning thumbs down on some programs, and up on others. You find some programs with pretty good ratings going down the drain because they're not reaching the right audience.

7   That happened with *Gunsmoke*. It was found that the audience that had listened to it for years and years was getting older and older. It wasn't reaching a young audience, and it wasn't reaching many women, and it was just reaching an old audience which was good for laxatives or some tonics. But they could be reached by news programs which stations felt they had to carry. There are lots of laxatives on news programs.

8   The networks actually provide agencies with the demographic statistics on who buys what product in exactly the same categories as Nielsen breaks down the program audiences. They suggest to the sponsors to match this up with the Nielsen demographics. Then they can say: We have just the programs to serve your needs.

9   Well, when it becomes as scientific as that, a sponsor no longer dares to go by hunch. He no longer dares to say, "That's a great program we watched last night, let's get behind that." Why would anyone stick his neck out that way? Instead he looks at Nielsen reports/demographics. He looks at a retail marketing index and demographic statistics on who buys what product. They match these up, and as long as you're going on this scientific basis no one can blame you if something goes wrong. You have ample scientific reasons for doing what you're doing. This becomes a kind of expertise which no longer has to do with whether you like a program.

10   You get into a situation where sponsor decisions do make programs rise in value to the network or make them less valuable to the network. That's where the sponsor

can't but help having a hand in the programming de-   *8*
cisions: to what extent is a program going to serve the
needs of the sponsors?

7

Arthur Nielsen, Jr., is the president of the A. C. Nielsen Company, the Chicago-based consumer research firm that has a television rating service. Thomas Birland is a free-lance writer.

This article originally appeared in volume 12 of TV Guide *on November 7, 1964, on pages 6–9.*

Nielsen Defends His Ratings

ARTHUR NIELSEN WITH THOMAS BIRLAND

1. Did you ever watch someone start on a bowl of soup? He stirs the liquid, lifts the spoon to his lips, and sips. He has just tasted a sample and rated it; whether he adds salt or not depends on that random spoonful.

2. You'll notice that he never denounces the spoon when there is too little salt.

3. Not so in TV ratings—despite the fact that rating techniques employ some of the most advanced statistical methods known, and some of the most sophisticated electronics.

4. Ratings are today's TV scapegoat: Shows with low ratings blame the raters; those who think television quality can and should be elevated blame the raters; and some owners of magazines and newspapers which lose advertising revenue to television attack the raters.

5. As the Nation's most listened-to rating, the Nielsen Television Index (NTI) often is the target of these attacks. After years of patience, I'd like to rise to its defense.

6. First, be sure you clearly separate *ratings* from *programming.* While one may affect the other, they are not the same. Ratings are television's batting averages—they indicate how many people programs are hitting. They are not critical measures of any program's intrinsic merit.

7. They observe, with objectivity and impartiality, the relative appeal of a given program by measuring how many households are tuned to it. Blaming the ratings when you don't like a popular program is like blaming the soup spoon.

8　　Those who would castigate commercial television, inci- 6
dentally, should remember that it is wholly supported by
advertising revenues. Advertising can be effective only if
it reaches people. That is why sponsors want programs
that attract the largest audiences containing the kinds of
people who might buy their products. Whether we like it
or not, weighty cultural, educational or artistic shows sel-
dom attract large audiences.

9　　A show's rating is an estimate of how many families
watch it. Nielsen ratings estimate how many households
have their TV sets tuned to which network shows.

10　　We keep tab by connecting automatic recorders (Audimeters) to a cross section of the Nation's TV sets. These
Audimeters are placed out of sight—in closets, basements,
etc.—and by electronic "photographs" on film, record
minute-by-minute whether the sets are on or off, and to
what channel they are tuned. This record is kept 24 hours
a day, week in and week out, and the film records are
mailed back to our production center twice a month, when
the sample home receives a fresh film magazine. 7

11　　In Chicago, the film records are run through large
data-processing departments, where information is in-
spected for errors that could mean broken equipment or
power failures. Typically, information from approximately
90 percent of the sample homes is included in each report.
(The rest may be eliminated because of home power failures, late mail-ins, etc.) Then the information is transferred to punched cards and matched against TV program
schedules. Finally, the information is fed into computers.

12　　If there were Audimeters in every American home
wired to a giant central computer, we could know instantly how many American households were tuned to
what at any moment. Unfortunately, there is no computer
large enough to do this job—and even if there were, it
would cost too much to get the ratings by this method.
More practical and far less expensive is the method we use
which gathers information from a scientifically selected
sample of homes.

13　　How a sample of homes (we use about 1100) can
properly reflect the actions and tastes of 52,600,000 homes
is completely mysterious to many people. I know because
this was a topic we went into thoroughly with a Congressional committee last year. Yet sampling is a basic part of
our lives.

14　　There's the man sipping soup; the doctor diagnosing
your illness after laboratory examination of a few drops of

blood; your gas-station attendant judging crankcase dirt 7
by the bit of oil on the dipstick.

. . .

15   Perhaps the best-known evidence that sampling is practical is found in political polling, where a sample of voters
is questioned. Polls, however, face a much more difficult
task because they are measuring *opinions* and *future action,* rather than precise matters such as whether a TV set
is on or off, or how many packages of a given brand have
been sold in a particular store. Despite these difficulties,
predictions of nationally known political poll-takers, in
recent years, always have been within a few percent of the
actual Presidential vote.

16   Unfortunately, there are no such figures as factory
shipments or final election results with which to check the
accuracy of television ratings. But our television rating
sample is selected by the same general principles as are
the retail store samples we use. We very accurately measure the sales of thousands of such products as soap, beverages, foods and drugs so it is reasonable to assume that
the TV ratings are similarly accurate.

17   We're all used to seeing such vital statistics as the U.S.
cost-of-living index or total unemployed. These statistics
were all obtained from samples. Like TV ratings they are 8
estimates—and are not *precisely* accurate. It is impossible
to know exactly what the *true* cost of living is or the *exact*
number of people who are unemployed. Yet these Government estimates based upon samples are very useful
and are accurate enough for the intended use.

18   How accurate are the Nielsen television ratings?

19   Let's take a program with a rating of 30. . . . When our
report says that the show has a rating of 30 we mean that
our best estimate is that 30 percent of all homes with TV
sets are tuned to the show. Now that's an estimate based
on our sample, of course. The truth could be higher or
lower. Statistical mathematics tell us that 19 times out of
20 such a rating obtained from a perfect probability sample will be off by less than 3 points—here between 27 and
33 percent.

20   The ratings could, of course, be made even more accurate by using a larger sample. But to cut the error in
half—say, from 3 points on a 30 rating to 1½ points—
would mean not just doubling the sample size, but increasing it *fourfold*. This in turn would make the ratings cost

nearly four times as much. While we would have no objec-   *8*
tion to increasing our prices 300 percent, we strongly
doubt that our customers would approve!

21   "Sampling errors" are inherent in ratings, cost-of-living
figures and other statistical estimates. There are also
other types of errors. But they are small and in all probability wouldn't change the rating user's decision about a
particular program.

22   For example, some people say that just because a TV set
is on does not mean anyone is watching it. This is true. All
of us may leave our sets on now and again when we aren't
viewing. But we have made thousands of phone calls to
homes to find out how often this happens. On the average
only about one set in a hundred is on with no one viewing
it. This can't affect significantly the accuracy of our rating.

23   Another criticism our ratings sometimes get from
nonstatisticians is that each Audimeter home represents
approximately 50,000 homes. . . .

24   Unlike the line you might pick out on your TV screen,
homes that have Audimeters are not selected haphaz-
ardly. They are part of the sample of the population systematically selected according to methods devised by top
statisticians, both in and out of the Nielsen company,
using data from the U.S. Housing Census.   *9*

25   Every housing unit in the country is assigned to a small
census area, technically known as an enumeration district. A computer picks the houses to be used in our sample
from these districts in such a way that every house in the
country has an equal chance of being selected. The computer selects say, every 10th house on a street but does not
supply the addresses. Hence, a special force of Nielsen
men must go out and get the street addresses of every
house chosen. This is how the Nielsen "Master Sample" is
developed—at a cost of more than $250,000.

26   But, the job still is not complete. Our regular field men
then travel to these computer-selected homes and ask to
install our Audimeter. The families are paid for this cooperation. Most households accept; alternates are selected
for those who don't.

27   Thus the sample, in many ways, reflects the actions of
the millions of viewers. One check, for instance, showed
that 26 percent of the sample families own Chevrolets and
2 percent own Cadillacs. National license registrations
show that 25 percent of American families own Chevrolets, and 2 percent own Cadillacs.

28   In other words, our TV ratings are reasonable estimates *9*
of the public's viewing habits. They are not represented to
be the *exact* number of homes tuning in a given program.
They are, however, very useful in indicating to broadcasters how certain shows are doing—in relation to other
shows and over certain periods of time to show trends in
viewing. Our customers tell us that the accuracy is about
right for their purposes.

. . .

29   TV ratings are a tool designed for a specific job. With
their limitations kept firmly in mind, their users get from
them valuable and highly useful information otherwise
unavailable. Just as you do when you sample a bowl of
soup. So, if a sponsor decides that his offering needs more
salt, don't blame the spoon!

30   And most important to the viewing audience, ratings
are the democratic way of counting the vote in terms of
number of homes watching. It's the broadcaster's way of
"giving the lady what she wants."

8

Les Brown writes about television for the New York Times.
*This book was published by Harcourt Brace Jovanovich in New York in
1971.*

From Televi$ion: The Business Behind the Box
LES BROWN

1 It was not through oversight that the networks, and local 60
stations, did not for years produce programs of specific
interest to the black population. The ghetto Negro was not
a target audience for most advertisers because, generally
speaking, he was a low-income citizen with scant buying
power. It was not that advertisers did not want to reach
Negroes but that they did not want to reach them *especially,* and it was assumed that the poor black, as a heavy
viewer of television, would be part of the audience composition of programs aimed at other segments of the
audience.

2 So little valued has been the black man as a consumer of
nationally advertised products that he was not properly
represented in the Nielsen sample of the American television audience. Although this was generally known in the
television and advertising industries there was no outcry,
no move to set it right, no show of conscience that the
ghetto black did not have a representative "vote" as a
member of the viewing masses. The Nielsen Company, as
well as the other, lesser, rating services, explained that it
was difficult to place their hardware in ghetto homes, difficult to get representative families to keep viewing
diaries adequately because of the high rate of illiteracy,
and even a problem in the telephone methods of audience
research because of the shortage of telephone homes in
the ghetto.

3 This sound explanation, given conventional advertising
priorities, seemed fair enough to everyone until it became

---

desirable to count the audience for *Sesame Street,* the non- 60
commercial children's show which had been designed for
the culturally underprivileged of the ghettos. The real
success of *Sesame* was not to be told in the total number of
persons reached but specifically in the total number of
slum children reached.

4 At approximately the same time, moreover, station
WTOP-TV in Washington, D.C., complained that its
black-oriented programing in a city whose population was 61
predominantly black was receiving no advertising support
because the rating numbers were slight for them, and they
were slight, the station charged, because black households
were not adequately represented in the rating samples.
Thus, it became a matter of one station's economic interest
and one conspicuous program's social value that the ghettos be adequately surveyed, and so far as is known correc-
tive action then began to be taken. . . .

5 Flip Wilson enjoyed far better luck. Establishing itself 292
quickly and decisively as the [1970] season's new rating
hit, even against the competition of a long-popular CBS
series, *Family Affair,* the new series was nevertheless no
more original or inventive than the others in its
framework.

6 Why did Wilson catch on, and not [Don] Knotts and
[Tim] Conway? First, because he had never been a second
banana and could conduct a show of his own without seeming out of character. Second, because his source of humor 293
was not white society but black, and in that sense it *was*
original for television, other Negroes in the medium having had to pretend the races had a common culture. Third,
he was a one-man repertory company, having developed
two characters outside his own stand-up comedy identity,
the Reverend Leroy of the Church of What's Happening
Now and the Harlem chatterbox Geraldine Jones, both
satirical types and so distinctly Negro they had no credible
co-ordinates in white society. Fourth, his comedy was not
an ethnic argument; rather than sentimentalizing Negro-
American culture it seemed to mock it. And fifth, it did
mock it.

7 The last may well have been the key. Wilson had performed his act before black audiences in segregated clubs
and theaters for many years before his first television exposure and, within the group, the satire was appreciated
for the healthy reasons. Irish can satirize the Irish, Jews
the Jews, and Italians the Italians. Within the respective

ethnic circles the stereotypical truths, although embarrassingly amusing, have a way of strengthening an individual's identification with the group and heightening his pride in belonging to it. But on television, with its vast and heterogeneous audience, the honest kidding of ethnic types becomes something else, tending to validate the stereotype as a true representative of a whole people and in that way contributing to prejudice.

8   *Amos 'n' Andy* was very popular even in television when the players were black (whites created the series for radio and did the voices), but it was driven off the air finally because its portrayal of Negro life fed, rather than dispelled, racial bigotry. Whites can be represented in comedies as bumbling, shiftless, or ignorant, and no one would conclude that all Caucasians are of that kind; but when the only series on black life in all broadcasting portrays the characters in precisely the way bigots imagine black people to be, it is insidious.

9   Flip Wilson's character Geraldine was funny because she yielded to her impulses and, in her shrill way, always *294* explained her waywardness with the running line, "The debbil made me do it." It was dependably the big laugh line. And the Reverend Leroy, taking up collections in the church, had his funniest moments whenever he had to explain away his possession of valuable goods, such as Cadillacs.

10   Flip Wilson was liked by the mass TV audience for positive reasons, because he was a lively and prepossessing personality, and loved for negative ones, because he substantiated a racist view of blacks. The show was defined a hit because the audience for it was great in size, and many who were drawn to it for negative reasons undoubtedly believed that their hour a week with a Negro, filtered through a TV screen, manifested their tolerance, their essential goodness as Americans.

11   But the Flip Wilson 40 per cent share of audience was accompanied by this curious development. Two television series headlined by blacks which had been popular the previous season suddenly and unaccountably lost their following. In the very year that Flip Wilson vaulted into the television top ten, Bill Cosby—who had been TV's favorite black the previous season—dropped to the bottom quartile of the ratings and was averaging only a 25 per cent share of audience. What made it harder to explain his decline in popularity was that his competition had not changed from

the year before; it was still Ed Sullivan and *The FBI*. Ex- *294* periencing a similar drop in the ratings was *Julia,* the first television situation comedy with Negro stars, Diahann Carroll and Marc Copage, which had done well for two seasons; and worth noting here was that it was losing to the most Southern cracker show on the networks, *Hee Haw.* The other Negro show in prime time, *Barefoot in the Park,* a new ABC entry, was a rating flop—and deservedly—from its first installment.

12   Flip Wilson had become the new pet Negro to a television populace that apparently could embrace only one at a time.

9

Martin Maloney, a professor of Radio and Television at Northwestern University, has also written radio and television scripts.

This article appeared in volume 15 of TV Guide *on December 2, 1967, on pages 7–10.*

The Big War in the Little Box
MARTIN MALONEY

1 Like millions of other Americans, I am disturbed by the 7 war in Vietnam. I am not a pacifist, although I think that war in this day and age may prove to be the ultimate disaster. I did spend some time in uniform 20-odd years ago, and in 1950 I thought that Harry Truman was probably right when he decided that North Korea had to be stopped.

2 But Vietnam is something else again. It's pretty hard to visualize the embattled citizen taking his old rifle down from the mantelpiece and going off to keep Ho Chi Minh's Asian legions from eating Texas chile in the White House. It's even pretty hard to see anyone resembling the old-fashioned conscientious objector in those mobs of demonstrators who occasionally heckle Hubert Humphrey and hiss Dean Rusk. I suspect that the demonstrators, along with many others, are people like me: namely, confused, upset—or, in the current lingo, bugged. I have begun to wonder whether I, at least, am not reacting to a combination quite new in human experience: something which I think of as TVietnam, the big war in the little box, the war brought to me by courtesy of pain-relievers, deodorants and low-cal beverages.

3 Let me make myself clear. In the first place, I think that TV coverage of the Vietnam war, in the United States, has been professional and conscientious. Given the war, the medium and a special way of handling news, the network news teams seem to me to have done an honest job.

4 In the second place, I don't mean to suggest that TV has *created* Vietnam out of whole cloth. The medium is not entirely the message in this case. Still, there may be a kind

of fatality in the fact that the first TV war is also the war 7
best—or worst—adapted to TV coverage.

5   There can be no question that Vietnam is *the* TV war.
The Arab-Israel conflict, of recent memory, was not really
covered at all while it lasted—partly because the Arabs
didn't know what was going on, partly because the Israelis 8
were busy and anyway preferred to leave the event to history. When Korea was fought, the coaxial cable was
hardly settled all snug in its bed. The European war of
1939–1945 was the first and last of the radio wars, and the
Pacific-Asian conflict of that period was so remote that it
was covered by the press only with difficulty and had to
wait on the postwar histories and memoirs for full reporting. But the Vietnam war came along in an age of television, of supersonic jets and satellite transmissions, and so
is the first—and so far, the only—true TV war. It may persist into a period when, as someone has noted, American
parents may sit comfortably before the box in the living
room and watch their sons being killed and wounded,
10,000 miles away, precisely while the event is taking
place.

6   If that time comes, I venture to suggest that the parents
so blessed by modern technology may react in a peculiar
way, simply because the experience is utterly new. They
may take these instantaneous images of terror, shock and
death as we take so many other images of the TV
world—with a sort of nagging, tortured, inward concern
which may force them to become participants in the agony
of the times. Previous wars were *presented* to us in the
press, on film, in books, even on radio—always well-
rationalized, and always after the fact. But a war processed through TV approaches simultaneity; it comes to us
now, as a kind of daily puzzle which we must ourselves
piece out and understand. This is a frustrating experience.
How does it work?

7   TVietnam is like all TV news: fragmented and repetitious. Any TV news broadcast segments the day into a
certain number of items, each presenting a more-or-less
dramatic and exciting high point in the diurnal history.
Where the event is particularly dramatic, and/or film
footage is available, the news broadcaster's narrative account will be followed by a film sequence which presents
the event in the most concrete dramatic terms. Naturally,
where a given crisis continues, or where a series of similar
events occurs, the TV version tends to be highly repetitive.

As a fairly consistent viewer of TV news programs, I some- 8
times get the nightmarish feeling that I have been trapped
in a 6 o'clock treadmill: There is nothing new about the
news.

8 The Vietnamese war has been processed through the TV
news machinery, and it has gone on for a long time. As a
result, it continues, over and over and over again, in a
series of vignettes, each one barely meaningful in itself,
each one echoing a hundred similar news items past, and
perhaps a thousand to come. And then there are the pictures, which effectively reduce the war to the dimensions
of a horrid Punch-and-Judy show.

9 Visually, TVietnam is a small, dim war, fought by
puppet-like figures. GI doll images appear in gray-on-
gray, struggling through swamps, riding atop toy tanks,
firing automatic weapons which go pop-pop-pop. Then 9
there are the omnipresent helicopters, strictly out of Dis-
neyland. Occasionally, we see the figure of the enemy, a
willowy, starved-looking mite; occasionally, too, the
figures of the dead or wounded, also small and usually
sacked up in stretchers or blankets. These scenes occur
again and again; the fight goes on forever, seemingly in
the same terms; the living, the dead and the wounded
are always caught in the same terrifying, miniaturized
drama, and they are always very small.

10 Unless my memory of a similar war, now 20 years past,
has betrayed me utterly, TVietnam differs from the
realities of combat as much as it does from the earlier
press, film, radio presentations of war. To the best of my
recollection, a major battle, if you are in it but not immediately involved, gives a feeling of enormous size—the
thud and shock of explosions, the roar of engines, stabs of
flame, smoke—which reduces you, the observer, to a minute scale. You are a midget in a huge universe of stink
and shock and blast. When you become involved—being
bombed, shelled, strafed, shot at, trying to find cover, trying to fight back, or hoping that *somebody* will fight
back—this universe contracts into an absolute hell of
noise and haze.

11 The response you make to it is frequently one of wild
exhilaration and excitement, and sometimes of absolutely
paralyzing fear; the experience of battle is a shocking,
shaking experience which cannot ever be forgotten. TV
reduces this experience to doll-scale and detaches the
viewer from it; the information is all there, but in a faint,

weak form, like the signal from a remote satellite. The 9
watcher needs a special scanner to pick up the information
at all, and a special amplifier to bring the signal up to understandable strength.

12   There are other profoundly disturbing aspects of TVietnam. For one thing, the war is almost inaccessible to the
human intellect. It appears to be the first multivalued war
in American history. In previous conflicts, one could always describe what was happening as a war between Us
and Them. But in Vietnam, We were not engaged in war-
fare at all for a long time (We simply had sent military advisors to the Good Guys), and even today it is hard to tell
whether We are at war or not, or with Whom.

. . .

13   There is also no geographical logic to TVietnam. In 10
World War II the British, Americans, Canadians and
others made beachheads at Normandy in 1944 and pressed
eastward, toward Berlin. At the same time, the Russians
came thundering westward, toward Berlin. Between the
two assaults Germany and her allies were crushed, Hitler
shot himself, and the war ended. It was a nice, linear,
well-oriented war, which made a lot of sense. TVietnam is
something else again. In the country proper, there are of
course a North and a South, and what is jokingly called a
Demilitarized Zone between; but if the war has actually
progressed from North to South, or South to North, or in
any other discoverable direction, you would never know it
from TV. The news broadcasters seem almost to have
given up on maps, and may be about to give up on place
names. (A mention of "Pleiku," for instance, even reinforced with a map, doesn't tell you how or where the war is
going.)

14   The final solution to the tangle seems to be to reduce the
whole war to simple numbers, and to report it rather like a
series of baseball games in an endless hot summer. Old
Walter, or Chet, or Harry, or somebody, comes on and
says: "This was an average fighting week in Vietnam. Opposition casualties: 2473. South Vietnamese: 417. Americans: 201." But the numbers don't mean anything, really;
they're like the scores in a game so remote and incom-
prehensible that you hardly know whether the stake is
matchsticks, or home runs, or human lives.

15   Maybe this explains some of the hypnotic fascination
which the war seems to exert on the American imagination, as well as the revulsion and horror. The war inside

the box is a monstrosity which every viewer must invent *10* for himself. M. R. James once wrote a short story about a wealthy collector who bought an antique doll's house, elaborately decorated and furnished, which turned out to be haunted in a strange way. Each night the new owner would awaken from sleep and find himself forced to gaze on his new possession, in which the dolls had come to life and were acting out a gruesome drama of greed, murder and spectral revenge. The happy fact about James's doll house was that, once the drama had run its course, the restless spirits which haunted it were appeased, and the device lost its power to fascinate and terrify.

16 But the war inside the box is never acted out in full; *this* drama continues, night after night, world without end. Who can seriously believe, watching TVietnam, that the war will actually end? The numbers keep coming in, but nobody knows what numbers, if any, will signal the end of the game.

17 Somehow, it does not surprise me that people exposed to the big war in the little box protest, complain, demonstrate, cry out. They are suffering the ultimate human discomfort; they need desperately to make sense out of one of the crucial events of the time, an event which eats at them—at their secure existence, at their children, at their sense of what is decent and proper, at the whole fabric of their lives. And the sense is not given them. It simply is not there.

18 Meanwhile, the news broadcasters, caught between necessity and habit, will continue to produce their box scores. Meanwhile, the discomfort will become more and more painful. The end is not in sight.

10

Newton N. Minow, who was federal communications commission chairman under John F. Kennedy, has written many books on broadcasting. John Bartlow Martin, former ambassador to the Dominican Republic, was an investigative reporter during the 1940's and 1950's. Lee Mitchell is an attorney specializing in communications law.

This book was published in New York in 1973 by Twentieth Century Fund, Basic Books.

From Presidential Television
NEWTON N. MINOW, JOHN BARTLOW MARTIN,
AND LEE M. MITCHELL

1   ON THE EVENING of July 15, 1971, a spokesman for the   3
Western White House at San Clemente, California told the three major television networks that President Richard M. Nixon had an announcement he wanted to make on nationwide television. The networks quickly cleared time for the announcement, which would interrupt their regular shows at 10:30: "The Dean Martin Show," a rerun of "NYPD," and a 1968 movie entitled *Counterfeit Killer*. But even after agreeing to the presidential preemption, the networks did not know the subject of the president's address. Network newsmen with the president in California received neither advance copies of his statement nor prebroadcast briefings; they were as much in the dark as anyone else at air time. Promptly at 10:30 P.M., from NBC studios in Burbank, California, the president's image appeared in 25 million homes across the country. "I have requested this television time tonight," he said, "to   4
announce a major development in our efforts to build a lasting peace in the world." He then told the American people he had accepted an invitation from Premier Chou En-lai to visit mainland China. At the same time, he revealed that his chief foreign policy adviser, Henry Kissinger, had secretly spent three days in China already.

Adapted from Chapter 1 of *Presidential Television,* by Newton N. Minow, John Bartlow Martin, and Lee M. Mitchell, © 1973 by the Twentieth Century Fund, Inc., Basic Books, Inc., Publishers, New York.

2

President Nixon's dramatic announcement of a major   4
reversal of U.S. foreign policy took the news media, the
American public, and the rest of the world completely by
surprise. And its impact was greatly increased because he
made it directly and personally to the American people.
One professional observer, calling this use of television
a "bombshell approach to major new announcements,"
wrote that such an approach almost guaranteed that the
first wave of news coverage would be extremely heavy and
would be limited to straight reporting, thus giving the
new policy powerful momentum—and momentum without
critical appraisal: "Surprise makes for confusion and,
at least initially, confusion does not make for valuable
analysis."[1]

3

Time and again, and in recent years with increasing
frequency, presidents have appeared on television to explain their policies, to mobilize support, to go over the
heads of the Congress and the political parties, and to
speak directly to the people for their cause—and their
reelection.

4

Television has made it possible for a president to appear
and speak directly before the entire American people. Not
speeches on the stump, not speeches from the rear plat-
forms of trains, not courthouse square handshaking, not
newspapers, not magazines, not books, and not even radio
can confront so many people with the president's face and
with his words at the moment he utters them. Television,
and only television, allows the president to exhibit his
plans, opinions, and personality to the eyes and ears of
unprecedented numbers of Americans—in their homes,
but in his own way and under his control. As a result, television has become an increasingly important part of the
complex power structure of presidential politics.

5

Television (complemented by radio) has come to play a   5
significant role in presidential politics because it is the
most effective communicator of ideas and images, with the
greatest potential for influencing public opinion, that
political man has yet developed. . . .

6

A congressional subcommittee has found that "broadcasting, and television in particular, has indeed become
indispensable to the political processes of our nation. This
has come about because the medium—for whatever
reason—has become the public's prime source of information."[2] One survey made in 1971 indicated that television   6
is the primary source of news for most people; according to

other surveys, people consider television the most objective and believable of all the mass media.[3]

7   Television's combination of ideas, moving pictures, and
easy accessibility is unmatched by any other medium.
Television and television alone has made the people
eyewitnesses to history: the muffled drums and riderless
horse at President Kennedy's funeral, Ruby shooting Oswald, the burning huts and crying children of Vietnam,
the first man on the moon, triumph and tragedy at
Munich's Olympics, the American president toasting the
Communist chieftain in the Great Hall of the People in
Peking. When Martin Luther King, Jr. was assassinated,
television so shortened reaction time that within hours of
the first televised civil disturbances, riots broke out in
more than a hundred cities.[4]
. . .

8   But television's most significant political characteris-
tic probably is its ability to present an image of a
politician—providing an indication of his character and
personality. An aspiring political leader today is likely to
rise faster and further if he "comes across" well on television. Citizens in the television age expect their leaders to
be reasonably pleasing to the eye and to be capable of a
confidence-inspiring television presentation. "As a result
of continual exposure to television," writes an experienced
political television adviser, "we have learned to project
characteristics of our television heroes to our political
heroes. We want them to be articulate and also look com-
petent. . . ."[5] Consequently, it is not unusual for politicians
at all levels to hire television advisers, speech therapists,
makeup artists, or other professionals to work on the
leader's television image. The electoral success of such   7
political figures as John and Robert Kennedy, Senators
Percy and Tunney, Governor Reagan and Mayor Lindsay
is often credited, at least in part, to their creation of a
favorable television image.

9   If a good television image helps a politician, a poor one
can hurt. Lyndon Johnson, for example, rarely appeared to
good advantage on television despite a great deal of personal effort and professional advice. When he appeared before the large television audiences, his image, in the words
of one critic, "stuck to the lens." But such is the power and
prestige of the presidency that each of his television appearances exposed that image to millions. When Johnson
finally announced on all three major television networks

simultaneously that he would not run for reelection, he 7
faced an audience of 75 million people. In comparison,
when George Washington made the same announcement
172 years earlier, his words, without any image, took four
days to reach New York in print and ten days to reach out-
lying regions.

10 Researchers still argue over whether television changes
or merely reinforces opinions, but they generally agree
that it can promote familiarity with an image or a personality, whether real or manufactured, with considerable
success. . . .

11 Recognizing the pervasiveness of television, its role as
the electorate's main source of political information, and
its ability to convey images, candidates for election to
public office have embraced the public airwaves with en-
thusiasm. By a television appearance, a politician may 8
place his views before a potentially enormous audience; by
appearing simultaneously on most major television channels, so that alternative viewing choices are sharply limited, he can assure that much of the potential will be
realized. . . .

12 Television's role in elections has become so important
that the *New York Times* assigned a reporter to cover the
1972 elections from in front of a television set. The paper
was acknowledging that the way the candidates appear on
television can be a critical factor in the election and that
much of the candidates' other activities—the traveling,
the dinner speeches, the factory and shopping-center
visits—are done as much to gain television news exposure
as for any other purpose.[6] Although social scientists and
political experts have yet to determine the precise effect of
television political advertising on the outcome of an election campaign, most candidates are not willing to take
chances.[7] As any television viewer can attest, candidates
do their best to saturate the airwaves with their messages.

13 But television advertising is expensive, and the candidates' rush to television has skyrocketed the cost of
running for office. In the 1970 nonpresidential elections,
candidates spent $58 million on political broadcasting,
almost doubling the broadcast expenses of the previous
off-year elections.[8] The three senatorial candidates in New 9
York spent an incredible total of $5 million, more than $2
million of it on television and radio broadcasting.[9] Even
running for such a modest office as congressman from the
First District in Utah requires at least $70,000.[10] These

enormous costs present a real danger to the political sys- 9
tem.... Certainly the high cost of campaign advertising
can allow a heavily financed candidate to dominate the
most important means of communication, adding credence to the cynics' view that politics is but a rich man's
game....

14   Growing public uneasiness about the money pressures
on candidates has led to two recent legislative reforms.
First, Congress adopted a law that will allow each citizen,
by marking his annual tax return, to contribute one dollar
to the party of his choice or to a general campaign fund
to assist in financing the campaigns of major party candidates for the presidency.[11] Second, Congress enacted a
requirement that broadcasters charge candidates only
their very lowest rates for political broadcasting time.
Congress also established a limit on the amount that
could be spent by candidates for the purchase of broadcast
time.[12] These two reforms are expected to reduce the
danger of abuse.

15   But the power of political television is not limited to individual candidates or to election campaign periods....
The success of candidates' use of television has given rise 10
to presidential television—the use of television (and radio)
by an already elected president to advance his legislative
programs and his political objectives. The public and Congress have turned their attention to financial and fairness
problems resulting from the use of television by candidates but have paid relatively little attention to the ram-
pant growth of presidential television. Yet presidential
television may damage democratic institutions even more
than campaign television.

16   The Constitution established a presidency with
limitations upon its powers—the need to stand for reelection every four years, checks that can be exercised by the
Congress and the Supreme Court. The evolution of political parties and a strong two-party system provided a rally-
ing point for opponents of an incumbent administration,
enhancing the importance of frequent reelection. An intricate set of constitutional balances limiting the powers of
each of the three government branches added force to the
separation of government functions. These political and
constitutional relationships served the country well for
many years. Television's impact, however, threatens to
tilt the delicately balanced system in the direction of the
president.

17   By transmitting information and images effectively, *10*
television influences public opinion; public opinion is the
key to the maintenance of political power. Plato reasoned
that because a leader must seek public support if he is to
govern effectively, the population of a city should be the
number of people who can hear the leader's voice.
Abraham Lincoln wrote that in politics, "public sentiment
is everything. With public sentiment, nothing can fail.
Without it nothing can succeed."[13] Professor Richard
Neustadt, whose model of a powerful presidency was
sought by President Kennedy, observed that "presidential
power is the power to persuade."[14] Because he can act
while his adversaries can only talk, because he can make
news and draw attention to himself, and because he is the
only leader elected by all the people, an incumbent president always has had an edge over his opposition in per-   *11*
suading public opinion. Presidential television, however,
has enormously increased that edge.

18   Presidential television means the ability to appear
simultaneously on all national radio and television networks at prime, large-audience evening hours, virtually
whenever and however the president wishes. It means
holding a news conference before a potential audience of
60 million people, or delivering light banter on the country's most popular entertainment programs. Presidential
television is the president's own explanation of his plans
and positions to politicians, legislators, and voters—the
national audience of millions. It is the carefully presented
presidential "image." It is the nationally viewed justifica-
tion of war, invocation of peace, praise for political allies,
damnation of opponents, veto of legislation, scolding of
Congress by a chief executive, commander-in-chief, party
leader, and candidate.

19   Presidential television is free use of an extremely expensive commodity. An individual or group wishing to
broadcast a half-hour program simultaneously on all three
major networks during evening prime time could pay
more than $250,000, exclusive of the cost of producing the
program, assuming that the time could be bought—which
in all probability it could not. But a president, as Senator
Fulbright has noted, can "command a national audience to
hear his views on controversial matters at prime time, on
short notice, at whatever length he chooses, and at no
expense to the Federal Government or his party."[15] Or
himself.

20 The continued ability of the opposition political party to 11
pose a realistic election threat, the continued ability of
Congress to withstand presidential pressure, and even the
continued ability of the Supreme Court to maintain its independence from political pressures, depend on keeping
the balance between them and the president. Given the
president's special access to television, it may be necessary
to give these institutions sufficient access of their own to 12
the public through television. Reviewing President Truman's seizure of the steel mills in 1952, the Supreme
Court noted that through public opinion the president
"exerts a leverage upon those who are supposed to check
and balance his power which often cancels their effectiveness."[16] Public opinion has historically enabled opposition
parties, the Supreme Court, and the Congress to act as a
rein on the executive and preserve the two-party political
system. "Public opinion," Clinton Rossiter has noted,
helps to check presidential power "when it encourages
Congress to override a veto, persuades an investigating
committee to put a White House intimate on the grill, stif-
fens the resolve of a band of Senators to talk until Christmas . . . and puts backbone in a Supreme Court asked to
nullify a Presidential order. The various institutions and
centers of power that check the President are inept and
often useless without public opinion."[17] If the president's
naturally preeminent position becomes a virtual monopoly of political communication, presidential television
can constitute a danger to democracy.

21 Other countries have experienced similar television
monopolies under circumstances that can only be considered ominous. Adolf Hitler, who employed his monopoly
over German radio with great effectiveness, was intrigued
by television's manipulative potential; his scientists, before being diverted by wartime urgencies, developed a
closed-circuit system that Hitler once used to broadcast an
announcement to an audience watching his image on a
large theater screen. Fidel Castro spent hours under klieg
lights during the months in which he consolidated his vic-
tory in the Cuban revolution. Gamal Abdel Nasser, too,
built a television system in Egypt to advance his political
fortunes. His technicians even developed battery-powered
television for use in villages lacking electricity. Nasser's
broadcasting was filled with subtle propaganda, but because he was afraid of overexposure, Nasser himself rarely 13
appeared on television.[18]

22   Unlike Hitler's Germany or Castro's Cuba or Nasser's   *13*
United Arab Republic, the problem in this country is not
that of a total monopoly. The Congress and the opposition
party are not completely barred from television. Far from
it. Network interview programs regularly feature political
and congressional leaders, and it is a rare newscast that
does not offer a glimpse of a party or congressional figure
voicing opposition to the president's viewpoint. Traditionally, responses to a presidential State of the Union
address are broadcast by one or more of the major networks. The networks also produce "specials" from time to
time that have presented reactions to presidential policy
statements. Nevertheless, newscasts and specials are not
the same form of access that the president enjoys. In appearances on presidential television, he controls the
programs; the opposition does not. Richard S. Salant,
president of CBS News, acknowledges that while the
president's political and congressional opposition is frequently heard on news and documentary programs, these
broadcasts generally are internally balanced and, unlike
presidential television, not intended to persuade. "Further, the participants in these . . . broadcasts do not have
the advantages which the president has—the live, un-
edited appearance, the direct presentation free of jour-
nalists' questioning, the simultaneous appearance on all
networks, and the control of timing and place in the
broadcast schedule."[19]

23   Congressmen supporting a move to override a presidential veto of legislation—a veto message delivered by a
president before millions of television viewers—are not
likely to be able to command free, prime, simultaneous
three-network broadcast time for their side of the issue to
quell the flow of constituent mail generated by the president's appearance; the leading opposition party figure is   *14*
not likely to be able to command free, prime, simultaneous
three-network broadcast time to state his position on an
issue discussed by the president in an appearance just
ninety days before a presidential election. As one interested group sees it, it is "as if the President has a
megaphone and a soapbox while everyone else is required
to whisper."[20]

24   Many believe too, that television has contributed to the
weakening of the political parties in the last decades. Before television, a candidate depended upon the party organization, especially on the precinct captains, to take

his cases to the voters. But today the candidate can *14*
speak directly to the voters in their homes. As a result, the
party label has become less important than the man who
wears it.

25 Of late, numerous small special-interest organizations
such as Common Cause have demanded television time to
raise new issues for national debate or to respond to issues
set forth in presidential television appearances. Each
group wants to present its views not through interviews,
panels, commentators, newsmen or network-produced
specials, but rather in broadcast time that, like the president's time, is under its own control. "In many places they
are called coalitions," says *Broadcasting,* the leading industry news journal. "In some cities they are, simply,
committees. But the aims of the members are the same: to
gain access to the broadcasting media, to help set the
agenda for American broadcasting."[21] . . .

26 Speaking to a group of broadcasters in 1971, the chair- *15*
man of the Federal Communications Commission re-
marked that "in a real sense, your industry is the victim of
its own success. It's a vital medium. The public wants in.
And a growing crowd of individuals and groups are *demanding* access."[22] The number and vociferousness of
these demands suggest that the public institutions designed to counterbalance the presidential appeal to the
power of public opinion are not adequately performing
their function. The fault does not appear to be theirs so *16*
much as it is the growing power of the presidency, aided by
presidential television.

27 Little less than fifty years ago, virtually all government
interest in broadcasting occupied but a small part of the
time of a House of Representatives' Committee on Merchant Marine and Fisheries; radio was primarily used for
ship-to-shore communication. Nevertheless, that committee dimly glimpsed broadcasting's future and, in an early
report, listed among the "possibilities and potentialities"
of the medium a substantial "political" role.[23] By the
1970s it was acknowledged that broadcasting, and particularly television, had become a powerful political
weapon in reaching elective office and in governing once
there. The chairman of the Senate Communications Subcommittee, which devotes almost all its attention to
broadcasting, observes that a political candidate easily
can reach more than 20 million voters—one-third of the
number that voted in the 1968 presidential election—with

one appearance on one television network for just one minute.[24] And once in office that candidate can use television to sell his program, his party, and himself.

NOTES

[1]John J. O'Connor, *New York Times,* August 18, 1971, p. 75.

[2]Special Subcommittee on Investigations, House Committee on Interstate and Foreign Commerce, Report, 91st Cong., 1st sess. (1969), p. 6.

[3]*Broadcasting,* April 5, 1971, p. 24, and April 10, 1972, p. 88.

[4]Ben H. Bagdikian, *The Information Machines* (New York: Harper & Row, Publishers, 1971), p. 13.

[5]Jay Weitzner, "Handling the Candidate on Television," in *The Political Image Merchants: Strategies in the New Politics,* ed. Ray Hiebert et al. (Washington, D.C.: Acropolis Books, 1971), p. 102.

[6]Early in the fall campaign of 1972, Sen. George McGovern, the Democratic nominee for president, confined his campaign almost entirely to three "media events" a day. That is, he did almost nothing but travel to three television population centers, often widely scattered, to read a statement or make an appearance calculated to provide good television pictures for the evening news. Once, for example, he traveled to Superior, Wisconsin, and Duluth, Minnesota, to make a statement about the sale of wheat to the Soviet Union that he could have made far more easily from his Washington headquarters. He went to Duluth-Superior solely to be photographed issuing the statement in front of a grain elevator (and, of course, because Wisconsin and Minnesota were states he hoped to win). Before long, however, newspaper reporters began to complain that McGovern was running a phony campaign of little substance, television reporters began to view his calculated performances skeptically, and his advisers concluded he must change his style. He did, addressing large political rallies and delivering serious half-hour speeches on major issues to the evening television audience. McGovern's experience led some observers to wonder whether the power of television in political campaigns was waning. Others concluded that McGovern simply used it too blatantly.

[7]See studies cited in The Twentieth Century Fund Commission on Campaign Costs in the Electronic Era, *Voters' Time* (New York: Twentieth Century Fund, 1969), pp. 55–58, nn. 1–2.

[8]*Washington Post,* June 18, 1971, p. A2.

[9]*Washington Post,* November 22, 1970, p. A1.

[10]*Time,* May 18, 1971, p. 18.

[11]Revenue Act of 1971 (Public Law 92–178, 85 Stat. 497).

[12]Federal Election Campaign Act of 1971 (Public Law 92–225, 86 Stat. 3).

[13]Quoted in William L. Rivers, "Appraising Press Coverage of Politics," in *Politics and the Press,* ed. Richard W. Lee (Washington, D.C.: Acropolis Books, 1970), p. 53.

[14]Richard E. Neustadt, *Presidential Power* (New York: John Wiley & Sons, Inc., 1960), p. 10.

[15]116 *Congressional Record,* S81612 (daily ed., June 2, 1970).

[16]*Youngstown Sheet & Tube Co.* v. *Sawyer,* 343 U.S. 579,   *202*
653–54 (1952) (concurring opinion by Justice Jackson).

[17]Clinton Rossiter, *The American Presidency* (New York: New American Library, 1962), p. 66.

[18]Wilson P. Dizard, *Television: A World View* (Syracuse, N.Y.: Syracuse University Press, 1967), p. 149.

[19]Address by Richard S. Salant, president of CBS News, before the Journalism Foundation of Metropolitan St. Louis, May 1, 1972.

[20]Committee for Fair Broadcasting of Controversial Issues, quoted in Comment, "Televised Presidential Addresses and the FCC's Fairness Doctrine," *Columbia Journal of Law and Social Problems* 7 (1971): 75, 79.

[21]*Broadcasting,* September 20, 1971, p. 32.

[22]Address by Hon. Dean Burch, Chairman, Federal Communi-   *203*
cations Commission, to the National Association of Broadcasters, Chicago, Illinois, March 31, 1971.

[23]House of Representatives Report No. 464, p. 3, 69th Cong., 1st sess. (1926).

[24]Remarks of Sen. John O. Pastore, Hearings on S.J. Res. 209, p. 2.

11

Martin Mayer is a free-lance writer who has written books and articles on education, music, and law as well as on television.
This book was published by Harper & Row in New York in 1972.

From About Television
MARTIN MAYER

1   . . . The first patents for a device to send pictures by wire   *16*
were issued in Germany in 1884, and by 1930 the Eng-
lishman J. L. Baird was selling television sets to the public for about $130 each and broadcasting video signals on
BBC transmitting equipment after the close of the radio
broadcast day. This was a mechanical system that involved a disc with pinholes and a light behind it; by syn-
chronizing the very fast spinning of the disc with varying
intensity of the light, a picture—well, a silhouette—could
be constructed. Similar systems were being tried out in
the United States, where Secretary of Commerce Herbert
Hoover appeared on a television transmission over wires
from Washington to New York in 1927, and General Electric telecast a play in Schenectady in 1928.

2   As early as 1923, however, Vladimir K. Zworykin, a
Russian refugee working in America, had won a patent on
a practical electronic television camera, though he never
got the thing working right until he joined RCA in 1929.
(Gilbert Seldes once speculated that if Zworykin had gone
to work in Hollywood rather than in New York the movie
industry rather than the radio broadcasters might have
controlled television.) And in Britain engineers working
for Electrical and Musical Industries developed an improved camera based on Zworykin's. The BBC in 1936 ran
a formal test of this "Emitron" as against the Baird system, alternating weeks of broadcasting in each. The EMI
system was an easy winner for picture quality, and was of-
ficially adopted. In 1937 the BBC televised the coronation

of King George VI, and in 1938 regular television broad- *16*
casts began, with a page of programs announcing the tele- *17*
vision schedule amidst the radio schedules in *Radio
Times*. American television first went to the public in
1939, when RCA put a few hundred sets in the stores at
$625 each for rich New Yorkers presold by the enthusias-
tic promotion for the new device that dominated the RCA
Exhibition Hall at the newly opened World's Fair. But the
license RCA held from the Federal Communications
Commission was for "experimental" broadcast only, and in
fact the system RCA used in 1939 was not what finally became the standard broadcasting system in America.

3   Technically, television required a great deal of
decision-making before service could begin; radio was
simple by comparison. Sound waves translate directly into
electrical terms in the broadcasting studio, and translate
equally directly back into speech or music in the radio at
home. But picture information is much more complicated,
and there were various ways to code it and to reconstruct
it from the code at the opposite ends of the broadcasting
system.

4   Very quickly and too simply: a television camera contains many dots of an element which is sensitive to light
and generates a tiny electrical charge when light hits it.
An electron beam in the camera scans these dots, moving
very rapidly from left to right in a pattern of parallel horizontal lines, and discharges the light-sensitive element.
At the receiving end, in the television set, a "cathode ray"
scans dots of a fluorescing element on the inside of the
television screen, making an identical pattern of lines,
causing each dot on the screen to light up or stay dark according to the charges carried on the electron beam in the
camera in the studio. Between the studio and the television set, of course, are interposed all the paraphernalia of
broadcast, generators, transmission towers, home anten-
nae and much else.

5   Obviously this system is going to work only if the camera in the studio and the set in the home can be
synchronized—the number of lines in the horizontal pattern, and the length of time required to complete each
"frame" of these lines (like the individual picture "frames"
in a strip of movie film) must be the same in both camera
and receiver. The simplest way to synchronize the length *18*
of time needed to complete the frame is to use the frequency of the alternating current that drives both camera

and receiver and all the other electrical appliances in the *18*
city. In Britain and on the European continent, the electrical current alternates at 50 cycles per second. The British and European systems make a separate frame for every two cycles of AC, or 25 frames per second. In the United States the current alternates at 60 cycles per second. American television also generates a separate frame for each two cycles of AC, so the American television standard is 30 frames per second.

6   The choice of the number of lines to be used in a television picture was an arbitrary decision. British television has been operating at 409 lines; the Europeans operate at 625 lines (and the British will slowly convert to 625 over the next decade); and American television operates at 525 lines (RCA's false start in 1939 had been at 441 lines). Every so often somebody publishes a magazine article about a glorious future in which satellites will send the same television picture to homes all over the world, but it can't happen. No American set, demanding a 525-line frame 30 times a second, can make any picture at all from a European transmission of a 625-line frame 25 times a second—or vice versa. In fact, American and European broadcasting companies can't use each other's videotapes. As late as mid-1971 there was only one machine in the whole world, in London, that could convert television signals from one system to signals usable in all other systems. Except for news, all television pictures that cross the Atlantic are sent on film. This is a great nuisance, but nothing can be done about it: each country is locked into its own system by the immense public investment in television sets.

7   Another technicality relating to frame speeds: professional Hollywood 35-mm. movies are made to play at a rate of 24 frames per second. In Europe this presents no serious problem: the movie projector is simply speeded up to show the television camera 25 frames per second, which is what the television camera needs; the pitch of the sound track rises very slightly, and the movie gets finished just a little quicker—a 1-hour, 12-minute movie plays in 1 hour, 7½ minutes. In the United States, however, the gap between the 24-frame standard of the movies and the 30- *19* frame standard of television transmission was too great to be bridged by speeding up the film.

8   Originally, nobody in television worried about this problem—it was just inconceivable to the pioneers of the

new medium that their glorious invention, with its unique *19* capacity to disseminate live action, live drama, live performances, would ever be employed simply as a carrier of film. Eventually, however, the engineers perfected the "telecine chain," which uses the fact that the 30-frame-per-second television picture is actually two 60-frame-per-second pictures with each frame repeated once. The aperture of the movie projector used in the telecine chain is geared to show one frame of the film for 2/60th of a second and the next frame for 3/60th of a second. The two frames together use up 1/12th of a second, and 24 frames a second pass the lens of the movie camera, making 30 frames per second on the television tube. The human eye is nowhere near fast enough to catch the deception. Indeed, the telecine system is so acceptable that movies and series made for television only—even commercials with no other imaginable use—are produced on film running 24 frames per second. The use of these same telecine chains to televise old silent movies on public television, however—as Pauline Kael complained bitterly in *The New Yorker* in fall 1971—produced a 50 percent speed-up of the action, because many silents were made originally to play at 16 frames per second.

9 One last technicality: the "channel." All broadcasting stations are distinguished from each other by the "frequency" of the "carrier signal" (i.e., the speed of alternation in the current the transmitter pumps into the air: the "information" needed to convert electrical impulse into sound or picture is carried as a modulation of that basic frequency). Because sound is relatively simple to broadcast, a narrow "band" of frequencies is all a radio station needs to deliver a sound without interfering with broadcasts from other stations. AM radio broadcasting operates at frequencies from 55,000 to 165,000 cycles per second, and stations with carrier frequencies only 4,500 cycles apart will not interfere with each other.

10 But the quantity of information needed to reconstruct a telecast picture requires a band width of 4.5 *million* cycles *20* per second, and the carrier frequency must be much faster than that. In 1945 the FCC approved for use in America some thirteen carrier frequencies, each with the exclusive right to 6 million cycles ("megacycles") of band width, falling in the range from 44 to 216 million cycles, which the engineers called Very High Frequency (VHF). These channels were to be shared with nonbroadcast radio-telephone use (police and firecalls, etc.). The Commission

recognized that over the long run these thirteen channels   *20*
might not provide enough stations, and set aside for possible future exploration an Ultra High Frequency (UHF)
range from 480 to 920 megacycles.

11   Radio waves at relatively low frequencies, like the AM
broadcast band, meander about and bounce off the layers
of the atmosphere and in general wander many hundreds
of miles from their transmitters, especially at night; the
FCC had learned that it could not authorize too many
broadcasters to use the same frequency, even in fairly
widely separated cities. But the VHF waves used for television go in straight lines, zipping out into space as the
earth curves inward—that's why KTHI in North Dakota
has to go so far up to garner a larger coverage area. In
theory the thirteen channels could be used over and over
again, all around a big country. Nor was there much worry
about nearby stations on adjacent channels interfering
with each other—though 4.5 million cycles of information
would normally generate a "sideband" on each side of the
carrier frequency, which would leave the FCC-allocated
6-million-cycle channel insufficient to prevent interference, the AM radio broadcasters had learned to "suppress"
one of their sidebands, and the FCC assumed that television broadcasters would be able to do the same.

12   If any of these technical decisions turned out to be
wrong, the FCC thought there would be plenty of time to
correct them. Emerging from the war, the nation was still
bound by a depression psychology, remembering the sharp
economic setback that had followed less than three years
after the end of World War I, and the catastrophes of the
1930s. Television sets were expensive, and the medium
was seen as a rich man's toy. The FCC announced that any
qualified company, including the radio networks, could be
awarded up to five local television licenses in the VHF   *21*
band, but CBS took only one—"an expensive gesture of
contempt," as Eugene Lyons wrote later in his biography
of David Sarnoff. "In due time CBS would buy these discarded licenses for telecasting stations for sums running
into tens of millions." Tom Coffin, now vice president in
charge of research at NBC, recalls that in the late 1940s,
as a professor of psychology at Hofstra University, he
sought the advice of CBS president Frank Stanton, himself a former psychology professor, on whether he should
take a research job in broadcasting. Dr. Stanton was
enthusiastic—but, he said, Coffin should stick to radio:
there was never going to be much money in television.

13　　　In mid-1947 only ten stations were on the air, and pro- *21*
duction of receivers was at a rate of only 160,000 a year.
Martin Stone, who then produced *Author Meets the Critics*
for NBC, remembers sitting around the two small offices
television then commanded, with the boss saying, "We
have $150 for Thursday night. What should we do?" Then,
very suddenly, television took off. Like the automobile before it, television appealed to a pleasure center deep in almost every man, regardless of age, education, social status
or nationality. In 1950 Americans would buy 7,355,000
television sets (in 1971, the record year, they bought
14,860,000, of which 7,250,000 were color sets). By December 1948 there were 127 stations on the air, and it had
become clear that the initial FCC technical decisions were
wrong.

14　　　The nonbroadcast services permitted in the VHF band
did interfere with television reception; they were barred
from Channels 2–13 and given exclusive use of Channel 1.
The geographic separations plotted in the original alloca-
tions turned out to be insufficient—VHF signals traveled
in straight lines, all right, but they could take queer
bounces off hills and sometimes off cloud formations and
get into other licensees' coverage areas. Worst of all, the
sideband suppressors could not be made to work properly.
Telecasting on Channel 2 or 10 interfered with the programs on Channel 3 or 11, even some distance away.
Through the latter part of 1948, the Commission studied
reports from the field as a dog might study a cobra emerging from a basket; and in December the Commission
panicked, and "froze" all construction of television trans- *22*
mitters, anywhere in the country.

15　　　Ostensibly, the reason for the freeze was the need to
consider the possibilities of color television. CBS had a
system which it said was ready to go, involving a whirling
disc (again) between the cathode ray and the screen; RCA
had an idea for a system not yet ready to go, involving
fluorescent dots of different colors on the tube, to be separately illuminated by separate cathode rays. The CBS system, unfortunately, was not "compatible" with normal
black-and-white television—i.e., a station broadcasting
color could not be received at all on a conventional set.
And even in the time of the freeze Americans were buying
conventional sets at a rate of almost seven million a year.
Color telecasts by the RCA system still gave atrocious
color (and inferior black-and-white: when RCA actually

began colorcasting in 1954, its first "color spectaculars" *22* were so deficient in black-and-white contrast that, "in a rare manifestation of the old pioneer spirit," as Gilbert Seldes put it, "millions of Americans walked all the way over to their television sets and tuned out the programs ... it was the worst case of betrayal of the public interest in the history of broadcasting"). But at least the RCA system was "compatible," and would not deprive customers of the benefits of their investment in monochrome television sets.

16   No color system should have been authorized in 1950, but under political pressure the FCC approved the CBS system, and authorized broadcasting to begin on November 20 of that year. Fortunately, controls on the civilian use of electronic components during the Korean War gave CBS an excuse not to try to exploit its triumph at the FCC, and late in 1953, without much complaint from CBS, the Commission reversed itself and authorized a slightly altered (but much improved) version of the compatible RCA system. Incidentally, the CBS system, inherently well adapted to computer processing techniques, returned to life in 1970 as the source of color pictures from the moon.

17   The freeze on the new stations was lifted before the end of the color controversy. In April 1952 the FCC announced a full national plan for the allocation of channels to localities—2,000 channels, divided roughly 550 in the *23* VHF band and 1,450 in the UHF band. The first UHF station—KPTV in Portland, Oregon—went on the air in September 1952. But the agency had again miscalculated. Nearly twenty million television sets which could not receive UHF transmissions were already in the hands of the public. "All-channel" receivers cost more than VHF-only receivers; in the absence of outstanding UHF programming the public was not disposed to waste its money; and in the absence of receivers advertisers were not prepared to support any programming (let alone outstanding programming) on UHF channels.

18   At best, moreover, UHF transmission was marginally inferior to that on VHF, more subject to interference, and not only in cities. "I ran a UHF in Ann Arbor," says David Connell, executive producer for *Sesame Street*. "In the winter, our signal got all the way to Ypsilanti. In summer, with the leaves on the trees, it wouldn't travel six miles." Britain is in process of converting all television to the

UHF band to free itself of the constraints a crowded Europe is forced to place on any one nation's use of the VHF range. Forty transmitters covered England and Scotland adequately in VHF broadcast, but for UHF the technicians now estimate a need for at least six hundred and perhaps a thousand "masts." Parliament is forcing BBC to share the towers with its commercial rival ITA for fear that otherwise, as an MP put it, "you'll turn this country into an upended hair-brush."

In 1962 Congress passed a law requiring all television set manufacturers to produce only all-channel receivers after January 1, 1964, but the horse was out the barn door. Even in television's *annus mirabilis* of 1969, nearly two-thirds of commercial UHF stations lost money. The total operating profits of 504 VHF stations in 1969 were just over $500 million; the total operating *losses* of 169 VHF stations were $43 million. It may be worth noting in this age of consumerism that between 1964 and 1971 the American people were forced by Act of Congress (incited by the FCC, the Ford Foundation and assorted critical commentators) to spend about $1.2 billion for UHF tuning capabilities the vast majority of them did not want and have never used.

12

Kas Kalba is the president of Kalba Bowen Associates, Inc., a communications consulting firm. He is also a lecturer on city planning at Harvard University's Graduate School of Design.

This article was published in Television as a Social Force: New Approaches to TV Criticism, *edited by Douglass Cater and Richard Adler, by Praeger in 1975 in New York. The article appears on pages 147–60 of the book.*

The Electronic Community: A New Environment
KAS KALBA

1   *Tomorrow's Electronic Community.* The last area of so-   147
cial and economic activity that the local neighborhood
continues to dominate is the provision of community services. For most households it remains the locus of the   148
school, the police and fire precinct, the access road, and the
garbage pickup. In some instances it is still the place
where commercial and professional services are
provided—for instance, banking, newspaper delivery,
shopping, and medical services. But it is also this area of
community services that is being prospected by the propo-
nents of the new communications technologies. As television matures into the home communications center of
tomorrow, they argue, it will be able to deliver many of
these same services directly to the home.

2   How will this extension of television's traditional powers occur? From a technological point of view, this question can be answered in a relatively straightforward
manner. (The answer in terms of social impact is, as I will
suggest further below, more complicated.) In essence, the
new communications media will extend television's
capabilities in the following ways:

1. *Channel Abundance:* Today's cable television systems
   are mandated by FCC regulation to carry 20 television

---

channels. Some systems already have the capability to *148* transmit over 30 channels, and more could be added in the future if needed. The point is that it is now possible to transmit more television to the home than simply by the over-the-air channels that are available in a given locality. Viewers can become more selective about when or what they watch.

2. *Audience Divisibility:* Programmers can also be more selective about who they reach. Through multiple head ends or special converter and scrambler devices, and ultimately through computer addressing of programs, programmers will be able to pinpoint the specific audience (by income, ethnicity, neighborhood, special interests, etc.) that they are most interested in reaching. Early forms of this capability are currently in operation in pay television experiments, medical programming for physicians, and local-origin programs that are aimed at a specific community rather than an entire metropolitan area.

3. *Display Alternatives:* Programmers will not be limited to transmitting video messages alone. The augmented television terminals of tomorrow will be capable of receiving a variety of data, sound, and video messages, including stop-frame displays of print, facsimile, stereo sound, and large-screen television. Various hybrid communication forms will undoubtedly emerge, involving simultaneously or in sequence still pictures, moving images, captions, textual printouts, or supplementary sound tracks.

4. *Feedback Mechanisms:* Some of the home devices will allow for inputs as well as outputs. The consumer or a surrogate (e.g., his electricity meter or home burglar alarm) will be able to send messages back to the pro- *149* gramming source, eliciting particular programs, registering opinions, or responding to questions regarding his banking transactions, shopping needs, or knowledge of early American history. Home response mechanisms are likely to be limited to data and possibly voice communication. However, full-scale two-way video conferences may also be feasible on a limited basis, for example, between business or institutions.

5. *Storage Capability:* Finally, both programmer and viewer will have access to increased storage capability. Data banks tied to the programmer will monitor and record various transactions between the viewer and the

programmer, storing these for future reference. The *149*
viewer, on the other hand, will be able to record television programs on video cassettes (or to acquire them
directly in that form) for playback at a convenient time.
In fact, repeated and selective playback will be possible,
as a result of which television will function more like
the audio record or the book and less like a mass broadcasting system.

3   These are some of the capabilities that will be introduced by the new communications media, in particular
by cable communications and a variety of ancillary
technological developments. All of these capabilities are
available in the laboratory today, and most of them are already being tested in selected areas. The questions that
remain are how rapidly will these developments permeate
our society and how desirable are they? What is no longer
uncertain, however, is that in the future, whether five or
ten or fifteen years from now, television will affect virtually all aspects of our daily lives.

4   The days of television as a spectator activity, during
which we passively witness the unfolding of a Sunday afternoon football game, a light comedy serial, a Geritol
psychodrama, or a national political convention, will be
replaced by a television through which we directly engage
in the act of learning, shopping, voting, and working.

5   The image of tomorrow's communications-supported
home learning facility that is usually presented in graphic
or film simulations is that of a child sitting in front of a
video display console with his or her hands on an adjacent
keyboard. At times the picture is that of an adult, since
presumably the console will also be used for learning practical information such as how to repair the plumbing or
how to plant tomatoes, as well as for continuing formal
education. In the film simulations there are usually some
shots of the actual operation of the console, showing how
the student can interact with computer-generated ques-   *150*
tions, can retrieve factual data or images on demand, or
can even create animated designs on the console. Interactive home learning, in short, will be to *Sesame Street* what
the dual-mode guideway (the Ford Motor Company's most
advanced concept in "people-moving") is to the Model T.

6   It is reasonable to assume that our learning ability will
be enhanced by the availability of such a home learning

facility. For example, curriculum choice will be expanded, *150*
since the user will have access to a considerably wider
array of programming than is true in the typical school today. Self-pacing in instruction will become more possible
in that the user will not have to adjust to the pace that is
set in a conventional classroom. And the new facility will
presumably be free of the human-relations biases that can
exist in the traditional teacher-student relationship,
whether due to race, sex, ethnic differences, or personality
characteristics.

7   But the notion of a home learning facility also raises
some difficult questions. How will this new communications medium affect educational objectives that have little
to do with factual learning? It is not likely to provide day-
care or socialization experiences, for example. Will it be
responsive to the communications differences of different groups, as defined by age, ethnicity, or cognitive proficiency? In reducing social bias will it also reduce effective contact and comprehension? Will interactive home
learning reduce our ability to deal with everyday problem
situations due to its inherent abstraction of the learning
process? Even though televised and computer-assisted
forms of instruction have proven to be effective learning
tools in the past, we have little knowledge of their impact
on overall learning and problem-solving capabilities at
the point that these tools become dominant (rather than
occasional) learning modes.

8   Considerable divergence of opinion exists concerning
how "home shopping" will actually operate, even among
the early promoters of this particular communications
service. The more rudimentary proposals call for the consumer to push a single button at the end of a commercial,
thereby indicating a desire to purchase the product. Alternatively, special shows may be produced to exhibit a
department store's or supermarket's wares, during which
viewers will be able to ask questions concerning particular
items. Or, in still another rendition, the remote purchasing process is compared to computer-assisted instruction,
where the consumer will be able to ask for information on
a class of commodities (e.g., rental housing, automobiles,
clothing, used furniture, etc.) and then through a series of
branching routines be able to determine the product that
meets his or her specific needs.[1]

9   It is also unclear how the product will be delivered once   *150*
the electronic purchase is made. It is unlikely that a slow
delivery process of the kind that is available today   *151*
through mail-order catalogues will be sufficient to launch
this new communications service. In fact, a whole host of
delivery, warehousing, and managerial questions arise as
one begins to contemplate seriously the establishment of
remote shopping on a widespread basis. The electronic ordering mechanism, it turns out, is only a small part of the
home shopping "system" that will be required. (The same
can be said for other home communications services,
whether remote burglar alarms, facsimile services, or
medical care.) After all, the retailing trend for the past
three decades has been away from home delivery and the
corner store to much more centralized outlets such as
supermarkets and regional shopping centers. Reversing
this pattern will take more than an electronic push-button
device.

10   But overlooking for the moment these practical problems, the appeal of an instantaneous home shopping facility, given the decline of neighborhood shopping, remains
nonetheless considerable. Added choice, greater consumer
information, convenience, and perhaps even cost savings
due to sales economies are values that could conceivably
be gained through home shopping. From a social viewpoint, the resulting decrease in shopping trips could help
reduce air pollution and energy consumption. And access
to commodities, which continues to be a problem in rural
areas as well as inner-city poverty areas, could be
equalized.

11   These are some of the potentially positive benefits. At
the same time, less desirable social and economic consequences could also occur. For example, shopping trips
today retain a quasi-social character. Even if market bar-
tering and social discussions with the grocer are disap-
pearing phenomena, shopping still involves a degree of
social contact; at a minimum, it is a change of pace in
day-to-day routine activity. As it is turned into a
mechanized decision function, this may reduce social involvement and increase alienation.[2] Similarly, the
economic base of the local pharmacy, the specialty shop, or
the downtown department store may be undermined, leaving us with unexciting cities and further disrupting the
urban economy and related social structure.[3]

12 An alteration of our political system is also likely to *151* occur in tomorrow's electronic community. Channel abundance will allow the home viewer to follow local town council or PTA proceedings. Feedback mechanisms will permit him to register an opinion at these proceedings or to vote in national referenda. And access to stored information will facilitate the collection of facts about candidates, agencies, and issues. As a result of these developments, the mutual cynicism that so often distorts relationships between citizens and government officials could be reduced through a more continuous information flow.

13 But once again the underlying impact of these technological capabilities is more difficult to pinpoint. *152* Will access to the political system be truly broadened or will new entry requirements be placed on such access? One problem is that the ability to interact effortlessly by means of a remote communications device may not be universal.[4] The costs of such a home voting service, unless covered by the government, could also restrict participation, thereby creating a new kind of second-class citizenship. And the feedback mechanisms might be centrally controlled, so that instead of fostering genuine participation and the raising of issues the voter's response would be limited to pre-structured agenda items and choices.

14 Both the effectiveness and impact of home voting systems will, in other words, depend on how these are actually designed and implemented. The inclination at present is to visualize them as conveyors of instantaneous national referenda. Yet there is some question whether the lack of such electronic plebiscites is a root problem of contemporary American democracy. Would having a national election every month or every week to contend with the latest political crisis improve the system or simply multiply its current deficiencies? Would it not be more fruitful to expand participation in the political resolution of more specialized issues, whether the problems of the handicapped, foreign import quotas, or airport expansion? This, however, may run counter to the incentives underlying "digital democracy," namely, to raise issues in which the largest number of individuals will want to participate. The old television economics of appealing to the widest audience may survive the new television technology.

15 Once we develop the technological capability and the psychological willingness to learn, shop, and engage in

politics by remote interactive communications, the final 152 step will be to connect the home to the work place. This will permit many of us to work at home, accessing files, secretaries, and corporate managers by means of remote communications devices. Since white-collar workers (the expanding sector of the economy) already spend much or perhaps most of their time in data-processing and communications activities, the notion of performing these same jobs on a highly decentralized basis is not necessarily utopian. Moreover, the ramifications on the tangle of social problems that are generated by daily commutation to work—that is, traffic congestion, air pollution, and energy consumption—could be very positive if home-bound work were to become an accepted practice.[5] At a minimum, work might be decentralized to a more local level, thereby cutting down on the length of the average commutation trip.[6]

16   This vision of "communicating to work," as Peter Goldmark has called it, is appealing both to the social planner and to the suburban employee faced with an hour-long drive two times each working day. But again a number of issues need to be examined before this new form 153 of employment can be generally prescribed. There are several practical concerns. Can the variety of communications tasks involved in the business world be converted to a remote communications mode? Some, of course, have already been converted to the long-distance telephone, remote facsimile, or on-line computer services. And the new technologies, such as two-way video conferences, will allow even more business functions to be handled on a remote basis. Still the suspicion remains that certain intricate business activities, in particular negotiations that precede major decision-making, require face-to-face contact. More importantly, such contact may be essential to the maintenance of corporate morale and as a stimulant to other employment functions.

17   The notion of home-based work also raises important social and psychological issues. At present the ritual of departing the home for work is a deeply-imbedded concept that governs the daily behavior of most workers. The physical separation of home and work place underlies our economic and cultural behavior. How readily can these habits be changed? Do we, as a society, want to change them? And what will happen to family life when formal work invades the private household?[7]

18   What generalizations can be drawn from this discussion *153*
of four separate dimensions of tomorrow's electronic community? One, at least, is that the electronic community
will not be a steady utopian (or counter-utopian) state in
which society and culture are transformed once and for all.
Rather it will be an evolving social process, during which
the practical and economic difficulties of engaging in fun-
damental community activities on a remote basis will be
worked out through trial and error, one at a time.

19   Similarly, the social impact of the new communications
tools that are brought into being will not always be
rapidly detectable, but over time, combined with other
societal developments, they could be profound. The home,
for example, is likely to become an even more intensive
center for activity than it is today, but whether it will gain
or lose in intimacy as a result remains to be seen. The
work place may become less dependent on the economies
of agglomeration that sustain today's cities and will be
free to locate its various functions in different locations
(including the home). But this may exacerbate rather than
resolve the social problems of the metropolis. And in general our contact universes, whether shopping, learning, or
work-related, will probably be expanded. In another sense,
however, they may be collapsed, in that the time we will
be able to accord to any one contact will be considerably
shortened.

20   In sum, it will be the manner in which the new
technologies are introduced and implemented that will determine their ultimate impact. This realization places a
major responsibility on individuals and organizations involved in the design, marketing, and regulation of communications innovations. It also calls for the emergence of
a new kind of television criticism, which, as I will argue at
the end of this essay, must begin to examine the overall
television environment that is being produced and not *154*
only individual programs. For in the future television's
role as a monolithic entertainment medium will be fragmented by the advent of the new technologies, much as
our cities have been dispersed through suburbanization.

21   *The Future of Television* Like the telephone and radio
which preceded it, television began as a relatively aimless
technical invention and as a luxury consumer commodity.
It had no content to speak of. Then gradually, borrowing
heavily in production techniques and programming concepts from media predecessors, it emerged into a mass-
entertainment medium. This, to a large extent, is the

television we watch today: part radio, part cinema, part *154*
theater, and part athletic event.

22   But even in establishing its identity as an entertainment medium, the roots of a more variegated communications medium were beginning to take hold. The TV box began to carry marketing messages, newscasts, educational programs, and morning and evening talk shows. It became a purveyor of social roles, attitudes, and information, as well as entertainment. Even the serials convey not only emotions and catharsis by specific images of how social roles can interact, how products satisfy, how institutions operate, and how values are fulfilled. These images have become as much a part of American reality as highways or frozen foods.

23   In short, television has already passed through several phases of transformation and is likely to continue doing so. It has become a complex social innovation, one that cannot be defined solely by its technical parameters, or by static concepts of economic demand. Both old and new technical properties of television interact with changes in business markets, government decisions, and social or cultural needs and preferences.

24   And the medium will continue to evolve in the future. But in what ways? How will the transition from today's mass medium to tomorrow's electronic community be accomplished?

25   One way in which television will evolve—and is, in fact, already evolving—is in the direction of more "selective" communications services. It should be noted in this regard that television viewing patterns have changed considerably over the past ten years. The typical household no longer has only one TV set. Various economic factors have encouraged this new multiple-set household to come into being, including increased discretionary income, the reduction in the price of TV sets, and the availability of color television. At the same time the more individualistic viewing pattern that has resulted has been caused by, and has as well contributed to, several larger social transfor- *155* mations, including the disappearance of traditional local forms of recreation (e.g., bars, neighborhood theaters, social clubs) and the fragmentation of entertainment and information pursuits within the family.

26   If these trends persist, television is likely to become an increasingly selective medium. While the members of the family household may continue to watch certain programs jointly, an increasing portion of their viewing time will be

consumed on an individual basis in a manner consistent *155*
with their different schedules, tastes, and information
needs. Selectivity, in this sense, is also likely to mean
diversity—not necessarily diversity as defined by traditional cultural critics, namely high-, middle- and low-
brow programming, but diversity of the following kinds:

(1) time diversity (i.e., the same program made available
at different times of the day, week or year in response
to the fluctuating demand and convenience of viewers)
(2) programming diversity (i.e., greater variety in sports
or movie programming, talk shows, news, children's
programming, etc.)
(3) functional diversity (i.e., availability of programs not
only for entertainment but for other uses as well,
whether self-education, hobbies, shopping, specialized
information, etc.)

27   The advent of multi-channel cable television and of pay
television will reinforce this trend, already apparent at
the margins of broadcast television (i.e., UHF stations,
morning and late-evening programs, etc.), toward a more
selective utilization of the medium. The viewer of tomorrow will have greater choice about when a program can be
viewed, what that program is, and the manner in which
television can be responsive to his or her needs. Cultural,
educational, and other forms of nonentertainment programming will begin to flourish.

28   At the same time, the fragmentation in television viewing resulting from this increased selectivity is likely to
have social and cultural consequences. If viewers watch
sports or local news instead of national news, this may affect our level of national integration, in which television
as a mass medium has played a major role. If viewers are
drawn more and more to programs that correspond to their
minority tastes, whether cultural, ethnic, or life-style related, this may create social, economic and possibly political tensions. And if within a given household TV viewing
becomes highly individualistic, the nuclear family will
experience further strains, leading possibly to a transformation of its current functions.[8]

29   It is the functional diversification of television that will *156*
produce the most obvious changes in the utilization of the
medium. Up to the present our common notion of television has been that of a medium which has little bearing on

ordinary, day-to-day life. It has been there to amuse and *156* entertain us after a heavy day's work; to take us away from boredom or frustration of daily housekeeping; to report on distant political events at City Hall, Washington, or Peking; or to enlighten us occasionally through cultural programming. Compared to the telephone, or even the daily newspaper, television's relation to our daily lives has been negligible.

30 Increasingly, however, television will begin to enter the daily activity patterns of our seasonal and life-cycle existence. It will cease to play solely a mythical, expressive, or cathartic role and will become an instrumental medium, helping us to learn, to shop, to make business decisions, and to engage in active leisure and community pursuits. In fact, the general lessening of distinctions between work and play, public and private space, and family and collective spheres will be reflected in tomorrow's "service video." We will tune in to get advice from a doctor, to find out how to fill out IRS forms, to learn how to play tennis or a musical instrument, to upgrade occupational skills, or to participate in a local zoning decision.

31 Another type of television diversity will accompany this evolution—*space* diversity. The selective use of television will not only expand in the home but also in other places, such as schools, hotels, hospitals, retail outlets, and workplaces. These will not be entirely new uses of television, since the medium has been utilized on a closed-circuit basis for educational, training, marketing and other purposes for the past two decades. But these specialized uses will become more commonplace. Moreover, the conceptual distinction between, for example, television used for monitoring purposes in a bank and television as a mass entertainment vehicle is likely to disappear. What will emerge instead is a notion of the spectrum of uses to which television can be put, some serving very specialized or local purposes, others involving widely dispersed but still selective audiences, and still others encompassing truly mass audiences.[9]

32 As it becomes more of a service medium, television will also become more of a hybrid medium. To begin with, the imaginary line that has traditionally been drawn between video and print and that is only transgressed by television when production credits are shown will be gradually eliminated. This will occur not so much because of a direct

infusion of print into the TV medium but because of the   *156*
emerging relationship between television and the computer. Computer-assisted instruction, for example, has always depended on the digitalized transmission of textual   *157*
content to a cathode ray tube or other visual display device. It is this type of communications capability that is
being incorporated into the interactive television experiments that are currently being launched.[10]

33   The relationship with print will be reinforced in other
ways as well. For example, Caravatte-Kleiman, "a video
publishing" firm, recently produced a video cassette that is
indexed like a book. Utilizing a video cassette machine,
the viewer can go forward to those segments (pages) that
are of relevance to an immediate information need. The
program can be "read" selectively or "re-read" like a book.
Can "speed viewing" be far behind? Another example of
media hybridization, involving television, print, and the
telephone, is the video reference service currently offered
by the public library in Casper, Wyoming. A cable television subscriber can call up the library by phone, request
the display of a textual or graphic item (e.g., menus,
statistics, maps), and view it over a television channel in
his home.

34   The matrix of possible relationships between television
on the one hand and the computer and printed, graphic,
and other audio forms of communications on the other, is
virtually infinite. This is particularly true as television
ceases to be simply a reception medium and becomes a
storage, recording, and interactive tool as well. The systematic exploration of this matrix will lead to many dis-
coveries which at present are hardly conceivable. It will
also raise new questions concerning "man-machine interaction" and the social and psychological impact of these
new communications forms, not all of which will be
equally accessible or equally manageable for the average
home viewer. Technical proficiency, or media literacy,
may limit the service benefits that tomorrow's television
can provide us.

35   How will the gap between today's passive consumer of
television and the active participant of tomorrow be
breached? This, ultimately, may be the overriding issue
that determines the character of tomorrow's electronic
community. Today our ability to utilize television in an
active mode is analogous to our ability to explore the
moon. We are at the point of departure, but only a very few
individuals have passed through the elaborate training

exercises required to perform the task—and even they *157*
must contend with biological, technological, and environmental barriers to achieve free movement on the lunar
landscape. Our ability to actively explore the television
medium is similarly constrained.

36   In part, the problem lies with our overall ability to
utilize technology and, more specifically, communications
media. Apart from voice, ball-point, and camera, the active utilization of communications media is, as a rule, reserved for specialists. Most of us, even today, cannot type. *158*
Many telephone users have never called the operator for
information. Most of us are frustrated by the UHF dial on
our TV sets. And most of us have never made a film, a videotape, or even an audio cassette recording. The prospects
for a society where active media utilization is the norm are
not high. Technical, psychological and economic barriers
stand in the way.

37   Fortunately, the first signs of the active utilization of
television are increasingly evident. The availability of
low-cost portable television recording equipment, and the
FCC requirement that all cable television systems provide
free "public access" time to an individual or organization
that requests it, are particularly significant developments
in this regard. Most large cities now have one or more
community video centers where the making of videotapes
by individuals, whether community organizers, artists, or
senior citizens, is encouraged and facilitated. And video
training and tape exchange programs are being organized
by schools, libraries, museums, church groups, and other
community institutions.[11]

38   As the time approaches when television will not only affect our spare time but our everyday activities, its significance as a communications medium will also change.
Television will no longer be solely a purveyor of consumer
products and social relaxation. More and more it will become a total communications environment, as complex
and variegated as the offices, schools, department stores
and neighborhood parks, where our social and economic
activities take place today. Increasingly important portions of our community life will occur on television,
through television, or as a result of television and the
other emerging electronic media.

39   The electronic community that will be created will at
times enhance community life as we know it today and at
times undermine it; more often than not it will compete

with it for our attention, our response, our resources and   *158*
values. As we have already seen, television today is capable of heightening our concern about safety in the streets;
tomorrow it may substitute for much of our need to use
these streets as community spaces. Television has already
started to short-circuit our schools and political institutions by creating a more palatable and accessible electronic medium for the consumption of educational and
political imagery. Tomorrow it may replace these institutions by interactive, multi-media linkages between central data banks and dispersed subscribers. And, as Martin
Pawley has recently suggested, it may lead to the further
privatization of both family life and national identity.[12]
The community of today may become a museum, a mere
archaeological referent for new electronically-supported
life-styles and social institutions.

40   The Luddites would, of course, prefer to shatter the electronic community before it is too late. The espousers of
technological utopia see its arrival as a new level of   *159*
human evolution. Both, however, recognize that the most
phenomenal aspect of the electronic community is its
developmental pace. In less than a quarter century its
foundations have been ubiquitously laid throughout our
society. In another quarter century it may become the
predominant environment in which we live.

41   In short, the challenge of ensuring that the electronic
community enhances the quality of life and encourages active and equitable involvement in this new community
sphere cannot be underemphasized. Our recent experience
with the physical and social environment in which we currently live has hopefully shattered our naiveté concerning
how a convivial yet complex living environment is
brought into being. The naiveté of the business firm that
claims it is only adding a new product or technology to the
marketplace; the naiveté of government that formulates
its policies in response to short-term political pressures
rather than long-range communications priorities; the
naiveté of the systems planner or engineer who believes
that a neatly-drawn blueprint can anticipate the needs of
a dynamic, pluralistic society; and the naiveté of the citizen who leaves decision-making about the future up to
others until that future impinges on his doorstep: these
are not adequate postures for the building of a new communications environment.

42　　　Fortunately, the deflation of naiveté has been one of the *159*
principal roles of the social critic. Clearly, the participation of such a critic will be crucial to the evolution of the electronic community, whose fabric remains to be determined by the numerous decisions that will guide and develop emerging communications technology. The problem that remains is that today's social critic may not be adequately prepared to take on this challenge.

43　　　Today's serious television critic generally falls in the tradition of the theater critic. He analyzes the thematic, aesthetic, or production values of a given event, that is, the single program or, at most, a series of programs. He is not likely to question the overall, environmental impact of television. By comparison, the journalistic critic may look beyond the values or effects of the latest TV special by examining the broader function of the media or by exposing the viewer (or reader) to the intricacies of judicial cases or federal regulations. But he is no more likely to probe into the subtle relationships that link technology, economics, and social change. Moreover, given the competitive tension between established media and emerging ones, he may be constrained in publicizing the advent of new communications services.[13]

44　　　Finally, the environmental critic, focusing on architecture, urban affairs, or the visual arts, may feel a distinct obligation to pursue the impact issues associated with high-rise projects, new highways and airports, or outdoor recreational programs. But ironically, television, because of the division of labor, has not been placed under his purview. *160* Nor is it clear that the environmental critic could easily contend with the environmental impact of television, even if given the opportunity. The fact that television may shape the physical form of cities, family life, leisure activities, and political and social attitudes does not correspond to the prevailing concept of environmental influences.

45　　　In short, there is need for a new kind of television critic, one who will explore the broader impact of tomorrow's television but who will also be familiar with the regulatory and production constraints that define the medium today. The role of this critic will be to follow technological developments as much as programming events; to ensure that the results of scientific research on the effects of television and of field and laboratory experiments with the

new technology are widely disseminated and understood; *160*
and to report on policy, business and educational delibera-
tions on how the new media can be utilized and developed.
Most importantly, it will be to stimulate us into deciding
what kind of electronic community we want to live in—
before technology decides for us.

FOOTNOTES *161*

¹ See, for example, "Toward a Market Success for CAI—An
Overview of the TICCIT Program," Mitre Corporation, (McLean,
Va., 1971).

² In most occasions when I have presented the concept of home
shopping to women's groups, the reaction has been negative. The
need to examine the product and "to get out of the house" were
among the reasons cited for hostility to the idea. I am not sure,
however, whether women who are formally employed would react
in the same way.

³ Subtle family arrangements regarding who has access to *163*
credit and who is responsible for the procurement of food and
household commodities could also be altered.

⁴ "Man-machine interaction" problems could arise with respect
to any of the home communications services. Many individuals
find manipulating the UHF dial on TV sets difficult or bother-
some; in comparison, the push-button consoles of tomorrow may
be much more difficult to operate. For example, a major problem
encountered in a recent home banking experiment was the difficulty individuals had in "talking to the computer" through push-
button telephones. Since the experiment took place in Seattle,
this problem presumably arose even in the case of technically-
trained aerospace workers. (See "New Inventions and a First-of-
a-Kind Service that Failed," *The New York Times,* December 29,
1973). For a home voting service to be effective it would have
to be mechanically manageable for a broad cross section of the
population.

⁵ Automobile travel is the single biggest consumer of energy in
our society as well as greatest source of air pollution, and com-
muting to work is in turn the most frequent reason why such
travel is undertaken.

⁶ I have projected the concept of decentralizing employment
sites to neighborhood "service parks" in "Telecommunications for
Future Human Settlements," *Ekistics,* Vol. 35, No. 211, June
1973, pp. 329–336. However, I also questioned the inevitability of
substituting telecommunications for transportation. In the past
whenever two offices, cities or continents have been linked by
communications technology, the effect has usually been an increase in travel rather than its reduction.

⁷ The fact that learning, shopping, and political participation
may also occur in the home of the future suggests that a new form
of household congestion will arise even if the traffic congestion
outside will have been eliminated. At a minimum, houses will

have to be redesigned to accommodate this multiplicity of ac- *162*
tivities, each of which may require a different kind of psychological and physical space.

[8] It is worth emphasizing that changes in television will be only
one factor in the tensions and demands with which national,
community and family institutions will have to cope in the future.
Nonetheless, tensions present due to other factors could be mag-
nified by the viewing patterns that tomorrow's television reinforces. For example, with respect to the family, the availability of
more sports, educational, hobby-related, women's and children's
programming may reinforce the separation between the adult
and child members of the family that is already apparent in some
families, according to Young and Willmont. Consequently, their
questions about the growth of non-family activities on children *163*
become more salient, given the television viewing patterns that
are being projected. Will tomorrow's children, ask Young and
Willmont, be "less subject to control at home, less bound by old
disciplines, more out of the thoughts of parents whose attentions
are engaged elsewhere, more emancipated, expected to become
little adults at an earlier age than they were . . . ?", *op. cit.,* p. 174.

[9] The Swiss communications scholar René Berger has referred
to these three dimensions of television as *micro, meso,* and *macro*
television. He presented these concepts at a conference on the future of television held at the Museum of Modern Art in New York
in January, 1974.

[10] These experiments are being supported not only by private
industry but also by the National Science Foundation, which has
recently funded several demonstration projects to examine the
use of two-way cable television in the delivery of government
services.

[11] Similarly, psychiatrists, architects, lawyers, and social
workers are experimenting with specialized uses of television
that pertain directly to professional practice. For an overview of
community and artistic innovations in video, see my previous
Aspen Institute Program on Communications and Society report,
The Video Implosion: Models for Reinventing Television, which
includes a bibliography of related publications.

[12] Martin Pawley, *The Private Future* (London: Thames and
Hudson, 1973).

[13] For example, the coverage accorded to cable television by the
broadcast media has not been exemplary when compared to the
attention placed on space, bio-medical, or computer technologies
or technology-related social issues such as automobile safety or
water pollution.

13

William Melody's work is the result of a study commissioned by ACT, Action for Children's Television.

This book was published by Yale University Press in New Haven in 1973.

From Children's Television: The Economics of Exploitation

WILLIAM MELODY

1   Advertising is a $4 billion-a-year industry, and more 59
than $400 million a year is spent to convince children to
buy. As noted in chapter 2, advertising agencies have become increasingly specialized, with time buyers and market researchers working to help budget these large sums
of money most efficiently. In children's advertising, specialized youth-marketing agencies are now probing youth
markets in great detail—going far beyond traditional ratings values—in developing detailed marketing and advertising placement strategies. *Mediascope* lists over fifteen
such agencies specializing in the youth market in New
York City alone. Robert B. Choate, chairman of the Council on Children, Media, and Merchandising, has recently
described the stated objectives and activities of these specialized youth-marketing agencies in testimony before the
U.S. Senate. He stated:

> Today, in motivational research houses across the country, chil-
> dren are being used in laboratory situations to formulate,
> analyze, polish, compare, and act in advertisements designed to
> make other children salesmen within the home. Armed with
> one-way mirrors, hidden tape recorders, and inobtrusive vid-
> eorecorders, professionally trained psychologists and experts in
> child behavior note every motion, phrase, and other indication of
> children's responses.[1]

2   The advertisements for children's audiences tend to be
loud, bright, and action-oriented, and are integrated as

From *Children's Television: The Economics of Exploitation* (New Haven: Yale Univ. Press, 1973), pp. 59–62, 141. Reprinted with permission.

closely as possible into the program in order to reduce the 59 probability of losing the child viewer's attention at the time of the advertising break. The traditional fade to black before commercials is often not used, so that the 60 child, who lacks the perceptual discriminatory power of the adult, will not recognize the difference between program and commercial. This process is facilitated, of course, if the program is designed and planned to merge with the advertisement. For example, animated advertisements are used with animated programs. Maximum impact is achieved by the ad when the child is deceived into believing that the promotion of certain products is simply part of his entertainment. Advises one youth-advertising specialist: "TV can be highly effective for the preschool group. With a good program and a good commercial, you can command 60 seconds of total interest—the child's eyes will remain riveted on the screen. But preschoolers are famous dial twisters. The program has to provide action and adventure, the way animated cartoons do, to involve the viewer, and so does the commercial."[2]

3   Children's advertising is also tailored to the market in other ways. The frequent repetition of ads reflects consideration of the relatively short memory spans of children.[3] The ads cater to peculiar needs, anxieties, and status concerns of children, exploiting peer group competitiveness to stimulate desires for the child to be the first, the best, the hero, the most popular, etc. For example, Helitzer and Heyel observe with regard to the status concerns of children:

Children, just like their parents, are highly status conscious. Commercials that appeal to the desire for stature in the child world are highly effective. Children respond to appeals that carry the promise of making them a better person, or smarter, or stronger, or someone that is growing up faster than the other kids. The infamous phrase, 'be the first kid on your block,' has 61 been subject to considerable criticism—both seriously and in not-so-funny jest. However, in the children's marketplace, this idea is a tested and proven persuader. Every child strives to get an edge on his contemporaries, to be first. One-upmanship is far from being an exclusively adult phenomenon.[4]

4   We have noted that the advertisers in the children's television market are heavily concentrated in such products as cereals, candies, snack foods, toys, and until recently, vitamins. This high degree of specialized marketing insures that the advertising on children's shows has

filtered down to specific products that have demonstrated 61
a unique capability for influencing the behavior of the
child viewer and the purchasing habits of his parents.

Both children's advertising practices and the types of
products advertised clearly indicate that the thrust of
children's advertising is toward an immediate impression
followed by a quick sale of the product. This, of course,
exploits the vulnerability of children's first impressions
and their immediate emotional responses. It has led to
substantial fluctuations in the demand for advertising
minutes, with the greatest demands preceding holiday occasions. It has created an unprecedented advertising boom
just before Christmas, when the combination of the holiday spirit and the normal techniques for children's advertising make child viewers and their parents especially
vulnerable, and therefore the probable effectiveness of
such advertising is at its peak.

The specialization of advertisers in children's television
also has become media specialization for some products
when some firms—for example, Nestle's Quik and some
toy companies—have come to spend extremely high pro- 62
portions of their total media advertising budget on children's television. The ability to reach a large number of
child viewers at a relatively low cost per thousand,
through "scatter plans" on network and local programs,
has stimulated an unusual degree of specialization in
these advertisers' media budgets. It clearly indicates substantial success in stimulating the child to serve successfully as a conduit to adults for purchase of the advertised
products.

NOTES 141

1. Robert B. Choate, "The Selling of the Child," testimony before Consumer Subcommittee of the Committee on Commerce,
United States Senate, Feb. 27, 1973, p. 5.
2. Helitzer and Heyel, *The Youth Market,* p. 218.
3. Ibid.
4. Ibid., pp. 181–82.

14

Susan Whittaker is program manager for WVFT–TV, the University of Florida station. Ron Whittaker is on the broadcasting faculty of the University of Florida.

This article appeared in the Spring 1976 issue of volume 20 of Journal of Broadcasting *on pages 177–84.*

Relative Effectiveness of Male and Female Newscasters

SUSAN WHITTAKER AND RON WHITTAKER

1   The broadcast industry has been dominated by males   *177* since the time of Marconi. This has been especially true in the area of broadcast news where employment practices have apparently been based on long-held but relatively untested assumptions about the relative lack of effectiveness and believability of female newscasters.[1] In 1971, Reuven Frank, President of NBC News, was quoted as saying, "I have the strong feeling that audiences are less prepared to accept news from a woman's voice than from a man's."[2]

2   Although such attitudes have been changing in recent years, employment figures on women working in broadcast news still point to a decided imbalance in the ratio of males and females in news departments. There has been very little research done in this area to either support or contradict the validity of these attitudes. Most of the studies that have been done have simply provided survey evidence that these attitudes generally exist on the part of broadcast news operations, and little experimental research has been done to discover whether broadcast audiences find women to be less believable, acceptable, or effective, compared to their male counterparts. These facts, together with the growing pressure on the broadcast industry from government agencies and citizen's groups   *178* over alleged discrimination by sex make research in this area especially significant.

3   Three previous studies were found which were related to this general research concern. In 1965, Kienzle, using a

survey approach, sent out questionnaires to newspaper editors and broadcast news directors in all 50 states to try to determine their attitudes about hiring women. In the broadcast area it was found that 73% of the news directors expressed a preference for hiring men in most newsroom jobs. This finding was supported by the fact that only 4.7% of the broadcast employees in the stations surveyed were women. When asked why they preferred to hire men, the reason most often given by the news directors was that men sound more "authoritative" while delivering the news.[3]

4   The result of these attitudes apparently was reflected by employment statistics gathered in a survey by the Radio and Television News Director's Association (RTNDA) in 1972, which followed in the wake of the National Organization for Women's (NOW) successful petition for amendment of section VI of various broadcast application forms. Effective February 4, 1972, FCC license renewal forms were amended to include discrimination based on sex as part of the Equal Employment Opportunity Program.[4]

5   Of the radio stations responding to the RTNDA study, 85% indicated they had no full-time females in their news departments. Only half of the responding television stations said they had full-time women on their news staffs. It was found, however, that practically all of the stations employing newswomen were using at least one woman regularly for on-air reporting.[5]

6   In 1972, Stone surveyed both news directors and a sample audience to see if, in fact, the attitudes of the news directors accurately reflected the attitudes of their broadcast audience. The researchers chose four available audience groups from contrasting generations and communities—university students and professors, fourth and fifth grade students in a small town, and the parents of the children.

7   Although TV news directors overwhelmingly thought their audiences would prefer a male in most reporting situations, at least half of every audience group surveyed said it did not matter to them what the sex of the newscaster was. In the area of "believability," TV news directors also overestimated the audience's preference for males. Although not more than one-fifth of any audience group said they would find a male more believable, over half of the news directors thought the majority of the audience would tend to believe a male newscaster more.[6] *179*

Studies such as this raise the question of whether news *179* directors in many cases are assuming biases among audiences that don't actually exist.

8   Three specific factors were selected for study for a male-female newscaster comparison: "effectiveness," "believability," and "acceptance." Although these three factors have the disadvantage of being inter-related with obvious subjective aspects, they were seen as representing three important criteria for judging the effect of a newscaster's presentation. Their selection was suggested, in part, by the results of a study by Orozco.[7]

9   Since the subjects of this study were to be as close as practical to "average adult listeners" and not news directors, the hypothesis was in keeping with the limited research findings on audience attitudes toward male and female newscasters; namely, that there would be no statistically significant difference between male and female newscasters in the areas of "effectiveness," "believability," or "acceptance."

10   A critical element in the design of a study such as this is to try to insure that a newscast delivery of controlled quality is presented for audience evaluation. Unequal performances reflecting different levels of competency or professional development could bias results along non-sexual lines. Thus, four network newscasters, two males and two females, were chosen on the basis of similar professional competency and stature. They were: Sylvia Chase (CBS News), Harvey Hauptman (WCBS News Radio), Robert Glenn (WCBS News Radio) and Sharron Lovejoy (CBS News). The selection of two newscasters of each sex reduced the chances of preference resting on such things as personality, reading style, etc. Each of the four recorded an audio tape which contained two versions of a newscast in "network style." Each newscast contained two categories of stories: factual and ficticious. Although the two versions of factual stories differed only in written style (and not in factual content), the fictitious stories were selected because they lent themselves to the alteration of central facts. The newscasts will be discussed in more detail below.

11   The subjects (Ss) used as sample audiences in the study were primarily members of various adult evening classes at a community college. However, in order to have representation from the over 65 age group, a small number of Ss

were added who were members of the Gainesville, Florida *179* Older Americans' Council. This sample audience totaled *180* 174 men and women who represented a rather broad age and socio-economic distribution. Of the total sample of 87 men and 87 women, 28% were general professional and technical workers; 27% were full-time students; 8% were elementary and secondary school teachers; 8% were clerical and kindred workers; 6% were in sales; 6% were housewives; 5% were in administrative positions; and about 12% represented other occupational categories. The range of ages for the sample was from 16 to 75, with over 75% of the subjects falling between the ages of 18 and 34.

12   The 174 subjects were tested in eight groups of 20 to 25 each. Each of the eight audience groups heard two newscasts; one delivered by a male and one delivered by a female newscaster. This introduced two major elements to be considered: the sex of the newscaster and the playback order of the newscasts. Although the sex of the newscaster is an obvious variable, the importance of controlling playback order may not be readily evident. The concern here was the effect of recency and primacy; would the Ss tend to recall or possibly believe more of what they heard last (recency) or would the first newscast make more of an impression (primacy).

13   After hearing the tapes, each of the eight subject groups was asked to fill out two questionnaires. The first was a multiple-choice instrument which included "right answers" for both newscast versions, along with some plausible wrong answers that would suggest that the subject couldn't recall information from either newscast. Since "none of the above" responses were not offered, the questionnaire represented a forced-choice situation with subjects instructed to select the answer which they *believed* to be correct. Since each of these stories was fictitious, the influence of prior knowledge was also controlled.

14   The second questionnaire was administered after the first one was collected to avoid "checking back" or changing answers for the sake of consistency. This questionnaire contained multiple choice and open-ended questions which called for subjective evaluations of each newscaster. If a subject recognized the voice of a particular newscaster, or even mistakenly identified a newscaster as someone he was familiar with, both of his questionnaires were deleted from the sample. This was to guard against the possibility that prior knowledge or feelings about a newscaster would

influence the evaluation. To offset a possible bias being in-   *180*
troduced by the experimenters, both a male and a female
test administrator were present at the test sessions, and
each played an equal part in explaining and administer-
ing the tests.

The experimental materials consisted of eight, four-   *181*
minute tape recorded newscasts. To make them appear to
be recordings of bona-fide newscasts, a standard broadcast
news format was used. Anglo-Saxon names were selected
in order to eliminate the possibility of ethnic bias. The stations' call letters, WKLY and WSLA, were also fictitious.
The newscasts were written in standard broadcast style,
but each story was written in two ways to represent individual style differences which would be associated with
different stations and newscasters.

The factual stories in the newscasts were based on the
following items: (1) aid to public schools; (2) Watergate
tapes; (3) salary hike for military doctors; (4) grain re-
serves; and (5) national health insurance. The important
key to the experiment, however, rested on three fictitious
stories. These were news stories related to: (1) a Florida
Supreme Court decision; (2) a local judge's ruling on a case
involving compensation payments to an injured athlete;
and (3) a Missouri bank robbery.

Whereas the factual stories were used to test retention,
the fictitious stories were included to determine relative
believability. For purposes of identification, the newscasts
were referred to as version A and version B. Both versions
opened and closed with the same basic stories. Each version also contained a "unique story," which provided information on relative recall. The remaining stories, which

TABLE I Playback Order

Group	1st position	2nd position
1	M-1-A	F-1-B
2	F-1-B	M-1-A
3	M-1-B	F-1-A
4	F-1-A	M-1-B
5	M-2-A	F-2-B
6	F-2-B	M-2-A
7	M-2-B	F-2-F
8	F-2-A	M-2-B

NOTE: F-1 and F-2 = female newscasters while M-1 and M-2 = male newscasters. The A and B indicate the version of the newscast.

did not appear in the same sequence in the A and B version, were basically common to each newscast. These stories had crucial fact discrepancies which were designed to significantly change the basic meaning, or "outcome," of the stories.[8] Each of the four newscasters recorded both A and B versions of the newscast and they were played back to the subject groups in the order shown in Table I.

18. The data from the two questionnaires were analyzed using cross-tabulations and chi square (χ^2) tests of independence through the Statistical Package for the Social Sciences (SPSS) computer program. The following briefly summarizes the findings of the study.

19. *Behavioral Believability* was checked by cross-tabulations between "right answers" on questionnaire one and the sex of the newscasters. No significant difference in relative belief between the male and female newscasters was found (p < .50).

20. *Verbalized Believability* was determined by the second questionnaire. There was no significant difference in the Ss stated response to which newscaster they thought was the more believable (p < .90).

21. *Acceptance* was determined by responses on the second questionnaire. There was no significant difference in the Ss acceptance of the male and female newscasters (p < .90). When Ss were analyzed separately according to their sex, there was still no significant difference in the acceptance responses for the male Ss (p < .50) or for the female Ss (p < .30).

22. *Effectiveness* was measured by a comparison of the retention rate on the "unique stories" when read by the male and female announcers. Once again the hypothesis was supported by the lack of a statistically reliable difference in the retention of these stories (p < .10).

23. *Preference* in the sex of a newscaster by Ss was approached by a question in the second questionnaire which asked which of the two newscasters the S would prefer to listen to. Compared on the basis of sex, there was no statistically reliable difference (p. < .80). A cross-tabulation of preference by Ss age indicated that there was no significant difference between the responses of the under 33 age group and the over 33 Ss (p < .80).

24. *Playback Order* of the newscast versions was found to influence believability. This primacy effect was demonstrated in both questionnaires. In questionnaire one,

59.7% of S responses favored the believability of the first *182*
newscaster, regardless of sex, compared to about 19% *183*
which favored the second newscast and 20% which resulted in no preference. In questionnaire two, 50.6% of Ss
stated a preference for the first newscaster, 31% preferred
the second newscaster, and 18.4% had no preference.

25   *Limitations:* Since subjects in this study constituted a
"captive audience" and were not necessarily in a "normal"
listening situation, the conditions under which the newscasts were evaluated could be considered as "unreal."
Slightly offsetting this limitation was the fact that considerable effort was made to present the newscasts as "real
recordings" which had been made off of the air a short
time before the study.

26   Based on an analysis of two types of questionnaires used
with a broad sample of 1974 subjects, the hypothesis that
there would not be a statistically significant difference in
the perceived acceptance, believability, or effectiveness
between two professional male newscasters and two professional female newscasters was supported.

27   Although there were no differences based on sex, it was
found that Ss tended to believe the first newscast they
heard, regardless of its content or the newscaster involved.
Perceived newscaster effectiveness or acceptance were not
found to be related to newscast order.

NOTES

[1]This study was funded by a research grant from the National
Association of Broadcasters.

[2]"The New Breed," *Newsweek* (August 30, 1971), pp. 62–63.

[3]Kathleen Johanna Kienzle, "A Study of the Employment Opportunities for Women in Broadcast News" (unpublished Master's
thesis, Ohio State University, 1965).

[4]32 FCC 2nd 708; 32 FCC 2d 831. Section VI of FCC forms 301,
303, 309, 311, 314, 315, 340, and 342 were amended to include
women. Prior to February 4, 1972 this section provided that licenses shall file equal employment opportunity programs designed to provide equal employment opportunities for Negroes,
Orientals, American Indians, and Spanish Surnamed Americans.
The Commission also added the Equal Employment Program
filing requirement to Commission rules 73.125, 73.301, 73.599,
73.680, and 73.793.

[5]Vernon Stone, "Radio and Television News Directors and Operations: An RTNDA Survey," Research report presented at the
International Conference of the RTNDA, Nassau, Bahamas, Nov.
27 to Dec. 2, 1972.

[6]Vernon Stone, Jill Geisler and Barbara Dell, "Attitudes *184* Toward Television Newswomen," paper presented to joint meeting of the Minorities and Communication Division and Radio and Television Division, Association for Education in Journalism, Southern Illinois University, Carbondale, August, 1972.

[7]Eloy Orozco, "The Relative Credibility of Discrepant Radio Newscasts as a Function of Announcer Professionalism," (unpublished Master's thesis, University of Florida, 1973).

[8]Copies of the newscasts and questionnaires used in this study are available from Susan Whittaker, WUFT, 311 STA Bldg., University of Florida, Gainesville, FL., 32611.

15

Horace Newcomb, former television critic for the Baltimore Sun, *teaches American Studies at the University of Maryland, Baltimore County.*

This book was published by Doubleday and Company in Garden City, New York, in 1974.

From TV: The Most Popular Art
HORACE NEWCOMB

1   . . . Sports, as games involving human beings, embody *192* almost every aspect of popular entertainment. The idea of conflict is central. Legitimate violence is present in varying degrees in all athletic contests. Ultimately the sporting event as game focuses on the aspect of problem-solving, that pattern we have seen in all the entertaining forms of the popular arts. But unlike the socially oriented problems that form the content of most television programming, the sports game is much more like combat. Instead of value conflicts, generational differences, and human interaction, we have the basic tests of skill and strength. To maneuver the team down the field without losing the ball, to control play so that the opposing team achieves no runs for its hits, to loop the ball into the basket as the last buzzer sounds—these are the conflicts that have thrilled vast numbers of fans in the most traditional ways and that thrill millions more on television.

2   Sport has never served as mere entertainment in American culture. From Little League through high school, sports activities have been cited as a means of self-identification for participants. For parents, supporters, cheerleaders, and bands, sports frequently serve as the center for community activity. These identifications expand into the local semipro teams and the regional professional organizations, and the whole structure of classes, regions, and leagues serves as a cultural framework. For a young male, growing up in New York meant for many

years a symbiotic relationship with one of the three major 192 baseball teams located there. The Yankees, the Giants 193 and the Dodgers took on symbolic, mythic proportions, and around the teams was built the whole mystique of gathering autographs, monitoring averages, and predicting success at the league or the "world" level. For millions of other fans far away from such centers of pure worship the teams were venerated via newspapers and radio, but always with the knowledge that the "home team" was a surrogate, embodying an ideal expressed far away in the elegant temples of competition. The idea that two American baseball teams were competing each year for the "world" championship title was a unifying concept. Sports offered cohesion and identity, the mythic model.

3   Because of the powerful visibility of the components of such a model, it has always been used as far more than either entertainment or cultural unifier. It is quickly transformed into a vehicle for cultural values, and we translate the playing field into an image for "real life." The virtues of practice, hard work, dedication, desire, competitive spirit, fair play, "good sportsmanship," and a host of other commodities are pointed out to generation after generation of young people. The language of the games, the initiations into rituals, the formalities of winning, are transformed into mystical moments. Sport is hallowed as holy text.

4   On the individual level all these virtues are located in the person and spirit of the sports hero. At the functional level he is simply a player who performs certain actions better than his colleagues and opponents, and is very much like the newscaster as conveyor of information. Because of his skill, however, he, too, becomes quickly translated into metaphor. Having accepted all the values associated with sport, and having practiced them with the 194 rigor of any devotee, he attests to their truth. So we point to the lives of Lou Gehrig, Babe Ruth, Mickey Mantle, George Halas, Bart Starr, or John Unitas and scores of other heroes as examples of what is possible in America. If the hero has overcome a physical handicap in order to reach his position, or if he plays only at the cost of great physical pain, then the process of sports becomes a metaphor for healing. If he has risen from economic hardship, the sport becomes the route for social mobility. If he represents an ethnic group that is generally oppressed,

then sports make obvious the equality of all Americans. If *194*
he becomes a millionaire, then sport is seen as a royal road
to material success. So we translate the biographies of the
heroes into children's books, into movies and television
specials for adults. We are entertained by the narrative of
their lives. We record the words they leave with us upon
retirement as definitions of what it is to be American, and
their humility on such occasions is marked down as
another positive character trait.

5   The parallels between such games and their heroes and
the structures and heroes of television are clear. Those fictional shows demonstrate the ability to solve problems by
working within a defined set of values. A highly similar
set of values is traditionally associated with sports, and
those who practice them win. The sports heroes, then, are
very conscious of their role as public figure and have generally behaved in a way that corresponds to the actions of
our fictional models. When they have visited hospitals
filled with handicapped children, they have done so con-
sciously, as representatives of virtuous kindness. It is not
so much that they teach us these values in the same manner as the fictional fathers, but that they stand as models
of those who have been taught. The traditional image of *195*
the athlete as somewhat less than bright works here, and
we see the sports hero accepting, without question, the obvious wisdom of the culture.

6   The pervasive power of television has changed much of
this traditional function for sports and sports heroes. With
television the regional or local identity of teams is destroyed. The man sitting in Arlington, Texas, can watch
and enjoy the successes of the Los Angeles Dodgers with
the same degree of interest as the man sitting in Brooklyn.
When Arlington becomes the home of the former
Washington Senators, the fan in Washington has the
same opportunity. In any case it is likely that none of
them can experience the degree of ecstasy once possible in
Ebbets Field. The talk of sports is filled with strange
names, and there is something bizarre about the massive
football machine from tiny Green Bay, Wisconsin, mash-
ing into submission its opponents from Chicago or
Philadelphia. Collegiate sports become the supply centers
for the professional camps, become professionally oriented
in their own activities. School spirit remains, but as an ad-
junct to the competition for the number one position in the

national polls, and the players on these teams are rated in *195* terms of professional draft choices rather than as campus heroes.

7　　The mystique of sport is gone, and as the pervasive eye of television turns onto the private lives of the players, the mystique of the sports hero goes, too. What are we to make of news items about our sports figures that do not appear on the sports page or in the sports segment of the evening news? Caught in such a media cross fire, fans and players alike are unable to respond consistently. The sports figure becomes a superstar, and as such may be unwilling to sac- *196* rifice his private life for the traditional image imbedded in the culture, defined by an almost fictional regard for the heroic position. The fans, on the other hand, are unwilling to see their heroes as anything less than mythic. The resulting conflicts create new attitudes toward sports and sports figures.

8　　What sort of taboo is violated when baseball players actually resort to a strike in order to get more money, better benefits? Something very deep is touched as we watch fans turn against the players to side with the powerful big-business operation of the management. Perhaps it is simply a feeling that the players are all rich enough. Or perhaps it indicates that we do not wish to admit that these players, these "characters," in the drama of sport have real and apparently self-serving needs.

. . .

9　　When viewers could actually see black athletes in *197* the 1968 Olympics standing with clenched fists and bowed heads during the playing of the national anthem, many were outraged. It was the sight as much as the idea, and the knowledge that millions of viewers were seeing the same act was annoying and frightening. It was a bad image.

10　　It was not bad because of its social criticism or because it reflected an individual choice. It was bad because it was *198* not in the script, it violated our expectations. The result is a clash of symbolic gestures. The athlete as symbol of accepted values cannot also be the symbol of revolution— especially not in the televised version of the event.

11　　There is a structure imposed on the raw event of sports activity, part of which is inherent in the idea of contest. Much more comes, however, from television's insistence on creating the dramatic frame within which the event occurs. As a result, the role of the sports announcer, many of

whom are former sports stars, takes on increasing impor- *198*
tance. The audience is told what to see and is told what it
has just seen. Each movement and series of actions is in-
terpreted by the announcers and commentators. Even before the games we are told what to look for. We are shown
historical sequences in which the teams demonstrated, in
past games, their techniques and specialties. After the
game we are treated to analysis of what has happened,
usually in the larger context of what the event will mean
in the larger structure of competition for postseason
prizes, bowls, ratings, series, and so on.

12 Central to this process is the role of the television
director. He must decide what we actually see, and the
cameras move skillfully to capture for us the moments
and movements of greatest importance. It is here that
the developing technology of television has played its
largest part, with the invention and perfection of instant
replay. Now we can see a single moment over and over; the
commentators can refine their remarks accordingly. We
can see in split screen and slow motion more of the action
than we thought possible only a few years before, and we
become increasingly sophisticated in our understanding of *199*
the skills involved in sports. As this happens, the narrative structures become more and more important. Now, in
the new super stadiums being built in many large cities,
huge television screens are being designed as part of the
necessary equipment. The fans who attend the games will
be treated to the same comforts of perception available to
the home audience. Action and instant replay are telecast
to the fans in the seats by closed circuit. This is not because they cannot see the live action on the field or court
before them. Rather it is provided so that they can see it in
certain ways and see it again. During time-outs and half-
time breaks the fans are offered commercials for the are-
na's own facilities and for upcoming events. The screens
also provide cartoon and film "entertainment," fireworks
and waving flags during the playing of the national anthem, and they explode into riotous color when the home
team scores. Such comforts have to do with the elements of
narrative and frame, and though part of this structure
comes from the games themselves, more of it comes from
our knowledge of the television version of those games.
That is the version that includes advertisement, directed
viewing of events, and the technological advantages of repeated viewing of action.

16

James Baldwin is a novelist and essayist. His first novel, Go Tell It on the Mountain, *deals with the coming of age of a young black man in Harlem. This article was published in the Spring 1960 issue of* Daedalus, *volume 89, on pages 373–76.*

Mass Culture and the Creative Artist
JAMES BALDWIN

373

1   Someone once said to me that the people in general cannot bear very much reality. He meant by this that they prefer fantasy to a truthful re-creation of their experience. The Italians, for example, during the time that De Sica and Rossellini were revitalizing the Italian cinema industry, showed a marked preference for Rita Hayworth vehicles; the world in which she moved across the screen was like a fairy tale, whereas the world De Sica was describing was one with which they were only too familiar. (And it can be suggested perhaps that the Americans who stood in line for *Shoe Shine* and *Open City* were also responding to images which they found exotic, to a reality by which they were not threatened. What passes for the appreciation of serious effort in this country is very often nothing more than an inability to take anything very seriously.)

2   Now, of course the people cannot bear very much reality, if by this one means their ability to respond to high intellectual or artistic endeavor. I have never in the least understood why they should be expected to. There is a division of labor in the world—as I see it—and the people have quite enough reality to bear, simply getting through their lives, raising their children, dealing with the eternal conundrums of birth, taxes, and death. They do not do this with all the wisdom, foresight, or charity one might wish; nevertheless, this is what they are always doing and it is what the writer is always describing. There is literally nothing else to describe. This effort at description is itself extraordinarily arduous, and those who are driven to

From *Daedalus,* 89, no. 2 (Spring 1960), 373–76. Reprinted by permission of Daedalus, the Journal of the American Academy of Arts and Sciences, Boston, Massachusetts.

make this effort are by virtue of this fact somewhat re- *373*
moved from the people. It happens, by no means infrequently, that the people hound or stone them to death.
They then build statues to them, which does not mean that *374*
the next artist will have it any easier.

3 I am not sure that the cultural level of the people is subject to a steady rise: in fact, quite unpredictable things
happen when the bulk of the population attains what we
think of as a high cultural level, i.e., pre-World War II
Germany, or present-day Sweden. And this, I think, is because the effort of a Schönberg or a Picasso (or a William
Faulkner or an Albert Camus) has nothing to do, at bottom, with physical comfort, or indeed with comfort of any
other kind. But the aim of the people who rise to this high
cultural level—who rise, that is, into the middle class—is
precisely for the body and the mind. The artistic objects by
which they are surrounded cannot possibly fulfill their
original function of disturbing the peace—which is still
the only method by which the mind can be improved—
they bear witness instead to the attainment of a certain
level of economic stability and a certain thin measure of
sophistication. But art and ideas come out of the passion
and torment of experience; it is impossible to have a real
relationship to the first if one's aim is to be protected from
the second.

4 We cannot possibly expect, and should not desire, that
the great bulk of the populace embark on a mental and
spiritual voyage for which very few people are equipped
and which even fewer have survived. They have, after all,
their indispensable work to do, even as you and I. What we
are distressed about, and should be, when we speak of the
state of mass culture in this country, is the overwhelming
torpor and bewilderment of the people. The people who
run the mass media are not all villains and they are not all
cowards—though I agree, I must say, with Dwight Mac-
donald's forceful suggestion that many of them are not
very bright. (Why should they be? They, too, have risen
from the streets to a high level of cultural attainment.
They, too, are positively afflicted by the world's highest
standard of living and what is probably the world's most
bewilderingly empty way of life.) But even those who are
bright are handicapped by their audience: I am less ap-
palled by the fact that *Gunsmoke* is produced than I am by
the fact that so many people want to see it. In the same
way, I must add, that a thrill of terror runs through me

when I hear that the favorite author of our President is Zane Grey.

5 But one must make a living. The people who run the mass media and those who consume it are really in the same boat. They must continue to produce things they do not really admire, still less, love, in order to continue buy- ing things they do not really want, still less, need. If we were dealing only with fintails, two-tone cars, or programs like *Gunsmoke,* the situation would not be so grave. The trouble is that serious things are handled (and received) with the same essential lack of seriousness.

6 For example: neither *The Bridge On the River Kwai* nor *The Defiant Ones,* two definitely superior movies, can really be called serious. They are extraordinarily interesting and deft: but their principal effort is to keep the audience at a safe remove from the experience which these films are not therefore really prepared to convey. The kind of madness sketched in *Kwai* is far more dangerous and widespread than the movie would have us believe. As for *The Defiant Ones,* its suggestion that Negroes and whites can learn to love each other if they are only chained together long enough runs so madly counter to the facts that it must be dismissed as one of the latest, and sickest, of the liberal fantasies, even if one does not quarrel with the notion that love on such terms is desirable. These movies are designed not to trouble, but to reassure; they do not reflect reality, they merely rearrange its elements into something we can bear. They also weaken our ability to deal with the world as it is, ourselves as we are.

7 What the mass culture really reflects (as is the case with a "serious" play like *J.B.*) is the American bewilderment in the face of the world we live in. We do not seem to want to know that we are *in* the world, that we are subject to the same catastrophes, vices, joys, and follies which have baffled and afflicted mankind for ages. And this has everything to do, of course, with what was expected of America: which expectation, so generally disappointed, reveals something we do not want to know about sad human nature, reveals something we do not want to know about the intricacies and inequities of any social structure, reveals, in sum, something we do not want to know about ourselves. The American way of life has failed—to make people happier or to make them better. We do not want to admit this, and we do not admit it. We persist in believing that the empty and criminal among our children are the

result of some miscalculation in the formula (which can be *375*
corrected), that the bottomless and aimless hostility which
makes our cities among the most dangerous in the world is
created, and felt, by a handful of aberrants, that the lack,
yawning everywhere in this country, of passionate convic-
tion, of personal authority, proves only our rather appealing tendency to be gregarious and democratic. We are very
cruelly trapped between what we would like to be, and *376*
what we actually are. And we cannot possibly become
what we would like to be until we are willing to ask ourselves just why the lives we lead on this continent are
mainly so empty, so tame and so ugly.

8   This is a job for the creative artist—who does not really
have much to do with mass culture, no matter how many
of us may be interviewed on TV. Perhaps life is not the
black, unutterably beautiful, mysterious, and lonely thing
the creative artist tends to think of it as being; but it is
certainly not the sunlit playpen in which so many Americans lose first their identities and then their minds.

9   I feel very strongly, though, that this amorphous people
are in desperate search for something which will help
them to re-establish their connection with themselves,
and with one another. This can only begin to happen as
the truth begins to be told. We are in the middle of an
immense metamorphosis here, a metamorphosis which
will, it is devoutly to be hoped, rob us of our myths and
give us our history, which will destroy our attitudes and
give us back our personalities. The mass culture, in the
meantime, can only reflect our chaos: and perhaps we had
better remember that this chaos contains life—and a
great transforming energy.

17

Tony Schwartz, who had a regular radio program on WNYC in New York City, has put together over five thousand radio and television commercials, among them twenty-five for Carter's 1976 Presidential campaign.

This book was published by Doubleday and Company in Garden City, New York, in 1973.

From The Responsive Chord
TONY SCHWARTZ

1

1   It is difficult to imagine a person who watched Jack Ruby *1* shoot Lee Harvey Oswald before live television cameras, turning to his wife or children and commenting, "That was an extraordinary *message* we just received." Yet someone analyzing Oswald's televised assassination, from a communication point of view, will be encumbered by such terms as senders, receivers, channels, and messages. In talking about communication, especially mass-media communication, we often find ourselves using terms or analytical models that distort or oversimplify the process. The vocabulary of communication theory consistently fails as a tool for analyzing the mass-media process.

2

2   It is not just that we lack adequate terms for describing communication. Our understanding of the communication process is hindered by deep-rooted perceptual and cognitive biases. We believe that communication takes place across large spaces, over a period of time, and primarily through one symbolic mode (words). Though the exchange of verbal messages (typically, written messages) constitutes only a small percentage of human communication, we generalize this one mode as the basis on which all *2* communication is structured. This bias is founded, in part, on Western society's problems in communicating during the five-hundred-year period prior to the development of electronic media, when print was the dominant means of non-face-to-face communication. The movement or transportation of messages across considerable distances in the

briefest period of time was the central and overriding 2
communication problem. Most of our communication
theories today are still structured around this issue.

3 A classic transportation model of the communication
process first discusses the source of communication, or the
sender. A sender experiences and formulates "meaning"
through his encounters with other people and objects in
his world. He codes this meaning into a symbolic form—
typically, words. He is now ready to send a message, but
first he must choose a way of packaging his message for
the trip. Writing words on paper could serve as the package, or transmitter, in such a model. Next the sender
chooses a channel of communication, such as a letter,
newspaper, pamphlet, or book. A channel of communication is often low in efficiency. It requires time to move information across a given space. It may also introduce noise
into the message. Newspapers can be censored; pamphlets
are written in various *styles,* and this may alter the meaning a sender intended to put into his words; and letters
may be damaged in transit.

4 At the other end of a communication channel is a re- 3
ceiver. He must decode the symbolic forms in the message,
assess the damage produced by noise in the channel, and
match the "meanings" in the message against his understanding of the world, in order to comprehend the meaning
intended by the sender. Communication may be said to
take place when the two "meanings" are alike, or to the
extent that they match.

5 The transportation model is not without value. It is a
useful guide in analyzing some forms of communication in
our society, and it is a good model for illustrating the
communication problems in Western society during the
print era. Before electricity, the available channels of
communication, such as drums, smoke signals, reflecting
mirrors, cannon shots, and lantern signals, were subject to
severe limitations in the physical environment. Cloudy
weather, darkness, trees, and mountains interfered with
vision. Animal sounds, wind, thunder, canyons, etc., interfered with auditory signals. Messages had to be formulated according to a rigidly precise code and were limited

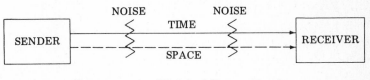

Transportation Model of Communication

to only the most crucial data—owing to the inefficiency of *3*
the transportation channel. "Getting the message across"
was the consummate problem. A military leader who
wanted to signal his allies through a system of pennants
by day or torches by night had to concern himself with
rain or wind extinguishing a torch or blowing over a pen-
nant, and thereby communicating the wrong battle instructions. The problem was compounded when a message
was to be sent over a long distance. Napoleon established a
network of 224 line-of-sight semaphore stations, spanning
over 1,000 miles. The coded message had to be repeated
accurately at each station for a correct message to get
through. The chance of an error was quite high. In addition, these vehicles for transporting messages were
single-channel systems. They lacked the multichannel
reinforcement of most face-to-face interactions (i.e., in
face-to-face encounters we see and hear a person simultaneously; both channels are likely to support the mean- *4*
ing he intends to communicate).

6   As Western culture developed more complex economic
and social structures, the quick and accurate movement of
information became more critical. Wars were often prolonged, and sometimes initiated, because of a breakdown
in the transportation of messages. Similarly, fortunes
were made and lost when one party gained a slight advantage in the time required to send and receive messages
across an ocean or continent. An English merchant who
discovered that the cotton crop in America was highly successful could undercut his competitors if he alone pos-
sessed this information.

7   As a result of these transportation problems, we came to
understand communication as the movement of information across space, over a period of time. We generalized the
problem area of communication as synonymous with the
process itself. A transportation theory of communication is
useful when the *movement* of information is a central
problem, but such issues are only a small area in the total
communication process.

8   When someone is overloaded with information, the
transportation theory ceases to be meaningful. In addition, transportation theory looks at communication from a
"message" point of view. It asks: How are messages
created? How do they move? How are they received? Most
human communication, however, involves the exchange of

so much information at any moment that it cannot be iso- *4*
lated as message units. The transportation theory is thus
inadequate in describing the human learning process, or
accounting for the dissemination and flow of information
in our society. Information flow is a much more complex
process than the mere transportation of messages.

9   The transportation theory of communication is the basis
of many formal models of communication as well as our
everyday conception of "sending messages." The way we
use a postal service to send a letter comes very close to our
commonplace analogy for all communication. We assume
that communication is difficult to achieve, and that a message encounters resistance at each step along the way.
This commonplace conception of communication is so basic   *5*
to our thinking that we have used the new electronic
media almost exclusively as message-sending devices. In
my childhood, for example, the telephone was used as a
surrogate for a telegram or letter, not as a new medium. If
our family was planning to visit relatives in New Jersey,
my mother would call long distance from New York to
New Jersey to tell them when we expected to arrive. Her
messages were short, loudly spoken, and to the point. She
used the phone as a vehicle for sending a message across a
space. Even when the line between New York and New
Jersey was clear, she spoke louder than necessary—
conscious of the space between them and using the phone
as if it were a tunnel through a chasm. She believed that
the phone, like a letter, was a low-efficiency vehicle for
communicating, and she was pushing to get her message
across. Today, my daughter often calls her friends to exchange giggles. They relate bits of news, giggle back and   *6*
forth a few minutes, then say goodbye. My daughter accepts the telephone as a communication system with no
resistance and no transformation. Communication for her
is what happens when you use a telephone, not something
that may occur if your message gets through.

10   Our misconception of communication as transportation
interacts with another deep-rooted bias: the identification
of print with "meaning." Only a tiny fraction of all communication takes place through print (the U.S. national
average for book purchases is .3 book per year, and this
represents an all-time high in Western culture), yet it
remains an idealized form of communicating the most
important information: "I'll believe that when I see it in

writing." More significant, print has helped foster a ⁶ narrow conception of communication that accepts perceptual information as meaningful only to the extent that it conforms to the patterning inherent in print communication. One cannot approach a viable theory of communication until he exorcises the "spirit of print" that has controlled our terms for learning, understanding, and communicating.

11   Print has dominated our non-face-to-face communications environment for the past five hundred years. During this period, the information most valued by Western societies was communicated in a fixed form, with words following one after another, left to right, on lines that proceeded down a page. All preserved knowledge, as well as those pieces of information that achieved high status throughout the society (e.g., laws) were recorded in print. The linear process, by which information was translated into print, took on a status unto itself. As a result, the linear process came to be valued in many areas of people's lives. Our language, for example, shows a marked dependence on linearity in the terms we use for clear thinking and proper behavior. A child growing up in our culture is taught to "toe the line ... keep in line ... walk the ⁷ straight and narrow ... don't make waves." Similarly, he is told that a good student is one who "follows a clear line of thought." And if someone really understands another person, we say he can "read him like a book." Our logic has been the logic of print, where one idea follows another. "Circular reasoning" is synonymous with unacceptable logic. And we know that you never accomplish anything by "running around in circles."

12   The linearity in our language is accompanied by a strong dependence on visual analogies to represent truth, knowledge, and understanding. Do you *see* what I mean? A really bright person—i.e. someone with hindsight, foresight, and insight—will see eye to eye with me. But a dull person, one who hasn't seen the light, won't agree with my point of view. Why, it's as clear as ABC.

13   If seeing was believing, listening and speaking were undependable elements in the communication process. It was a common view that children should be seen and not heard. If you played it by ear, you were not very sure of yourself. And to be recognized as a trained musician, you

had to be able to read a score and write notes on paper. In 7
the courtroom, unreliable evidence, whether of a written
or spoken variety, may be discarded on the grounds that it
is "hearsay." Similarly, a scholar could look back on history, and a prophet could see into the future; but if someone crudely imitated another performer, we said he was a
weak echo or that he was mouthing something that had
been done better. Even the early radio operators indicated
that they were receiving a strong signal by saying, "Read
you loud and clear."

Even after we recognize the predominance of linear
analogies in our language, it becomes important only
when we understand that many non-linear patterns in our
present communication structure are described and
analyzed as linear patterns. Our linear bias also prevents
us from understanding preliterate auditory cultures. Few
readers of the passage in Genesis, "In the beginning was 8
the Word," recognize that it refers to a spoken word. Jesus
said, "It is written but I say unto you" to assert a new
world order based on his spoken words. Linearity and a
strong visual orientation are not endemic to all cultures. A
society that depends on auditory communication for the
exchange of messages will organize their "world" in a very
different way from our own. Space, time, the concept of
self, etc., take on very different meanings when auditory
patterns replace a linear, visual orientation.

. . .

In many ways, we are today experiencing a return to an
auditory-based communications environment. However,
lacking the terms to describe this shift, as well as a perceptual orientation to recognize it, we often fail to understand what is happening. If one keeps his ears to the wall, 9
he will begin to hear this new base echoed in the language
of the young. Here, people in agreement are "on the same
wavelength" or "on the same frequency." A person learns
by "getting around." Someone who "plays it by ear" is open
to new possibilities that may emerge in a situation. Truth
is conveyed by "telling it like it is." An individual who
learns how to behave properly in a situation "tunes in on
what's happening." And effective communication "strikes
a responsive chord."

Our social organization clearly reflects the shift from a
predominantly linear to an acoustic base in communication structure. Lines are disintegrating all around us. The

NBC "Today" show has a one-handed clock that indicates   9
minutes past the hour. Since the program is viewed simultaneously in different time zones, it makes sense to tell the
audience, "It's ten minutes past the hour" and assume that
they know which hour, rather than to state, "It's ten past   10
eight in the Eastern Standard zone, ten past seven in the
Central Standard zone," etc. This sharing of information
across time zones demonstrates how time *lines* have lost
significance. Indeed, two western states have petitioned to
change their time zone because they receive most television programming from stations in border states with a
different time zone. Also, Congress is considering a redis-
tricting of congressional zones to match media districts.
Similarly, instantaneous information has reduced the
need for datelines in newspapers. One of the corner-
stone assumptions in the transportation theory of
communication—that a period of time is required for information to move across space—has been undermined by
the near-instantaneous speed of electronic communication.

17   The line, as a means of social organization, is being replaced by acoustic space principles. The "Party line" no
longer explains patterns of voting behavior. The railroad   11
line no longer explains transportation patterns in our society. Even the lines or rows that organized seating patterns in schools, churches, and theaters are giving way to
new patterns. Theater-in-the-round has returned. Conference tables and classroom desks are organized in circular
patterns. And recently, the governor of a large eastern
state defined his role as "Trying to *tune* government to the
needs of citizens."

18   Television and film, as well as radio, tapes, and records,
have contributed to a radical transformation in our perception of the world—from a visual, print base to an auditory base. Each of these media conditions the brain to
receive and process all information in the same way it has   12
always processed information received via the ear. The ear
receives fleeting momentary vibrations, translates these
bits of information into electronic nerve impulses, and
sends them to the brain. The brain "hears" by registering
the current vibration, recalling the previous vibrations,
and expecting future ones. We never hear the *continuum*

of sound we label as a word, sentence, or paragraph. The   *12*
continuum never exists at any single moment in time.
Rather, we piece bits of information (millisecond vibrations) together and perceive the entire three-stage pro-   *13*
cess as "hearing."

19   As a wider range of new material reached the public
through telephone, radio, film, records, and television, we
developed a stronger orientation toward the auditory
mode of receiving and processing information. A greater
percentage of the information that affected our lives was
reaching us in auditory form. This was true not only for
sound, but also for electronically mediated visual information, which is patterned like auditory information. Man
had never before experienced a world of visual sensation
patterned in an auditory mode.

20   Film transmits visual information by projecting a series
of still pictures in rapid succession. Each still frame is
projected for approximately one fiftieth to one seventy-   *14*
fifth of a second. Following each frame, the screen is black
for a nearly equal length of time. The same frame may
then be projected a second time, or the next frame may be
shown—depending on the projector. But in any one-second
period, the screen is black approximately half the time.
The brain "sees" motion by registering the current still
picture, recalling previous frames, and anticipating future
frames that will complete the movements. This differs
considerably from visual experience in everyday life,
where the eye is bombarded with a continuous stream of
information, which is always emanating from the sources
we are observing.

21   On film, the everyday visual experience is fractured,
and the brain must function in a new way to "reconstruct"
a continuous visual image. On television, the real-life visual image is fractured in a far more radical way. If we
were to set up a series of two thousand still cameras fo-
cused on a TV, each shooting at one two-thousandth of a
second and firing sequentially (so that we would cover a
one-second time span completely), no single camera would
record a picture. *The image we "see" on television is never
there.* A still camera, shooting at one two-thousandth of a
second, will capture only a few dots of light or perhaps a
single line across the television. In everyday visual experience, of course, a still photograph of a landscape shot

at one two-thousandth of a second will capture a complete visual image of the landscape.

22   A television set creates a visual image by projecting dots of light, one at a time, onto the front screen. The succession of dots moves across the screen and down alternate "lines." In all, there are 525 such lines on American television sets. During each one-fifteenth of a second, the scanning process will have completed two sweeps, once on each alternate set of lines.

23   In watching television, our eyes function like our ears. They never see a picture, just as our ears never hear a word. The eye receives a few dots of light during each successive millisecond, and sends these impulses to the brain. The brain records this impulse, recalls previous impulses, *16* and expects future ones. In this way we "see" an image on television. The process differs from film in that it requires much faster processing of information and more visual recall:

1. With film, the brain has to process twenty-four distinct inputs per second. With television, the brain has to process thousands of distinct inputs per second.
2. On a film screen, we always see a complete visual image, even if only for a brief instant (one fiftieth to one seventy-fifth of a second), but the presence of a visual image alternates with periods of nearly equal length in which no image is present. On a television screen, we never see a complete image, since there is never more than a dot of light on the screen at any one time.
3. With film, the brain does not "fill in" the image on the screen—it fills in the motion between the images. With television, the brain must fill in (or recall) 99.999 percent of the image at any given moment, since the full image is never present on the screen.

24   Watching television, the eye is for the first time functioning like the ear. Film began the process of fracturing visual images into bits of information for the eye to receive and the brain to reassemble, but television completed the transition. For this reason, it is more accurate to say that television is an auditory-based medium. Watching TV, the brain utilizes the eye in the same way it has always used the ear. With television, the patterning of auditory and visual stimuli is identical.

25   There has been a great concern about the effects of TV on children. If we found more violence only by children

against other children, or by children against adults, there might be reason to investigate the harmful influence of TV on children. But the increased violence in our world is *17* among all groups, including adults to other adults, adults to children, and by our society toward other societies. If there is a relation between TV and violence, it must be on a broad societal level, not just in relation to children.

26   Specific content on TV, in itself, does not foster violence. There has been a good deal of research attempting to show a stimulus-response relation between seeing an act of violence on TV and imitating that behavior in real life. Although some psychologists have managed to create this effect in a controlled laboratory situation, there is no evidence in society's laboratory that supports such a conclusion. There is no increase in the number of gasoline stations robbed the day after thirty-six million people watch such a robbery on "Ironside." And the news coverage of a skyjacking or murder does not *cause* others to imitate this behavior.

27   TV fosters violence, first, by conditioning people to respond instantly to stimuli in their everyday lives, and by focusing people's attention on the current moment. On TV, the only thing that exists is the current, momentary dot of light or sound vibration—each exists for a millisecond. People develop an orientation to everyday life based on the patterning of electronic information. We become very impatient in situations where information does not move at electronic speed. And we process new information instantly, rather than think out decisions. The increased violence in our society is generated by *impulsive reactions* to stimuli in a situation. This is largely a perceptual problem. We seek meaning in the world that conforms to the perceptual patterning of electronic media.

28   Second, *constant* exposure to TV over a period of time, and the *sharing* of TV stimuli by everyone in the society, creates a reservoir of common media experiences that are stored in our brains. In a group situation, commonly shared media experiences may overpower the previous nonmedia experiences of each member of the group as the basis on which a collective response will be formulated. The same is true for interpersonal encounters that must later be communicated to many people. It is easier to ex- *18* plain or justify action based on some experience we share with others. For example, in a political demonstration, there may be a flare-up between a policeman and one

demonstrator. Seeing this, other demonstrators may refer *18* the incident to the body of stored personal experiences where similar incidents took place. Their previous personal experiences will all be different, and therefore are not likely to foster an instantaneous collective response. However, if they refer what they see to previous media experiences of seeing demonstrations (commonly shared by all who watch TV), a collective reaction is more likely. Furthermore, since TV tends to show violent moments in demonstrations, the stored media experiences of people in the crowd makes violence commonly available to everyone in the group—as an appropriate collective reaction.

29   In addition, media depiction of *the good life* as *typical* throughout our society contradicts the everyday experiences of many people. This can be an element conducive to violent behavior, when people who do not experience *the good life* attempt to get *what everyone has.* Here too, constant exposure to TV makes certain solutions to this dilemma *commonly available.* The important point here is that we will get nowhere if we try to establish a direct cause-and-effect relationship between TV and violence in society. TV has a very mild effect in one sense—it makes certain knowledge available to us. The strength of the effect lies in TV's ability to make this knowledge available to everyone.

30   Truth, as a social value, is a product of print. In preliterate tribal cultures, the truth or falsity of a statement is not as important as whether it conforms to the religious and social beliefs of the society. Similarly, during the greater part of the Middle Ages, an imprimatur by the Church superseded any question of truth or validity re- *19* garding printed material. As print became a mass medium, literacy emerged as a social value. In order to learn about the world and communicate this knowledge to others, a person had to be literate. But men soon realized that print information, unlike other sensory data, could be true or false, fiction or nonfiction. Philosophers and *men of letters* spent a great deal of time and energy on this question, and truth emerged as an important social value (though the "white lie" was reserved for those occasions when another social value took precedence over truth). They did not recognize that truth is a particular problem in one medium of communication: the printed word.

31   No one ever asked of a Steichen photograph, "Is it true or false?" And no one would apply a truth standard in

analyzing a Picasso painting. Yet no one would argue that *19* a painting or photograph cannot communicate important and powerful meaning. Likewise, the question of truth is largely irrelevant when dealing with electronic media content. People do not watch "Bonanza" to find out about the Old West. So it makes no sense to ask if the program is a true depiction of that historical period. And we could not ask whether a children's cartoon program is true.

32   We can and should ask about the effects of television and radio programming. Electronic communication deals primarily with effects. The problem is that no "grammar" for electronic media effects has been devised. Electronic media have been viewed merely as extensions of print, and therefore subject to the same grammar and values as print communication. The patterned auditory and visual information on television or radio is not "content." Content is a print term, subject to the truth-falsity issue. Auditory and visual information on television or radio are stimuli that affect a viewer or listener. As stimuli, electronically mediated communication cannot be analyzed in the same way as print "content." A whole new set of questions must be asked, and a new theory of communication must be formulated.

33   The problem of applying a truth-falsity paradigm to *20* electronic communication is illustrated most clearly in the case of advertising. Periodically, the Federal Trade Commission clamps down on advertisers, demanding that they substantiate the truthfulness of their claims. How, they ask, can three different headache remedies claim to get into the bloodstream the fastest? And how can *every* brand of toothpaste claim to make teeth whiter than *any other* brand of toothpaste? Advertising agencies, forked tongue in cheek, respond by assuring the FTC that truth is essential if they are to convince the public to buy a product. Ironically, the ad agencies are very much concerned with truth, but they simply want to *appear* truthful. However, both the FTC and the agencies are dealing with an irrelevant issue. Neither understands the structure of electronic communication. They are dealing with TV and radio as extensions of print media, with the principles of literacy setting the ground rules for truth, honesty, and clarity.

34   Many advertising agencies believe that if a claim is accepted as true, the product will be considered better than all others in the field, thus increasing sales. The continuing proliferation of words like "best," "most," "cleanest,"

"purest," "whitest," etc., testify to the agency proclivity for 20
leaning on a truth image. For years, the agencies produced
ads that made incredible claims for products, and that
created arbitrary product differences where none in fact
existed. The effect of such advertising was to produce a
general cynicism in the public mind regarding all radio
and television advertising. Perhaps to combat this, many
large agencies recently adopted a policy of faking
"straight talk" in commercials. That is, since the effect of
their commercials was to create a negative attitude
toward the product being advertised, maybe they could
use a tone of voice that would sound truthful. Of course,
the result has not been "straight talk," but announcers
who sound like they are faking "straight talk."

35   The only important question for the FTC and advertising agencies alike is: What are the effects of electronic
media advertising? For an advertiser, the issue of concern 21
should center on how the stimuli in a commercial interact
with a viewer's real-life experiences and thus affect his
behavior in a purchasing situation. Here the key is to connect products to the real lives of human beings. As long as 22
the connection is made in a deep way, and as long as the
experience evoked by the commercial is not in conflict
with the experience of the product, purchase is possible, or
probable. At the moment, agencies could skirt an end run
right around the FTC by producing commercials that get
to the heart of the human use of products. People take aspirin because they need relief from a headache, not because it has monodyocycolate in it. People enjoy soup for
much simpler reasons than the Heinz commercials would
lead one to believe. Eating Heinz soup does not give one
the feeling that he is part of a 102-piece band riding on top
of a gargantuan can of Heinz soup. Commercials that do
not connect and resonate with real-life experiences build
an incredibility gap for everyone who uses the medium.

36   From the FTC point of view, "telling the truth" should
be the least important social concern. If electronic communication deals with effects, then government agencies
responsible for safeguarding public well-being should
concern themselves with understanding the effects of a
commercial, and preventing those effects that are not in
the public interest. A recent television commercial for
children's aspirin was 100 percent truthful by the most
rigid FTC standard, but the *effect* of the commercial was to

make children feel that aspirin is something to take when   *22*
they want to have a good time. The commercial clearly
demonstrates that truth is a print ethic, not a standard for
ethical behavior in electronic communication. In addition,
the influence of electronic media on print advertising (particularly the substitution of photographic techniques for
copy to achieve an effect) raises the question of whether
truth is any longer an issue in magazine or newspaper ads.

37   At present, we have no generally agreed-upon social
values and/or rules that can be readily applied in judging
whether the effects of electronic communication are ben-
eficial, acceptable, or harmful. Our print-based conception of electronic media prevents us from making social
decisions based on a correct understanding of our new
communication environment.

38   In discussing electronically based communication pro-   *23*
cesses, it is very helpful to use auditory terms. Words like
*feedback . . . reverberation . . . tuning . . . overload . . . re-
generation . . . fading* describe many of the characteristics
of social behavior in relation to electronic media. Similarly, the elements of electronic auditory systems serve as
useful analogies for social communication problems. In a
public address system, for example, too much output produces feedback. This "fed back" sound becomes ream-
plified until the system overloads, producing distortion.
Someone using such a system must learn to control the
output and anticipate feedback. In mass communication,
we experience a parallel problem. The interaction of program output with audience feedback can easily produce an
information overload.

39   These analogies suggest a new theory of electronic
communication, based on the patterning of information
inherent in auditory communication. Transportation theory assumes that communication is difficult to achieve
and that a message encounters resistance at each step in
its movement across space, over a period of time. In our
electronic communication environment, it is no longer
meaningful to assume that communication is a low-
efficiency process, or that messages must be pushed across
a vast chasm in order to be received and understood. The
space between phoning from one room in a house to
another room in the same house is equivalent to the space
between a caller in New York talking to someone in London. In both instances, space has no effect on the flow of

information. Similarly, time is no longer relevant when   23
communication takes place at electronic speed, and editing of film, sound, and video tape replaces the linear sequence of events *in time* with events juxtaposed in a time
relationship established by the communicator.

In formulating a new theory of communication, it is
valuable to build on Ray Birdwhistell's finding that a state
of communication is nearly always present in our environment. This state of communication is like an electric   24
circuit that is always turned on. The juice is present in the
line, and our problem is to make the current behave in
such a way as to achieve the desired effect. Today, there is
a nearly constant flow of information at all times. Indeed,
one has to expend considerable effort hypothesizing a
situation in our culture in which communication does not
regularly occur. We take in electronically mediated auditory and visual information as part of our life process. It is
part of our immediate physical surround, and we sit in it,
absorbing information constantly. The vital question to be
posed in formulating a new theory of communication is:
What are the characteristics of the process whereby we organize, store, and act upon the patterned information that
is constantly flowing into our brain? Further, given these
processes, how do we tune communication to achieve the
desired effect for someone creating a message?

In electronically mediated human communication, the
function of a communicator is to achieve a state of resonance with the person receiving visual and auditory
stimuli from television, radio, records, etc. Decoding symbolic forms such as pennants, drums, lantern signals, or
written words is no longer our most significant problem.
Words transform experience into symbolic forms. They
extract meaning from perception in a manner prescribed
by the structure of the language, code this meaning symbol-
ically, and store it in the brain. But the brain does not
store everything in this way. Many of our experiences
with electronic media are coded and stored in the same
way that they are perceived. Since they do not undergo a
symbolic transformation, the original experience is more
directly available to us when it is recalled. Also, since the
experience is not stored in a symbolic form, it cannot be
retrieved by symbolic cues. It must be evoked by a
stimulus that is coded in the same way as the stored information is coded.

42 The critical task is to design our package of stimuli so *24*
that it resonates with information already stored within
an individual and thereby induces the desired learning or
behavioral effect. Resonance takes place when the stimuli
put into our communication evoke *meaning* in a listener or *25*
viewer. That which we put into the communication has no
meaning in itself. The meaning of our communication is
what a listener or viewer *gets out* of his experience with
the communicator's stimuli. The listener's or viewer's
brain is an indispensable component of the total communication system. His life experiences, as well as his expectations of the stimuli he is receiving, interact with the
communicator's output in determining the meaning of the
communication.

43 A listener or viewer brings far more information to the
communication event than a communicator can put into
his program, commercial, or message. The communicator's
problem, then, is not to get stimuli across, or even to package his stimuli so they can be understood and absorbed.
Rather, he must deeply understand the kinds of information and experiences stored in his audience, the patterning
of this information, and the interactive resonance process
whereby stimuli evoke this stored information.

44 The resonance principle is not totally new or unique to
electronic communication. It has always been an element
in painting, music, sculpture, and, to a limited degree,
even in print. However, resonance is now a more *opera-
tional* principle for creating communication because much
of the material stored in the brains of an audience is also
stored in the brain of a communicator—by virtue of our
shared media environment. Also, the *process* of evoking
information is quite different today. It is much like the difference between riding a motorcycle under or over ninety
miles per hour. Under ninety miles per hour, a driver
should turn into a skid. Over ninety miles per hour, he
should turn out with the skid. The physical forces working
on a skidding motorcycle are reversed as the cycle crosses
this speed barrier, so the driver has to reverse his behavior
to pull out of the skid. Similarly, in communicating at
electronic speed, we no longer direct information into an
audience, but try to evoke stored information out of them,
in a patterned way.

Appendix A *Bibliography and Note Forms*

This appendix contains variations of the basic bibliography and note forms that you are likely to need for research papers in first- and second-year college courses. The entries are divided into three categories: Books, Articles in Periodicals, and Nonprint Sources. Until you learn the order within each category, you may use the index to find the form you need. Each entry appears as it would on a bibliography page and a note page of a research paper. The bibliographical forms should be consulted for making bibliography cards as well as bibliography-page entries. Consult Appendix C for the meaning of any abbreviations unfamiliar to you.

Books

1. Book with a single author (basic form)

Bibliography

Williams, Raymond.   Television: Technology and Cultural

    Form.   New York: Schocken Books, 1975.

- Author entry appears last name first (for alphabetization) followed by a period.
- Title entry includes any subtitle on the title page, underlined and followed by a period.
- Facts-of-publication entry includes city of publication followed by a colon; name of publishing company, which can be shortened as long as the name remains clear, followed by a comma; and the date of publication or copyright followed by a period.
- Brackets indicate additional information, such as the name of the library and call number or a short description of the book.

Note

    [1] Raymond Williams, Television: Technology and

Cultural Form (New York: Schocken Books, 1975), p. 76.

• Author's name in normal order preceded by a raised number for consecutive numbering of note-page entries and followed by a comma.
• Subtitles *may* be omitted.
• A space (without punctuation) separates title and facts of publication.
• Facts of publication are in parentheses followed by a comma.
• Abbreviation for page (p.) or pages (pp.) indicates the exact pages of material cited.
• A period ends the entry.

2. Book with two or three authors

Bibliography

Schramm, Wilbur, Jack Lyle, and Edwin B. Parker. Tele-

vision in the Lives of Our Children. Palo Alto:

Stanford Univ. Press, 1961.

• Only first author appears last name first.
• Names appear in the order they have on the title page. The entry is alphabetized in card catalogs and bibliographies by the surname of the first author.

Note

[2] Wilbur Schramm, Jack Lyle, and Edwin B. Parker,

Television in the Lives of Our Children (Palo Alto: Stan-

ford Univ. Press, 1961), pp. 81-89.

3. Book with four or more authors

Bibliography

Chester, Giraud, et al. Television and Radio. 4th ed.

New York: Appleton Century Crofts, 1971.

• Et al., the abbreviation of the Latin phrase *et alii* ("and others") is italicized in older publications, but not in recent ones.

• All authors *may* be listed, in which case the rules for number 2 would apply.
• See number 15 for explanation of "4th ed."

Note

   3 Giraud Chester et al., Television and Radio, 4th ed. (New York: Appleton Century Crofts, 1971), p. 38.

4. Book with author and collaborator

Bibliography

Rather, Dan, with Mickey Herskowitz. The Camera Never Blinks: Adventures of a TV Journalist. New York: William Morrow, 1977.

• Collaborator does not have author status.

Note

   4 Dan Rather with Mickey Herskowitz, The Camera Never Blinks (New York: William Morrow, 1977), p. 97.

5. Book with a corporate or group author

Bibliography

Roper Research Associates. A Ten-Year Attitude Study towards Television and Other Mass Media: 1958-1968. New York: Television Information Office, 1969.

• Name of the group, committee, or organization publishing the report or study is treated like an author's name in the bibliography.

Note

   5 Roper Research Associates, A Ten-Year Attitude

Study towards Television and Other Mass Media: 1958-1968,
(New York: Television Information Office, 1969), p. 17.

6. Book with an editor

Bibliography

Rosenthal, Raymond, ed. McLuhan: Pro and Con. Balti-

   more: Penguin Books, 1969.

• When the alphabetized name is not an author, an appropriate abbreviation indicating role follows.

Note

   [6] Irving J. Weiss, "Sensual Reality in the Mass

Media," in McLuhan: Pro and Con, ed. Raymond Rosenthal

(Baltimore: Penguin Books, 1969), p. 40.

• Note refers to specific page of one article in a collection.
• Abbreviations for titles accompanying names (for example, ed.) precede names when the name is not the first entry.
• Notes generally start with the smallest unit and work to the largest; for example, (1) article (2) in a book (3) in series of books on a subject (see number 14 for works in a series).

7. Book with author, editor, and translator

Bibliography

Artaud, Antonin. Antonin Artaud, Selected Writings.

   Ed. and intro. Susan Sontag. Trans. Helen Wea-

      ver. New York: Farrar, Straus, and Giroux, 1976.

Sontag, Susan, ed. and intro. Antonin Artaud, Selected

   Writings. Trans. Helen Weaver. New York: Farrar,

   Straus, and Giroux, 1976.

Weaver, Helen, trans. <u>Antonin Artaud, Selected Writings</u>.

Ed. and intro. Susan Sontag. New York: Farrar,

Straus, and Giroux, 1976.

• Entry can begin with the author, editor, or translator depending on emphasis. If the name of the editor begins the entry, the emphasis is on the editor's selection of the author's writings; if the emphasis is on a particular translation of a foreign work, the translator's name comes first.
• Author's name is not repeated in second and third examples because it is part of the title.

Note

[7] Antonin Artaud, <u>Antonin Artaud, Selected Writings</u>.

ed. and intro. Susan Sontag, trans. Helen Weaver (New

York: Farrar, Straus, and Giroux, 1976), pp. 82-91.

[7] Susan Sontag, ed. and intro., <u>Antonin Artaud,</u>

<u>Selected Writings</u>, trans. Helen Weaver (New York: Farrar,

Straus, and Giroux, 1976), pp. 82-91.

[7] Helen Weaver, trans., <u>Antonin Artaud, Selected</u>

<u>Writings</u>, ed. and intro. Susan Sontag (New York: Farrar,

Straus, and Giroux, 1976), pp. 82-91.

• Choice of format may depend on the portion of the work referred to in the body of the paper.

8. An anonymous book

Bibliography

<u>Cable Television Sourcebook 1975</u>. Washington, D.C.:

Broadcasting Publications, n.d.

• Entry is alphabetized by the first word of the title excluding articles.
• See number 19 for an explanation of "n.d."

Note

[8] <u>Cable Television Sourcebook 1975</u> (Washington, D.C.: Broadcasting Publications, n.d.), p. 11.

9. A work in several volumes or parts

Bibliography

Barnouw, Erik. <u>A History of Broadcasting in the United States</u>. 3 vols. New York: Oxford Univ. Press, 1966–70. Vol. I. <u>A Tower in Babel: A History of Broadcasting in the United States to 1933</u>. 1966; Vol. II. <u>The Golden Web: A History of Broadcasting in the United States, 1933–53</u>. 1968; Vol. III. <u>The Image Empire: A History of Broadcasting in the United States from 1953</u>. 1970.

• When each volume is titled individually, individual titles and dates follow the title for the entire work and the facts of publication for all volumes.
• Internal punctuation for each volume is the same as the basic book form.
• Arabic numerals are used when the whole work is considered and for the total number of volumes; roman numbers are used for individual volumes.

Note

[9] Erik Barnouw, <u>A Tower of Babel</u>, Vol. I of <u>A History of Broadcasting in the United States</u> (New York: Oxford Univ. Press, 1966), pp. 37–39.

• For material taken from pages of one specific volume that is part of a larger work, see items under Note, number 6.
• See number 1 regarding shortening titles in notes.

10. A work in a collection of pieces by different authors

Bibliography

Tumin, Melvin. "Popular Culture and the Open Society."

Mass Culture: The Popular Arts in America. Ed.

Bernard Rosenberg and David Manning White. New

York: The Free Press, 1957, pp. 548-56.

• Inclusive pages of work given since the reference is to one article rather than the entire collection.

Note

[10] Melvin Tumin, "Popular Culture and the Open

Society," in Mass Culture, ed. Bernard Rosenberg and

David Manning White (New York: The Free Press, 1957),

p. 554.

11. A work reprinted in a collection of pieces by different authors

Bibliography

McDonald, Dwight. "A Theory of Mass Culture." Diogenes,

3 (Summer 1953), 1-17. Rpt. in Mass Culture: The

Popular Arts in America. Ed. Bernard Rosenberg

and David Manning White. New York: The Free Press,

1964, pp. 59-73.

• Information about the original publication, if available, should be given preceding the information about the reprint.
• See number 20 for an explanation of the first part of the entry.

[11] Dwight McDonald, "A Theory of Mass Culture," Diogenes, 3 (Summer 1953), 1-17; rpt. in Mass Culture, ed. Bernard Rosenberg and David Manning White (New York: The Free Press, 1964), p. 60.

12. Articles in encyclopedias

Bibliography

Fink, D. G.   "Television."   The New Encyclopaedia Britannica, Macropaedia.   18 (1974), 105-22.

• Volume number, date, and page numbers are treated as they are in basic book form.
• Place of publication and name of publisher need not be given if the reference work is well known.

Note

[12] D. G. Fink, "Television," The New Encyclopaedia Britannica, Macropaedia, 18 (1974), 109.

13. Articles in reference works, unsigned

Bibliography

"Chou En-lai."   Who's Who in Communist China.   Hong Kong: Union Research Institute, 1966, pp. 137-42.

• Standard book form is followed for one-volume reference works.
• When the work is not well known, all facts of publication are necessary.

Note

[13] "Chou En-lai," Who's Who in Communist China (Hong Kong: Union Research Institute, 1966), p. 142.

14. A work in a series

Bibliography

Tuchman, Gaye, ed. The TV Establishment: Programming

for Power and Profit. The American Establishment

Ser. Englewood Cliffs: Prentice-Hall, 1974.

Note

[14] Gaye Tuchman, "Assembling a Network Talkshow,"

in The TV Establishment, ed. Gaye Tuchman, The American

Establishment Ser. (Englewood Cliffs: Prentice-Hall,

1974), p. 122.

15. A reprint of an older edition

Bibliography

Metz, Robert. CBS: Reflections in a Bloodshot Eye.

1975; rpt. New York: New American Library, 1976.

• The original date followed by a semicolon should precede the
facts of publication about the reprint.
• Books originally issued in hardcover and reissued in paperback are considered reprints.
• Books once out-of-print and then republished are reprints.

Note

[15] Robert Metz, CBS: Reflections in a Bloodshot

Eye (1975; rpt. New York: New American Library, 1976),

p. 57.

16. A new edition

Bibliography

Spiller, Robert E., et al. Literary History of the

United States. 3rd ed. New York: Macmillan, 1963.

• All editions except the first must be indicated by a number.

Note

[16] Robert E. Spiller et al., <u>Literary History of the United States</u>, 3rd ed. (New York: Macmillan, 1963), p. 921.

17. A pamphlet

Bibliography

<u>Color as Seen and Photographed.</u> 2nd ed. Kodak Publication No. E. 74. Rochester, N.Y.: Eastman Kodak, 1972.

• Pamphlets are treated like books.
• In the preceding example, there is no author (see number 8), the edition is not the first (see number 16), the pamphlet is part of a series (see number 14), and the abbreviation for the state (New York) is added to avoid ambiguity about the place of publication.

Note

[17] <u>Color as Seen and Photographed</u>, 2nd ed., Kodak Publ. No. E. 74 (Rochester, N.Y.: Eastman Kodak, 1972), p. 21

18. A government publication

Bibliography

U.S. Cong. House. Committee on Interstate and Foreign Commerce. <u>Hearings on Deceptive Programming Practices.</u> 90th Cong., 2nd sess. Washington, D.C.: GPO, 1968.

Great Britain. Dept. of Education and Science. <u>A Lan-</u>

guage for Life. Report of the Committee of In-

quiry appointed by the Secretary of State for Edu-

cation and Science under the Chairmanship of Sir

Alan Bullock FBA. London: HMSO, 1975.

U.S. Public Health Service. Television and Social Be-

havior, Reports and Papers. The Surgeon General's

Scientific Advisory Committee on Television and

Social Behavior. 3 vols. Washington, D.C.: GPO,

1972.

• The order is: (1) country, state, or city; (2) name of agency; (3) title; (4) author or editor; (5) additional information about edition, volumes; (5) facts of publication (as for a book).

Note

[18] U.S. Cong., House, Committee on Interstate and

Foreign Commerce, Hearings on Deceptive Programming

Practices, 90th Cong., 2nd sess. (Washington, D.C.: GPO,

1968), p. 5.

[18] Great Britain, Dept. of Education and Science,

A Language for Life, report of the Committee of Inquiry

appointed by the Secretary of State for Education and

Science under the chairmanship of Sir Alan Bullock FBA

(London: HMSO, 1975), p. 531.

[18] Monroe M. Lefkowitz et al., "Television Vio-

lence and Child Aggression: A Follow-up Study," in Tele-

vision and Adolescent Aggressiveness, ed. George A.

Combstock and Eli A. Rubinstein, Vol. III of <u>Television</u>
<u>and Social Behavior</u> by the Surgeon General's Scientific
Advisory Committee on Television and Social Behavior
(Washington, D.C.: GPO, 1972), pp. 39–40.

• Third example refers to one article in one volume of a multivolume work, each with author, editor, or corporate author (see item under Note, number 6).

19. A book without place of publication, publisher, date of publication, or pagination

Bibliography

Williams, Raymond.   <u>Television: Technology and Cultural</u>

   <u>Form</u>.   n.p.: Schocken Books, 1975.

Williams, Raymond.   <u>Television: Technology and Cultural</u>

   <u>Form</u>. ⁚ New York: n.p., 1975.

Williams, Raymond.   <u>Television: Technology and Cultural</u>

   <u>Form</u>.   New York: Schocken Books, n.d.

• Meaning of "n.p." is determined by its placement in the entry.

Note

   [19] Raymond Williams, <u>Television: Technology and</u>
<u>Cultural Form</u> (n.p.: Schocken Books, 1975), p. 76.

   [19] Raymond Williams, <u>Television: Technology and</u>
<u>Cultural Form</u> (New York: n.p., 1975), p. 76.

   [19] Raymond Williams, <u>Television: Technology and</u>
<u>Cultural Form</u> (New York: Schocken Books, n.d.), p. 76.

   [19] Raymond Williams, <u>Television: Technology and</u>

<u>Cultural Form</u> (New York: Schocken Books, 1975), n.

pag.

Articles in Periodicals

20. Articles in periodicals collected in volumes (basic form)

Bibliography
Baldwin, James.   "Black Man in America."   <u>WFMT Per-</u>

    <u>spectives</u>, 10 (Dec. 1961), 25-30.

• Author entry appears last name first and followed by a period.
• Title entry is followed by a period and enclosed in quotation marks.
• Name of periodical is underlined and followed by a comma; volume number in arabic numerals; the date—day, month (abbreviated) or season, and year—is placed in parentheses and followed by a comma; inclusive page numbers without abbreviation for *page(s)* are followed by a period.

Note
    [20] James Baldwin, "Black Man in America," <u>WFMT</u>

<u>Perspectives</u>, 10 (Dec. 1961), 26.

• Author entry appears in normal order for a name.
• Parts of the entry are separated by commas; a period ends the entry.
• Page number refers to exact page from which material cited was taken.

Alternate forms:

Bibliography
Wall, J. M.   "Planning Television's Future."   <u>Christian</u>

    <u>Century</u>, 92 (1975), 867-68.

Note

[20] J. M. Wall, "Planning Television's Future,"

Christian Century, 92 (1975), 867.

• When a periodical has continuous pagination throughout a volume—that is, each issue continues the pagination of the previous one—the entry for the date may include only the year.

Bibliography

Zajonc, Robert. "Some Effects of the 'Space' Serials."

Public Opinion Quarterly, 18, No. 4 (1954), 367-74.

Note

[20] Robert Zajonc, "Some Effects of the 'Space'

Serials," Public Opinion Quarterly, 18, No. 4 (1954),

370.

• When a periodical does not have continuous pagination, the issue number should be used when the season or month is not known.

Bibliography

Duggan, E. P. "Children at the Television Set." (London) Times Educational Supplement, No. 2112 (1955), p. 1165.

Note

[20] E. P. Duggan, "Children at the Television Set,"

(London) Times Educational Supplement, No. 2112 (1955),

p. 1165.

• When journals do not have a volume number, the issue number alone should be used.

21. Article from a periodical published weekly (or more often) or lacking a volume number

Bibliography
Arons, Stephen, and Ethan Katsh. "How TV Cops Flout the

Law," <u>Saturday Review</u>, 19 Mar. 1977, pp. 10–18.

• Date appears without parentheses in the following order: day, if given, is followed by the month (abbreviated); month is followed by year; year is followed by a comma.
• Because no volume number is given, *p.* or *pp.* precedes the inclusive page numbers.

Note
  [21] Stephen Arons and Ethan Katsh, "How TV Cops

Flout the Law," <u>Saturday Review</u>, 19 Mar. 1977, p. 12.

• Page number preceded by *p.* or *pp.* refers to exact page of material cited.

22. Article from a newspaper, signed

Bibliography
Vanocur, Sander. "'It has set us free'—A Defense of

Television." <u>The Sunday News</u> (Detroit), 5 June

1977, p. 11-B, cols. 1–4.

• If the city of publication is not part of the newspaper's title, it is added in parentheses following the title.
• Page reference includes information regarding section and column.
• See number 21 regarding date and page entry.

Note

[22] Sander Vanocur, "'It has set us free'—A Defense of Television," The Sunday News (Detroit), 5 June 1977, p. 11-B, col. 2.

• Note refers to material taken from column 2 only.

23. Article from newspaper, unsigned

Bibliography

"Congress to Study Many Free Services It Gives News Media." New York Times, 9 June 1977, p. A16, cols. 1-3.

• See number 8 for the explanation of an anonymous work.

Note

[23] "Congress to Study Many Free Services It Gives News Media," New York Times, 9 June 1977, p. A16, col. 1.

24. Article from newspaper, in a special category such as letter or editorial

Bibliography

"Rebuilding the Bridge to Cuba." Editorial. Los Angeles Times. 3 June 1977, pt. II, p. 4, cols. 1-2.

• Category follows title.
• See number 8 for the treatment of an anonymous work.

Note

[24] "Rebuilding the Bridge to Cuba," editorial, Los Angeles Times, 3 June 1977, pt. II, p. 4, cols. 1-2.

25. Reviews, signed and titled

Bibliography

O'Connor, John J. "TV: Crusading Scientist is a Pro-

file of Feisty Linus Pauling." Rev. of Crusading

Scientist. Prod. by Robert Richter. New York

Times, 1 June 1977, p. C22, cols. 1-2.

Note

[25] John J. O'Connor, "TV: 'Crusading Scientist' is

a Profile of Feisty Linus Pauling," rev. of "Crusading

Scientist," prod. by Robert Richter. New York Times, 1

June 1977, p. C22, col. 2.

26. Review without title

Bibliography

Harrington, Stephanie. Rev. of The Plug-In Drug by

Marie Winn. New York Times Book Review, 20 Mar.

1977, p. 8.

• Abbreviation for *review* is same as that for *revision;* context
and placement determine meaning.

Note

[26] Stephanie Harrington, rev. of The Plug-In Drug

by Marie Winn, New York Times Book Review, 20 Mar. 1977,

p. 8.

27. Review unsigned, untitled

Bibliography

Rev. of Television: Technology and Culture by Raymond

Williams. *Times Literary Supplement*. Dec. 1977, p. 1422.

• Alphabetized by "Rev."

Note

[27] Rev. of *Television: Technology and Culture* by Raymond Williams, *Times Literary Supplement*, Dec. 1977, p. 1422.

28. Unpublished notes

Bibliography

"NBC Policies and Operating Procedures." (Mimeo) n.d.

• If the material has been reproduced, the method should be mentioned.
• See number 19 for an explanation of "n.d."

Note

[28] "NBC Policies and Operating Procedures," (mimeo), n.d., p. 4.

Nonprint Sources

29. Unpublished lecture or speech

Bibliography

Cronkite, Walter. William Allen White Lecture. Univ. of Kansas. 10 Feb. 1969.

• If the speech has a title, it follows the speaker's name.

Note

   [29] Walter Cronkite, William Allen White Lecture,

Univ. of Kansas, 10 Feb. 1969.

30. Films

Bibliography

   Lumet, Sidney, dir. Network. Writ. by Paddy

      Chayefsky, Paramount, 1976.

• Additional information about writers, actors, or producers
follows title.

Note

   [30] Sidney Lumet, dir., Network, writ. by Paddy

Chayefsky, Paramount, 1976.

31. Theatrical performance

Bibliography

Wagner, Jane, and Lilly Tomlin, dirs. Appearing

      Nitely. With Lily Tomlin. Biltmore Theatre, New

      York. 31 May 1977.

Note

   [31] Jane Wagner and Lily Tomlin, dirs., Appearing

Nitely, with Lily Tomlin, Biltmore Theatre, New York,

31 May 1977.

32. Radio and television programs

Bibliography

"Crusading Scientist /Linus Pauling7." Writ. and prod.

by Robert Richter. *Nova* ser. Public Broadcasting

System. 1 June 1977.

• Network (or local station) information may be given.
• Researcher's addition is in brackets.

Note

[32] "Crusading Scientist," writ. and prod. by

Robert Richter, *Nova* ser., Public Broadcasting System,

1 June 1977.

33. Records and tapes

Bibliography

Rubinstein, Artur, pianist. Three Favorite Beethoven

Sonatas: Moonlight, Pathétique, Appassionata.

RCA. LSC-4001, 1962.

Beethoven, Ludwig Van. Three Favorite Beethoven Sonatas:

Moonlight, Pathétique, Appassionata. Pianist Artur

Rubinstein. RCA. LSC-4001, 1962.

• Composer/author or artist may be first entry depending on emphasis.
• Publishing company, numbers identifying work, and date are given.

Note

[33] Artur Rubinstein, pianist, Three Favorite Bee-

thoven Sonatas, RCA, LSC-4001, 1962, side I, band 2.

[33] Ludwig Van Beethoven, Three Favorite Beethoven

Sonatas, pianist Artur Rubinstein, RCA, LSC-4001, 1962,

side I, band 2.

34. Personal letters

Bibliography

Nin, Anais. Letter to author. 6 June 1969.

Note

[34] Letter received from Anais Nin, 6 June 1969.

35. Personal interviews and telephone interviews

Bibliography

Kaminska, Ida. Personal interview. 8 Aug. 1973.

Schechner, Richard. Telephone interview. 9 Sept. 1975.

Note

[35] Personal interview with Ida Kaminska, 8 Aug. 1973.

[35] Telephone interview with Richard Schechner, 9 Sept. 1975.

Appendix B *Documentation in the Sciences*

Documentation systems in the fields of science and technology differ greatly from those used in the humanities and social sciences. Most often notes are replaced by short parenthetical citations in the text; these citations refer the reader to a bibliography or reference section at the end of the paper. The MLA describes three principal methods of parenthetical citation used in scientific and technical writing: an author-date system, an author-title system, and a number system.

Author-date system:

Studies of the temperature at which liquids change to solids are relatively recent. (Swinney, 1969, 321-22.)

Author-title system:

Studies of the temperature at which liquids change to solids are relatively recent. (Swinney, "Critical Phenomena," 321-22).

Number system:

Studies of the temperature at which liquids change to solids are relatively recent. (21, 321-22).

Each work in the bibliography is numbered and the number for the work cited appears underlined to distinguish it from the page numbers that follow the comma.

Each discipline has its own style sheet. The following are commonly consulted in the fields indicated:

Biology

Council of Biology Editors, Committee on Form and Style. *CBE Style Manual*, 3rd ed. Washington, D.C.: American Inst. of Biological Sciences, 1972.

Chemistry	American Chemical Society. *Handbook for Authors of Papers in the Journals of the American Chemical Society.* Washington, D.C.: American Chemical Soc., 1967.
Engineering	Engineers Joint Council, Committee of Engineering Society Editors. *Recommended Practice for Style of References in Engineering Publications.* New York: Engineers Joint Council, 1966.
Mathematics	American Mathematical Society. *Manual for Authors of Mathematical Papers.* 4th ed. Providence, R.I.: American Mathematical Soc., 1971.
Physics	American Institute of Physics, Publications Board. *Style Manual.* Rev. ed. New York: American Inst. of Physics, 1973.
Psychology	American Psychological Association. *Publication Manual of the American Psychological Association.* 2nd ed. Washington, D.C.: American Psychological Assn., 1974.

Appendix C *Abbreviations*

The abbreviations below are those you may encounter in your reading or need to use in your research paper. When you use abbreviations, be certain that you use them correctly and consistently. Notice that abbreviations may require italics (underlining), periods, separation of the elements with spaces, or no spacing. Current trends emphasize the use of English equivalents of Latin terms. Thus, while you may encounter Latin terms in your reading, you should generally avoid using them.

A.D. (*Anno Domini*)	"in the year of the Lord"; abbreviation precedes numerals (A.D. 1066)
anon.	anonymous
app.	appendix
art., arts.	article, articles
b.	born
B.C.	"before Christ"; abbreviation follows numerals (19 B.C.)
bibliog.	bibliography, bibliographer, or bibliographical
biog.	biography, biographer, biographical
bk., bks.	book, books
c	copyright
c., ca. (*circa*)	"about"; used only with approximate dates (c. 1776)
c.f. (*confer*)	"compare"
ch., chs. *or* chap., chaps.	chapter, chapters
col., cols.	column, columns
comp., comps.	compiled by; compiler, compilers
cond.	conducted by, conductor
Cong.	Congress (United States)
Cong. Rec.	*Congressional Record* (United States)
d.	died
DAB	*Dictionary of American Biography*
dir., dirs.	directed by; director, directors

DNB	*Dictionary of National Biography* (British)
doc., docs.	document, documents
ed., eds.	edited by; editor, editors; edition, editions
e.g. (*exempli gratia*)	"for example"; set off by commas
et al. (*et alii*)	"and others"; used for more than one author or editor
f., ff.	and following; exact references are preferable (pp. 43–44 instead of p. 43f. and pp. 43–49 instead of p. 43ff); appropriate when pages of an article are dispersed throughout a magazine or newspaper
fig., figs	figure, figures
fn.	footnote; n is preferred
GPO	Government Printing Office (U.S.)
hist.	history, historian, historical
HMSO	Her (His) Majesty's Stationery Office (British)
H.R.	House of Representatives (U.S.)
ibid. or ib. (*ibidem*)	"in the same place"; refers to the single title stated in the note immediately preceding
i.e. (*id est*)	"that is"; set off by commas
illus.	illustrated; illustrated by; illustrator; illustration, illustrations
introd.	introduction; introduction by
l., ll.	line, lines
L.C.	Library of Congress (U.S.)
loc. cit. (*loco citato*)	"in the place cited"; used when citing the same passage cited in a recent note
ms, mss; MS., MSS.	manuscript, manuscripts; capitalized and followed by a period when referring to a specific manuscript
n., nn.	note, notes; p. 36n means "note on p. 36"; 12n means "note number 12"

narr., narrs.	narrated by; narrator, narrators
N.B. (*nota bene*)	"take notice, mark well"
n.d.	no date of publication
no., nos.	number, numbers
n.p.	no place of publication, no publisher
n. pag.	no pagination
NS *or* N.S.	New Series; New Style (calendar after 1752)
OED	*Oxford English Dictionary*
op.	opus; a work
op. cit. (*opere citato*)	"in the work cited"; used when citing a different passage (one on a different page) of a work cited in a recent note; see loc. cit.
OS *or* O.S.	Old Series; Old Style (calendar before 1752)
p., pp.	page, pages
passim	"throughout the work, here and there" (pp. 78, 111, et passim.)
par., pars.	paragraph, paragraphs
prod., prods.	produced by; producer, producers
pseud.	pseudonym
pt., pts.	part, parts
q.v. (*quod vide*)	"which see"; used for cross-reference
rev.	revised; revised by; revision; review; reviewed by
rpt.	reprinted by, reprint
S	Senate (U.S.)
sc.	scene
sec., secs.	section, sections
ser.	series
sess.	session
sic	"thus so"; usually in brackets; used after an error in a quotation to indicate awareness of the error by the person writing out the quote ("It was there [sic] turn.")

st., sts. *or* St., Sts.	stanza, stanzas; Saint, Saints
supp., supps.	supplement, supplements
s.v. (*sub verbo*)	"under the word or heading"; used in libraries for classifying
trans.	translated by, translator, translation
v. (*vide*)	"see"
vol., vols.	volume, volumes; capitalized when referring to a specific volume (Vol. II of the 4 vols.)

Index